Building a Discipling Culture

Legacy Edition

Mike Breen, Ph.D.

Discipling Culture Publishing

Building a Discipling Culture
Legacy Edition: April, 2025
© 2025, Mike Breen
© 2025, Discipling Culture Publishing an imprint of 3DM Publishing
© 2025, 3DM Publishing

All Scripture quotations, unless otherwise noted, are taken from the Holy Bible, New International Version® (NIV). Copyright © 1973, 1978, 1984, 2011 by International Bible Society. Used by permission of Zondervan Publishing House. All rights reserved.

First Edition 2009
Second Edition 2011
Third Edition 2017
Legacy Edition 2025

ISBN: 978-0-9998981-3-0

Dedicated to all my faithful friends.

Table of Contents

Introduction from Sally Breen 9

Prologue 13

Part I: Understanding Discipling Culture

1. The Call 19

2. The Challenge 35

3. Jesus' Way of Connecting 47

4. Community 63

5. Investing Capital like Jesus 87

6. Finding a Way to Imitate 101

Part II: Language Creates a Discipling Culture

7. A Language that Creates a Discipling Culture 115

8. The Circle: Learning from Life 127

9. Rhythm of Life: The Semi-Circle 151

10. Deeper Relationships: The Triangle 173

11. Relational Mission: The Person of Peace Strategy 201

12. Multiplying Life: The Square 215

13. Personal Calling: The Pentagon 241

14. Definitive Prayer: The Hexagon 271

Part III: Huddles Sustain a Discipling Culture

15. Using Huddles to Disciple People 287

16. Huddle Launch Guide 305

17. Sample Huddle Outlines 321

Appendix

Appendix 1. Triangle Questions for Up/In/Out 349

Appendix 2. The Temptations of Jesus and the Enneagram 355

Appendix 3. Spiritual Health: The Heptagon 361

Appendix 4. Relational Mission: The Octagon 375

Appendix 5. Fivefold Ministries Questionnaire 381

Letters to the Reader

A Personal Word 399

Letter 1 401

Letter 2 405

Letter 3 411

Letter from Restoration Team 415

Introduction from Sally Breen

For the longest while after the crisis hit our family in fall 2023,[1] I wanted to retreat and hide. I am a naturally more private person than Mike, and running away is one of my basic instincts. Adding to this already very difficult situation, much of what was said online and publicly about Mike was untrue and unkind, and it deeply affected me and our children. I felt the shame and the guilt and the pressure of it all.

The days moved into months, and with that gift of time and lots of prayers, good therapy, some hard deep conversations, and long walks holding Mike's hand absorbing the goodness of the wonderful and ever-changing countryside that surrounds us here in the U.K., I began to emerge. And as I did, I emerged with a new belief and understanding of the importance of *Building a Discipling Culture*.

One of the biblical principles I hold very close to my heart and talk about often is the call from the writer of the Psalms to the people of God to remember: to remember God's faithfulness and his help in times of trouble, and the need to keep reminding

---

[1] This crisis, as I assume you have heard, stemmed from Mike's inappropriate relationship and moral failure which became public at this time. Mike provides much more context in *A Personal Word* found at the end of this book.

those around us of the past because it informs and illuminates our future and our faith.

In time I began to remember where the tools in *Building a Discipling Culture* had originally come from and why Mike developed them.

I looked back and remembered the first time in our cramped kitchen in inner city London that, as toddlers tugged at my heart and clothes, Mike processed how he could help our urban and mainly non-literate congregation understand and engage in discipleship.

Mike being dyslexic gave him important insights into the frustrations connected with not being able to read and in being thought of as stupid. He knew instinctively that shapes would be easy to remember, and so began to explore how these could be used. Mike started with a circle and the rest of the shapes followed from there .

I feel it's important to understand that these tools were created to give access and understanding. They were never designed originally to be an academic teaching instrument or only to be used by experts. They came from the poorest of streets and were first given into the hands of the most marginalized group of individuals. The fact that they found them helpful and useful to understand Jesus better and how to help others to do the same is why this book is in existence today.

Forty years on from that kitchen table, these shapes have been used around the world in every type of community, and disciples of every kind have found them to be extremely useful tools for discipling others to disciple others.

Even though many colleges now teach *Building a Discipling*

Introduction from Sally Breen

Culture as part of their curriculum, and even though and pastors and people from Nepal to Uganda use them to form the basis of church planting in the Himalayas and the source of the Nile, your community and family—as unique as it is—will be able to use each tool yourselves. Of course you can use them in any order you like and use only the ones that are helpful. It's entirely up to you.

Mike got his Ph.D. looking into the patterns of imitation (mimesis) in the ways people learn. He loves a good meme because they help people learn. And many of you have heard him say, "People need a living example, not a perfect example".

Mike will quickly agree that he is not a perfect example, but that doesn't mean that the tools he's developed are broken or irrelevant. For me it just shows me more clearly that I should look to the Biblical principles that inform these teachings and tools, and to Jesus, rather than to the man that God used to create them.

We never could have done this alone and our children have been instrumental every step of the way.

They were the ones who got the raw and unfinished tools first hand as children, and they were the ones who would veto things and tell us when anything became too complicated or irrelevant.

They sat in coffee shops with us around the world while Mike drew shapes out on napkins and scrappy pieces of paper as the process to start and develop 3DM grew.

They have walked the walk, talked the talk, and they definitely got the t-shirt and the Starbucks mugs! We are forever proud and thankful for them and their families.

We have also heard from so many of you over the years as to how life-changing this book has been for you, and we are both grateful and humbled by those testimonies.

I am now very excited that we get the opportunity, despite the difficulties we have experienced these last few years (or maybe because of those trials), to release the final version of *Building a Discipling Culture*.

It comes with lots of love and lots of history, and we would love to hear new stories from you of how it's being used today.

Prologue

A few years ago, I was driving from Charleston, South Carolina, back to my home at Pawleys Island. The 40 or so miles of road between these two towns on Highway 17 is a four-lane highway with a divided median in between, and it is quite deserted and dark for much of the drive because it goes through a national forest.

I was driving my Ford F-150 truck on this familiar road, and perhaps because of the familiarity, I began to relax during the drive and then fell soundly asleep. I woke up with a start to see a curtain of green water covering not only the windshield, but the entire sunroof as well. Clearly, the wave I had created was incredibly high!

Somehow, I woke up enough to switch from two-wheel drive to four-wheel drive, which allowed me to drive out of the waterlogged median in the center of the divided highway. I drove back on the road and then pulled over safely on the shoulder, coming to realize how close I had come to death. Somewhat shakily I popped the hood and began to pull large swaths of vegetation from inside the engine compartment. I drove home wide awake from the fright of it all.

Of course I reflected very deeply on what was going on in my life for such an extraordinary thing to have happened. This was a warning that I hadn't just fallen asleep at the wheel of my car, but in many ways at the wheel of my life. All my rhythms were out of balance, and something had to change. I had been wrestling with a lot of relational conflict in my team and coming to terms with the death of some hopes I had for my ministry. All of that had begun to take its toll.

I was bumping along the bottom of my physical and emotional capacity. I was losing track of where to go and what to do. This vulnerable moment—this *kairos* moment—provided a breakthrough of clarity that something had to change in my life.

You may not have fallen asleep at the wheel of your vehicle or driven into a waterlogged median, but almost all of us have had the unsettling feeling of realizing that we've been slumbering through important moments of life. It can happen in many ways and can affect different things, but it causes a unique kind of vulnerability when we realize we have lost our sense of direction and have disconnected from the vision and hopes we have for our lives.[2]

Have you ever experienced this moment of vulnerability? Maybe you have looked at those people close to you and realized you've not been attentive to them in the way you should. Perhaps your work has suffered because you have lost your sense of purpose. In my world of pastoral ministry, I have heard from many pastors who have looked out at a weekend worship gathering and realized that, although the music and

---

2   I have experienced this in my own life, through a recent inappropriate relationship and a moral failure. I discuss this in much more detail in the Personal Word found at the end of this book.

teaching were right and good, their Sunday ministry didn't actually make disciples in the way Jesus did. With church leaders this can happen because we confuse the task of gathering people for worship with the task of making disciples, and the realization can prove to be quite a shock—like ending up waterlogged in the median was for me!

During the 2020 pandemic so many of us were awakened to the frightening discovery that we were ill-equipped and ill-prepared for shutdowns and restrictions. Sunday worship went online, but we had little idea of how we were going to disciple our children, witness to our neighbors, lead in our businesses or serve in the community effectively without a regular in-person Sunday service. Perhaps more than any other experience, COVID revealed how unprepared we are to function effectively as followers of Jesus. It took a pandemic to awaken us to the principal call of Jesus—the call to be and to make disciples.

Making disciples is still the call of Christ. Whether we have maintained our place on the road or have fallen asleep at the wheel, we all need to be stirred afresh by the call of Jesus to make disciples. All of us need to know how to build a discipling culture. That's what this book is all about.

For nearly 20 years, the earlier editions of this book have helped hundreds of thousands of people around the world build disciple-making cultures in their context. I hope that you'll find this new fourth edition equally useful and that it aids you in joining me to awaken the church so that together we can obey the call of Jesus to be disciples who make disciples.

Part I

Understanding Discipling Culture

1. The Call

I can remember the day quite clearly. I was walking through the Royal Exchange in Manchester—a beautiful building in the center of Manchester, England, within which a theater in the round had recently opened. I was home from seminary, and by chance I saw one of my former youth leaders in the coffee shop. We started talking, and he quickly revealed that he had changed his views on Christianity and no longer believed.

I remember how I felt—so conflicted and confused, but mostly just sad. I understood he was responsible for his own life, but I still found myself wondering if I could have done more for him in his struggles with faith. He was such a great person, but somehow he was unable to connect a sincere belief with the personal and relational conflicts he encountered. He just couldn't work out how to be a follower of Jesus every day. And so he gave up.

That experience marked me deeply, and it was one of many that set me on a course to discover how I could be better equipped to be a disciple of Jesus and how I could more effectively make disciples who could keep going through everything that life brings.

A disciple is someone who learns by following the example of another. And so if we want to be disciples of Jesus, we have to start by looking closely at his life and how he offered his life as a pattern for others to follow. Grasping this will be vital.

Over the first section of this book, we are going to do just this—look closely at Jesus' life and the pattern he demonstrated. Let's begin.

The Spirit Descends

At that time Jesus came from Nazareth in Galilee and was baptized by John in the river Jordan. As Jesus was coming up out of the water, he saw heaven being torn open and the Spirit descending on him like a dove. And a voice came from heaven:

> *You are my Son, whom I love; with you I am well pleased.*
>
> *Mark 1:9-11*

Jesus' work began with the sky being torn apart! This monumental moment in history would change everything.

As the Holy Spirit descended on Jesus, a permanent connection between heaven and earth was made. Now when people met Jesus, the Holy Spirit made it possible for ordinary people to encounter heaven and be changed forever.

Jesus put it this way:

> *The Spirit of the Lord is on me,*
> *because he has anointed me*
> *to preach good news to the poor.*

1. The Call

*He has sent me to proclaim freedom for the prisoners
and recovery of sight for the blind,
to release the oppressed,
to proclaim the year of the Lord's favor.*

Luke 4:18-19

Then he rolled up the scroll, gave it back to the attendant and sat down. The eyes of everyone in the synagogue were fastened on him, and he began by saying to them:

"Today this scripture is fulfilled in your hearing."

Luke 4:21

In Jesus a portal was opened between heaven and earth—a portal that remains open to this day.

And through that portal the gifts of heaven flow—good news, freedom, vision, and favor—for everyone, starting with "the poor"—those whom society considers the least!

The descent of the Spirit on Jesus marks a gigantic shift in the world—a shift that signifies that, whatever other changes we see around us, the goodness of heaven is available to everyone through Jesus. This should give us enormous confidence as we move through our world.

Yes, there may be turmoil around us—but the way to heaven is open, and the portal through which the goodness of heaven touches the world is permanently available. The Holy Spirit descending on Jesus means that we see in his life all that our Father in heaven wants us to receive. Following Jesus means that we are always in close proximity to this transforming power. We don't even have to understand it—following Jesus means we are connected to the portal of heaven every day in every circumstance.

When I think about my former youth leader, the one I met in the coffee shop in Manchester, I wonder whether he would still be walking with Jesus if he had experienced this!

A World of Seismic Shifts

We live in a world of seismic shifts.

And the tremors are coming more and more frequently.

In the old days, the Ages of human culture developed and changed at a glacial pace. The Stone Age, the Bronze Age, the Iron Age, the Middle Ages all took hundreds of years to develop and evolve into new Ages.

Then came the Industrial Revolution, after which Ages were measured not by centuries but by generations. The Machine Age, from 1880 until the end of the First World War. The Atomic Age, from 1945 to around 1970. And of course the Information Age, starting in 1970. Some suggest that we are currently embarking on a new, yet-to-be-identified Age—perhaps the AI Age or the Experience Age.

Change is occurring more quickly than ever before. It was once a novelty that we could email anyone around the world. Now we speak, face to face, at the touch of a screen on a mobile device. Before long, our smartphones and wearable devices will be augmented by the products of the metaverse and virtual reality.

1. The Call

These are big shifts in our experience of life, and they can leave us reeling in their wake. Beyond this, social and political upheavals around the world, heralded by every news outlet and recorded on every social media platform, only serve to further enhance the uncomfortable feeling of breathtaking change. Perhaps the most common reaction to this level of upheaval is to find the comfort of like-minded people who give us a sense that we are not alone with our unsettling feeling that the world is out of control. But as we find like-minded souls who experience the world as we do, we so often underline and enhance the social and political divisions happening all around us—the divisions that made us feel insecure in the first place.

As Christians we have to deal with these seismic shifts like everyone else, and of course we also have to deal with the same desire for security we find in the groups we belong to. But no matter where we fall on the spectrum of faith (Protestant. Catholic. Conservative. Mainline. Evangelical. Postmodern. Emergent. Neo-reformed. Neo-orthodox. Fundamentalist. Ancient Future. Neo-monastic. Seeker-sensitive. Seeker-aware. Bible-believing. Charismatic. Dispensationalist. Progressive. Deconstructionist.) one thing connects us—Jesus and our desire to follow him.

Endless things divide us theologically, philosophically, practically. Some of those divisions are very real and quite important. But for all of the things that divide us, the culture around us is a shared experience, and our desire to follow Jesus as his disciples unites us.

The Challenge of the Call

Several years ago, my team and I commissioned a study to get to the heart of the questions that keep Christian leaders up at night. Our goal wasn't to figure out what divided us. We wanted to figure out what we are all experiencing together as Christian leaders.

What we found wasn't that surprising, but the singular voice with which these questions were asked was nothing short of stunning. The questions that surfaced were:

- What does the church of the future look like?

- How do we reach people who don't know Jesus?

As we dug deeper, continued to listen carefully, and pieced together what people were saying, another question surfaced.

It was a question that people tiptoed around and found difficult to articulate explicitly. Yet so many responses indicated the desperate need for an answer to this question. No one asked the question out loud, perhaps because no one had the courage to ask it out loud. Frankly, it seemed that no one wanted to admit to not having the answer.

But it's the question that everything else hinges on.

And the answer to this question leads to the future of the church. It's the answer that teaches us how to reach people who don't know Jesus. It really is the answer to everything.

This is the question, and of course you know what it is: *How do we make disciples?*

For some of us, the issue is that either we haven't realized

1. The Call

we should be asking this question, or we can't seem to push ourselves to ask it. It's almost as if it's embarrassing to even mention it, because we feel it's something we should have figured out by now. After all, aren't we the most educated people who have ever lived? So why are we wrestling with such a simple question, and why don't we have good answers for it? After all, this question is at the core of every other question we ask about the church and our world.

Christian research organizations[3] in recent years have investigated how the church is recovering from the COVID shutdowns, and the questions being asked by church members and leaders sound very familiar:

- How do we grow the church of the future?
- How do we include children in the church?
- How do we make sure the church of the future survives?
- How do we reach people who don't know Jesus?
- How do we reach the next generation?
- How do we change things for the better in our society?
- How do we reach those parts of society marked by evil and oppression?

The answer to all these "How do we....?" questions is the same: By making disciples.

And it doesn't only apply on a macro level; it is just as relevant in our specific contexts and our everyday lives.

And that begs a follow-up question: if so many questions are

---
3   The Barna Group has led the way in this research

answered in the call to make disciples, how do we do it?

There Is No 'Plan B'

The problem is that most of us have been educated and trained to serve, build and lead the organization of the church. Most of us have actually never been trained to make disciples.

Church classes, training seminars, and seminary degrees teach us to grow the number of volunteers, develop new systems of member assimilation, and lead Sunday morning programs. They train us to teach classes and preach sermons.

But we have been educated and trained for a world that no longer exists. The seismic shifts have changed everything.

None of us were trained to make disciples through online worship in a pandemic, or in the upheavals caused by the cries for social justice, or during wars that have impacted everything from gas prices to world hunger.

And yet when we read the Gospels and examine the life of Jesus, the call is clear. It never wavers and never changes: Make disciples.

Here's the thing that can be difficult to wrap our minds around:

If you make disciples, you always get the church.
But if you make a church, you rarely get disciples.

Most of us have become quite good at the church thing. But recent experience underlines the realization that making disciples—the thing that Jesus cares most about—is an art that

1. The Call

most of us have never really learned.[4] It's not about church attendance or budgets or buildings. Jesus wants to know if we have learned to do the thing he gave all of his time and energy to achieve—how to make disciples.

Many of us serve in or attend or even lead in churches where we have hundreds or even thousands of people showing up on Sunday. But in all of this, we have to honestly answer this question: Do the lives of the people in my church look like the lives of the people we see in Scripture? Do they look like disciples?

Are we just good at getting together once a week and maybe into a small group, or are we actually good at producing the types of people we read about in the New Testament? Or have we shifted our criteria for a disciple to someone who shows up to church, gives money, and occasionally feeds poor people?

Jesus made disciples and got the church, and so we can definitely conclude that effective discipleship builds the church, not the other way around. We need to understand the church as the effect of discipleship and not the cause. If you set out to build the church, there is no guarantee you will make disciples. It is far more likely that you will create consumers who depend on the spiritual services that religious professionals provide. Rather we should make disciples and see the emergence of the most glorious thing—the church of Jesus Christ!

Do We Have A Missional Problem?

For almost a generation, "missional" was a buzzword in and around the church. This led to self-declared missional

---
4   We'll unpack this idea in more detail throughout this book.

churches or missional programs or even missional small groups and an upsurge in the multiplication of all kinds of missional communities. In some ways, the overuse of this word combined with its poor definition resulted in it falling out of favor. But it's worth asking whether this over-usage led to greater missional impact on society. Do we see growth in outreach to the margins of society? Do we see the church making breakthroughs among the under-resourced and underrepresented? Is society being impacted by the message of Jesus more today than it was in past years?

The thing is, I don't believe we have a missional problem or even an outreach problem in the Western church. We have a discipleship problem. If you know how to disciple people well, it will always result in a Jesus-centered mission. Always. Because mission and discipleship are inseparable, Jesus wants us to "go" (on mission) and "make disciples." Somewhere along the way, we started separating being on mission from being a disciple, as if somehow the two could be separated. Granted, we should focus the mission on people who don't know Jesus yet. But Jesus himself gave us the model for doing that: Disciple people. If you actually know how to make disciples, you'll reach people who don't know Jesus. Because that's simply what disciples do. That was Jesus' whole plan: you make disciples, those people do mission in their everyday comings and goings. And as the Spirit works through those people doing the things he did in the life of Jesus, the church emerges.

It All Starts With Making Disciples

Jesus has not called you to build his church. In fact, in all of the Gospels he mentions the church only two times. One time

1. The Call

he mentions it, and it's about conflict resolution. The other time? To say that he will build his church.[5] Our job, our only job and the last instructions he gave us, was to make disciples.[6] And out of this we will get the church. Out of this the future will emerge, and out of this will come a missional wave the likes of which we have never seen.

Clearly we need to learn how to build a culture that naturally multiplies disciples, trusting that all the necessities of building a church are taken care of by Jesus. And then we need to learn how to lead that culture, removing the obstacles to growth and spiritual fruitfulness, adding the necessary spiritual nutrition to aid our collective learning, fulfilling the call to teach and preach. This pattern of building a culture and then leading it is what this book and its companion *Leading a Discipling Culture* are all about.[7]

What It Feels Like

This book features a lot of practical tools, but if you look at it as a how-to book, your chances of success are frankly not great.

You could start with chapter 2 and go all the way through the last appendix, put everything you read to work, and still find it difficult to make disciples.

---

5   Matthew 16:18

6   Matthew 28:18-20

7   Many people have asked that I write an accessible book on how to lead a culture of discipleship. In the past I have created separate resources to discuss multiplying missional leaders, establishing missional communities, and leading Kingdom movements. Now these resources are combined into one volume, *Leading a Discipling Culture*, that serves as the companion to the book you're reading now.

That's because making disciples requires texture, not just structure.

Think of it this way: which would be more fruitful?

Trying to grow a vegetable garden in a damp, dark basement

Or growing a vegetable garden in a yard with plenty of sunlight and rainwater

You have to have the right environment, the right soil or culture, for the garden to thrive.

Just as garden plants thrive in the culture of abundant sunlight and rainwater, the culture in which discipleship thrives is family. Certainly the soil is important to the fruitfulness of any seed if the parable of the sower[8] is anything to go by!

For more than 30 years, I have done missional discipleship and have trained thousands of people around the world in it too. Time and time again, I've seen it takes more than the right structure to really make disciples. What really mobilizes discipleship—what fertilizes discipleship and helps it grow—is the texture of family.

In the movement of discipleship and mission worldwide, we have come to talk about this in terms of Family on Mission. It's the texture of discipleship that allows the structure to do its job. Family on Mission is the music to the lyrics of discipleship. Family on Mission is how we stop thinking of discipleship as a task that we do and start living out discipleship as a way that we are. Family on Mission is how we stop doing discipleship as a class, program, or curriculum, and start living it as a way of life.

---

8   Matthew 13:1-23

1. The Call

Family has become a front-and-center concern in the emerging generation as they wrestle with the experiments of past generations that has emerged in the artifacts of culture in movies, games, and media of various kinds.

I have been fascinated by the popularity of various dystopian dramas and the emergence of superhero franchises like *The Walking Dead, The Hunger Games, Divergent, The Avengers, Guardians of the Galaxy,* and *Black Panther's* Wakanda. So often there is a self-described extended family constructed of blood and non-blood relationships that can only survive in a perilous world if everyone contributes and works together. Parental figures are no longer seen as threats, but more as flawed mentors who are fun and productive to have around. The children no longer spend all their energy to compete for affection; rather, they collaborate for common goals.

The dystopian worlds of *The Walking Dead*, *The Hunger Games* or *Divergent* may be overdone, but the emerging generations genuinely fear that the overconsumption of the Boomers and the inactivity of Gen X have left them with starkly uncertain futures full of uncontrollable problems. Even a cursory glance at the most recent offerings of the gaming, TV, and cinematic industries suggests that the emerging generations believe that we may need heroes and heroic families to meet the challenges of the coming day. In a world full of change and uncertainty, we all need the stability and strength that only a team or family can provide.

Wherever they can, the emerging generations are seeking the succor and security of the extended family, even if these are chaotic and dysfunctional in nature. From missional communities to homesteading, "framilies" to blended families, and collectives to collaborations, the emerging generations show a distinct desire to shake loose the rampant consumerism and deconstructionism of the past and move toward a reconstruction of the extended family—using the human and relational tools from the past and the present.

The pandemic appears to have prompted a greater acceptance of a trauma narrative in defining our lives, and with our reliance on the nuclear family being called into question in recent years, we have instinctively turned to the extended family as the best place for achieving our goals and healing of the hidden wounds we all carry. What this creates is a way of viewing our life from the perspective of what happened to us rather than simply describing life in terms of what we have done. In itself this does not appear significant, and yet if we recognize that discipleship is essentially about learning how to hear what God is saying in our past and present and making decisions about how we are going to respond in the relationships he has given us, then this new emphasis can enormously enhance our work as disciple-makers.

All of this tells me that, if those of us who seek to build our lives around the call to disciple-making will do so in the context of Family on Mission, we will push on a door that the emerging generations are only too willing to open, according to recent Barna research into Gen Z's openness to spiritual conversation. We will lift up something they are longing to see. We will do something they are already deeply committed to emulating. And so I'm very encouraged, and what I see in my current work only adds to this sense of confirmation.

I talk at length about how we have created this kind of Family on Mission in my book of the same name, so I won't

1. The Call

cover that ground again here. But I can't help but note how vital this concept is as I talk about how we make disciples.

What It Looks Like

In the upcoming chapters of this book, I'll share the vehicles, language, and basics of how I have learned to make disciples over the past 30-plus years. I learned to do this in the crucible of post-Christian Europe. These ideas and practices sprang up in an environment where less than 1% of people were attending church, and still a missional revolution began. What I have found over and over again is that if we will disciple people, it always leads to mission. I've seen this in Europe, in Africa, in South America, in Asia and yes... in the United States. So many different vehicles have emerged for this disciple-making movement. Today it can be face-to-face work in church groups or one-on-one in the "third place" of the coffee shop. It can even function in the virtual space of the online meeting connecting people from divergent cultural and geographical backgrounds.

But in all of this reflection let me be clear:

I am convinced that Jesus' model for seeing heaven touching earth, for seeing the Kingdom of God advance in community, for seeing the world put to rights, and for seeing people becoming his followers and included in the family of God, was discipleship. Period.

That was his whole deal. So if you're counting converts, budgets, or buildings first and foremost, you're not counting the things that Jesus counted, and you're not counting the thing that will change the world: Disciples.

Of course I'm not saying that what you find in this book is the only way to disciple people or even the best way. This method has worked in shaping me and teaching me how to be a learner who learns from Jesus, and has now successfully shaped and transformed communities all over the world. It isn't a perfect system, because there are no perfect systems (which is particularly true when you realize discipleship is a relational endeavor depending on broken people depending on the grace of God!). To put it another way, this is a description of disciple-making, not a prescription of the only way to do it. I simply and humbly offer this book and my journey as a possible way of moving forward and once again taking seriously Jesus' call to make disciples.

2. The Challenge

The call to make disciples is clear. But the challenge that keeps us from making disciples is not really a misplaced focus on weekend gatherings or even a misunderstanding of mission.

The challenge is within me. The challenge is within you.

This foundational principle is clearly revealed in the story of Jesus. Scripture make it clear that Jesus lived a sinless life in which he recapitulated the entirety of human experience, and in so doing revealed the things that we need to attend to first. Jesus begins his ministry by submitting to baptism, and in this he hears the affirmation of his identity, the confirmation of his heavenly Father's call, and the manifestation of the Holy Spirit's empowering presence. From his baptism, the Holy Spirit leads him into the wilderness to be tested by the Devil, who brings to him the fundamental temptations faced by all human beings. Having overcome the enemy in this initial battle, Jesus emerges from the wilderness full of the power of the Spirit, declaring and demonstrating the kingdom of God.

Jesus was tempted in the wilderness of Judea, an incredibly challenging environment in which to live. As with Jesus, it is often in challenging environments—when we are most under stress—that we find ourselves most tested. For us this is where we discover our personality traits, behavioral tendencies, and individual weaknesses. Many of these things are deposited into our lives as the result of past trauma. Trauma functions like an erosive force in our lives, leaving behind sedimentary layers that weigh on us emotionally, relationally, intellectually, and spiritually. Over time these layers can become stratified within us, often influencing and at times shaping the way that we connect with others and with God.[9]

For me, the layered effect of past trauma has often been shaken or even broken up in times of challenge, giving me opportunity for personal renewal and an experience of new life. The fault lines produced in these layers of past trauma through my times of personal shaking have offered an access point for God's Spirit, so that my testimony is like that of Paul when God said to him:

"My power is made perfect in your weakness."

2 Corinthians 12:9

For all of us, these times of personal shaking reveal much of how we need to grow as followers of Jesus, because such times reveal the internal obstacles we face to being and making disciples. Of course, our enemy will seek to exploit these frailties and try to tempt us off the path of discipleship. He tried to do it to Jesus, as he sought to distract him from following the Father's mission. We can be sure that if he tried it with Jesus, he'll definitely try it with us—whenever he gets the opportunity.

---

[9] You will see how this happened in my life in the Personal Word at the end of this book, along with what I'm learning from my weakness exposed by trauma.

2. The Challenge

What Keeps Us From Becoming Great at Making Disciples

A few years ago, my wife Sally and I felt sure we should decentralize our work with 3D Movements and release the movement to be resourced and led from local churches around the world. Although we had lots of confirmation for this move, we had significant opposition from some within our own team. This, when added to the fairly continuous hatred and opposition we received online and the prospect of significant personal financial loss, caused us real internal conflict and, for me in particular, the painful feelings of isolation and abandonment. These layers had built up over many years of challenge and trauma.

The devil had a field day! I found myself tempted in all kinds of directions I had not experienced before. I felt terribly vulnerable. The most common temptation was to defend myself from the personal attacks in emails, blogs, social media posts and even old-fashioned letters in the post. The Lord had made it very clear to me that I was to trust him for our future—not to defend our actions, but to trust him for both financial security and personal defense.

Of course I desperately wanted everything to work out for all concerned, but I also discovered a deep need I had not recognized before—the need for the approval of others, especially those who didn't like what I was doing. The need for personal approval daily tempted me to move off the path of obedience. It was a deeply troubling and painful time for both Sally and I. Sometimes we did well with the temptation; other times we didn't. So it was a great comfort to know that Jesus trod this path before us. He was able not only to meet us in our pain, but also give us an example of how to move forward following him.

> *For we do not have a high priest who is unable to sympathize with our weaknesses, but we have one who has been tempted in every way, just as we are—yet was without sin.*
>
> *Hebrews 4:15*

We can see in the life of Jesus how important it is for us to take hold of the nature of temptation as we follow his example and learn to be his disciples. No sooner had he been announced to the world and projected onto the stage of world history in his baptism than he began to wrestle against the devil's wiles.

At once the Spirit sent him out into the wilderness, and he was in the wilderness forty days, being tempted by Satan. He was with the wild animals, and angels attended him.[10]

As we join the animals and angels in the wilderness with Jesus, we learn about the temptations he faced and how he overcame them. We are able to follow his example in tackling the biggest challenge to *building a discipling culture*—the challenge of each person, of me and of you.

The tendencies that make us susceptible to temptation sit at the core of our being. We must understand the nature and power of temptation if we are to become great at making disciples. Thankfully, Jesus shows us how.

In the beginning, when the world was still young, the Lord looked upon the crown of his creation—the first man and the

---

10   Mark 1:13-14

2. The Challenge

first woman—and did three things: he gave them his Approval, he satisfied their Appetite, and he gave them a task that could capture the Ambition he had given them. In Genesis 1:28-29, the Lord blessed them (approval), gave them everything they needed (appetite), and established them as his representatives to rule on his behalf (ambition).

As the Son of God incarnate as a human being, Jesus becomes our representative, forerunner and guide. In his baptism, Jesus, the Second Adam, heard the same three things the Father communicated to the First Adam[11]:

- The Father's approval: "this is my son"

- The Father's commitment to protect and provide: "whom I love"

- The Father's pleasure in Jesus' plans and intentions, expressed by saying that he was "well pleased"—that is, he is proud with what his son is and what he intended to do.

These three things:

- Approval

- Appetite

- Ambition

---

11   Luke 3:22

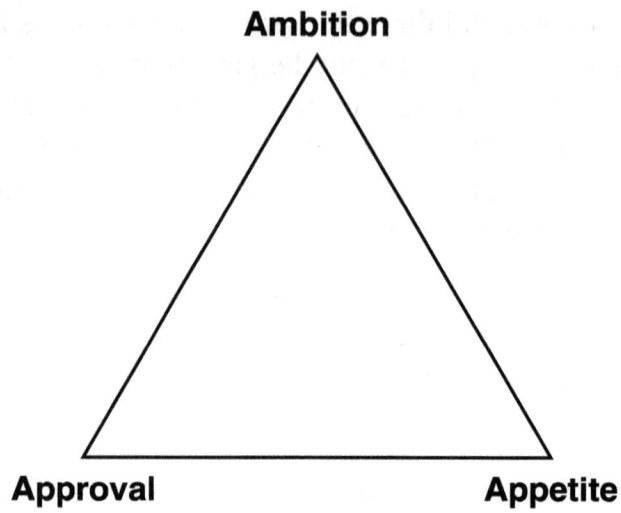

These are the defining marks of our humanity—the humanity that Jesus came to share. We need God's Approval, and our Appetites need to be satisfied by him as we recognize their presence in our lives and surrender them to him. In the same way, Ambition needs to be directed by God so that we can fulfill our heaven-given destiny as his children.

The heroic lives of the Desert Fathers and Mothers in the fourth and fifth century, inspired by the life of their spiritual forerunner Anthony the Great—as recorded by the remarkable theologian Athanasius around 360 A.D.—gave themselves over to prayer and solitude to battle in prayer on behalf of themselves and others with these three fundamental temptations.

Approval, Appetite and Ambition under-gird our existence, and so of course Jesus embraced these three things as he recapitulated our story and restored these expressions of our humanity and put them in their rightful place. To do this he was willing to be tested, tempted, and tried. Jesus entered the wilderness—a picture of what the world had become

2. The Challenge

since Adam and Eve left the Garden of Eden—and the devil did his best to subvert him as he had subverted the first man and woman.

"Turn these stones to bread," the devil said. In other words: "Rely on yourself for the needs that are so obvious to you, now that you're hungry." Appetite.

"Throw yourself from the highest point of the Temple." Or: "Demonstrate God's affirmation of you as his angels catch you on your way toward the ground." Approval.

"Take over all the kingdoms of the world; just let me stay on the throne of the world," the devil said. He meant: "You can easily fulfill your desire to reach every nation—just do it my way." Ambition.

I'm sure that like so many others, you and I wrestle with these basic temptations—we all struggle with them and often fall victim to them. So let's see how following Jesus' example and listening to Jesus' words in the desert help us face, fight, and redirect these temptations.

Appetite

"Man does not live on bread alone but by every word that comes from the mouth of God."

Matthew 4:4

In these words Jesus revealed that he trusted in God's word as a means of his personal sustenance.

Creation is the means of our physical support, and it depends on God speaking it into being. Jesus said he would wait for God's word and trust in the Father for all the provision he needed. In other words, he wouldn't try to make anything happen, and he wouldn't allow his needs or his natural human desires for self-preservation and provision to define his behavior.

How often have we made things happen— turning stones into bread—and missed the miraculous provision of God in our mission?

I can remember being convicted when I asked a rich man (who liked me) for money to help with my work in an inner-city community. I knew that I was not trusting God but was trying to turn stones into bread. I called this man and asked for his forgiveness. I didn't want to use any influence gained by friendship or leverage I might have had with a kindhearted Christian who wanted to do good. I felt convicted to trust in God and what he wanted to bring about and not myself. By waiting and trusting that God would supply all the needs of the mission, I saw a much more valuable thing emerge in the desert of that inner-city parish—the local community getting behind the work of the mission in their neighborhood. That episode helped me learn a lot about turning my appetites over to Jesus.

Approval

For me the internal battles that surround the issues of approval are just as foundational to an effective life on mission.

The Devil took Jesus to the highest point of the Temple and challenged him to demonstrate his special relationship with God by jumping off, expecting God to send angels to catch Jesus.

2. The Challenge

The Devil was bold enough in this challenge that he even used scripture to support his argument![12] Such a demonstration of the Father's favor would have certainly secured the approval of the crowds. Jesus rebuffed this temptation telling the devil that no one should put God to the test. In this challenge, Jesus dealt with the tendency we all have to seek the approval of others before that of God.

In his first temptation, where the Devil tempted him to turn rocks into bread, Jesus established that he would be dependent on what God said rather than anything else. In this temptation, Jesus affirmed that he believed the Father's approval was never in doubt.

If Jesus had failed this essential test, he would never have been able to challenge the religious hierarchy of Israel or be free from the expectations of the crowds who followed him. Jesus lived in the certain knowledge of the Father's approval and so was able to fulfill his mission.

Being on mission with Jesus will always place us in a position where other people's approval of our behavior could be in doubt. As I've already revealed, I've certainly felt this pressure in my own life of mission.

At times I have come to dread the all-too-common questions like, "Have you seen what was written about you in that blog?" Or "Have you seen what they're saying about you on Facebook and Twitter?"

The unkind and often untrue things that other Christians, seeking to function as self-appointed church watchdogs, have said have been deeply wounding and traumatizing. It's one thing

---

12   Psalm 91:11-12

for someone to disagree with my theology; it's an entirely other thing to be accused of intentionally dividing or destroying other people's congregations. Of course I tried to ignore or make light of such accusations as my initial strategy, but in time the signs of heightened anxiety became my close companions—sleepless nights, irritable behavior, constant dry mouth, and even heart palpitations—became so common that I barely noticed their presence until they were eventually relieved. In the end it felt like the only option available to me was to abandon certain social media platforms entirely and not to read anything online that referred to me by name.

Knowing the Father's approval and being free from the need for other people's approval is the key to being free to find the right method, the right word, or the right action in our missional context.

Hearing the Lord's approval ringing in our hearts—"you are my child whom I love"—orients our inner lives toward him. His whispered words of love keep our internal compass fixed in his direction.

Without this internal security, we will find it difficult to see the breakthroughs that will only come when we risk other people's disapproval.

Ambition

There is such a thing as godly ambition, and there's also such a thing as ambition that is the opposite. The problem with the latter is that it's usually hidden. But just because it's hidden doesn't mean it's not there!

2. The Challenge

During the temptations of Jesus, his ambition was tested. He wanted his Kingdom to rule the world—he still does. The devil (the current "prince" of "this present darkness") offered him that very thing, just as long as he was allowed to remain in his position of authority and power.

People have often wondered whether worshiping the devil[13] was really a temptation for Jesus. The old English word from which we derive the modern word worship simply means to give honor and worth. What the devil really wanted was to remain hidden behind the veil of human activity as the architect of the world's systems. The offer to Jesus was still to fulfill his ambitions, good as they were, as long as the devil was able to fulfill his.

But, of course, Jesus did not come to compromise or to collude with evil but to conquer. Conquer with love.

Jesus expressed his ambition to his first disciples as he commissioned them to replicate and multiply his mission.[14] This is our ambition—and it's good. But we will always be tempted to hide other ambitions beneath it—for example, the ambition to be rich, or powerful, or beautiful. In and of themselves, these ambitions may not be particularly heinous, but when hidden behind a godly ambition, they become the controlling motives of what we do.

In 2 Corinthians 10:4-5, Paul said that these kinds of thoughts should be taken captive, and the arguments and pretensions upon which they are built should be demolished.

Fulfilling our call to participate in the mission of God will

---

13   Matthew 4:8-9
14   Matthew 28:18-20

always require ambition, but a healthy spirituality will hold us on the path of transparency and keep us from too quickly colluding with our more base desires.

Perhaps, like me, you need to hold yourself accountable to others in the ambitions that you embrace. As someone who has led countless discipleship huddles down through the years, I have found these words from Psalm 139 particularly helpful:

> *Search me, O God, and know my heart; test me and know my anxious thoughts. See if there is any offensive way in me, and lead me in the way everlasting.*
>
> *Psalm 139:23-24*

These three temptations of appetite, approval, and ambition are the best strategies our enemy the devil has to offer. He tried his best to tempt Jesus from his course and he uses the same temptations in our lives individually and collectively.

Of course with Jesus, the devil failed. With us? Not so much.

For most of us one of these great temptations represents our fundamental point of weakness, and our underlying brokenness. For me it is ambition. Which one is it for you?[15]

---

15 In Appendix 2, I dive deeper into these three temptations, specifically in how they connect to the Enneagram personality types.

3. Jesus' Way of Connecting

When viewed from the perspective of social history, it's quite clear that the early church had a huge impact on the culture and social fabric of the Roman empire. Rodney Stark in his various publications on the subject suggests that as much as 50% of the Roman empire's population had become Christians by the time of Emperor Constantine in the early fourth century. It's also clear that the vehicle of this mission was the Christian household. The model for how the Christian household became so effective is found in the ministry of Jesus, as he joined the family of Peter and Andrew; and visited the household of Lazarus, Martha, and Mary.

As much as anything that Jesus did in his earthly ministry, he was a community builder. Using the raw materials of human relationships, he constructed the infrastructure of a community of mission that would change the world.

The relationship-building methods of Jesus have not always been the subject of intellectual inquiry, yet it would seem quite obvious that, along with studying the inspired words and the miraculous works of Jesus, we should become familiar with his way of doing things if we're to understand how he made disciples. Interestingly, the first name given to the early church was "The Way," indicating that the first followers of Jesus understood that being in a journeying community imitating the life of Jesus was essential to the life of a believer.

From the outset Jesus made disciples by building relationships that formed a community committed to his mission of kingdom transformation. And he did this in a particular way—a way we can imitate. To help us understand how he did this, let me use an illustration drawn from an entirely different time and place.

Monty Roberts spent his youth in the high prairies of the United States rounding up wild mustangs. He'd watch his abusive father tie the new horses to a post with a bridle and rope, then frighten them with a blanket so they would attempt to run away. By repeating this process over and over, his father was eventually able to break the spirit of the horse and control it in any way he wanted. As with another popular way to break a horse, by tying it to a tree or post and beating it until its will was broken, submission to the master was key.

Recognizing that what he was observing was the same abusive method his father used in disciplining him, Monty began to believe there had to be another way to train a horse. Compelled by his own trauma and internal wounds, he sought something more effective and more compassionate.

So he took to the plains.

Monty observed how the wild horses communicated with each other, particularly observing how the lead mare behaved as a new horse attempted to join the herd. Even when a young stallion—with greater physical attributes than the mare—attempted to join the herd, the lead mare would turn toward

3. Jesus' Way of Connecting

him, flatten her ears and look directly into his eyes: the language and posture of challenge. At this the stallion would stop his approach toward the herd. After the challenge, the mare would then turn her flank toward the new horse and lift her ears, offering invitation. This was a distinct posture of vulnerability, because when she exposed her flank, she exposed the part of her body that predators could more easily attack. It was a position of trust and openness. The young stallion, given this invitation, would inch closer. Then the lead mare would turn toward the young stallion, flatten her ears and make direct eye contact: Challenge again. After repeated invitations and challenges the new horse would adopt the posture of a juvenile horse, a foal, pawing the ground and bowing in submission.

This process of invitation and challenge would continue until the two would eventually touch (an exhilarating moment that Monty called join-up), and at that point, the young stallion would be admitted to the herd.

Monty began exploring whether he could replicate the process of alternating between invitation and challenge in training a horse. He found that when he acted like a lead horse, the other horses adopted a submissive posture. When he squared his shoulders the horse stopped when he exposed his flank, the horse inched closer. He simply imitated what he saw the lead mare doing.

Monty was able to fully train even the most abused horse in minutes, observing the process can be a deeply moving experience. His gentle "horse-whispering" was in marked contrast to his father's harsh and abusive control.[16]

---

16 See the documentary *Monty Roberts: A Real Horse Whisperer*, Ridiculous Pictures, 1998.

Now, this type of horse-whispering approach of invitation and challenge is used to rehabilitate prison inmates. In Wyoming, a program to care for wild horses teaches inmates nearing release to "gentle" horses. As the inmates are invited to work with horses, they are challenged to learn to better respond to their lives–to learn a better way to live from another's example. They don't call this program discipleship, but it sure looks a lot like it to me.[17]

Invitation and Challenge

In less than three years, Jesus was able to disciple a group of men and women, most of whom no one else would have chosen, and teach them to be and do like him in such a way that, when released, they changed the course of human history.

How was Jesus able to do this without breaking them and having them all running for the hills? How did the call to change the world not absolutely overwhelm them?

Simply put, Jesus built community by being the ultimate horse-whisperer. He was able to create a community of discipleship in which there was an appropriate mix of invitation and challenge and in which his disciples were able to flourish. After many months of building trust and community through the careful calibration of Invitation and Challenge, Jesus was able to usher in moments of remarkable breakthrough.

This is beautifully illustrated in Matthew 16 as Peter receives the revelation that Jesus is the Son of God:

---

17 "The Wyoming Honor Farm," *60 Minutes*, first aired March 12, 2023, https://www.cbsnews.com/news/wyoming-honor-farm-wild-horses-60-minutes-2023-03-12/

3. Jesus' Way of Connecting

Jesus replied:

> *Blessed are you, Simon son of Jonah, for this was not revealed to you by man, but by my Father in heaven. And I tell you that you are Peter, and on this rock I will build my church, and the gates of Hades will not overcome it. I will give you the keys of the kingdom of heaven.*
>
> *Matthew 16:17-18*

In affirming Peter, Jesus is inviting him to draw closer. But Jesus takes it even further. Jesus gives him the name "little rock." (Peter, when translated from the Greek word Petras, appears to mean "little rock"). At the end of the Sermon on the Mount, in the Parable of the Wise and Foolish Builder, Jesus referred to himself as the Petra... the "big rock." Jesus is the big rock; Peter is the little rock. Jesus was sharing his identity with Peter as a covenant partner with God.[18] The same relationship that Jesus has with his Father, Peter now has with the Father. Peter was being invited into a deeper relationship with Jesus, even to the extent that he was offered the keys to the Kingdom and by that given access to Jesus' authority and power. It must have been an incredible moment for Peter. In the words of Monty Roberts, this is a real join-up moment!

Probably emboldened by the depth of relationship that Jesus was offering, Peter took Jesus aside and suggested that he stop speaking about dying in Jerusalem. In response Jesus brought challenge:

---

18 From my book *Covenant and Kingdom: The DNA of the Bible*

> *You are a stumbling block to me; you do not have in mind the things of God, but the things of men.*
>
> *Matthew 16:23*

Time and time again, we see Jesus functioning as a classic horse-whisperer, inviting his followers into an intimate relationship with him while at the same time also initiating a direct challenge to behaviors he knew were either wrong or unhealthy. In his love for them, he drew his disciples closer, but also gave them the opportunity to accept the responsibilities of discipleship.

Invitation and challenge was the method Jesus adopted to build his discipling culture. He constantly calibrated both to produce disciples who could imitate his life. For instance, in Matthew's Gospel, Jesus says:

> *Which of you, if his son asks for bread, will give him a stone? Or if he asks for a fish, will give him a snake? If you, then, though you are evil, know how to give good gifts to your children, how much more will your Father in heaven give good gifts to those who ask him!*
>
> *Matthew 7:9, 11*

Being promised good gifts to those who ask is definitely an invitation.

> *If anyone would come after me, he must deny himself and take up his cross and follow me. For whoever wants*

3. Jesus' Way of Connecting

to save his life will lose it, but whoever loses his life for me will find it.

Matthew 16:24-25

Of course, all the talk about losing is most certainly a challenge.

Invitation: In John's Gospel, Jesus says:

In my Father's house are many rooms; if it were not so, I would have told you. I am going there to prepare a place for you.

John 14:2

Challenge: Responding to Philip's question about this, Jesus says:

Don't you know me, Philip, even after I have been among you such a long time? Anyone who has seen me has seen the Father. How can you say, 'Show us the Father?'

John 14:9

This is an example of a deeper truth in the work of invitation and challenge demonstrated by Jesus—the tight connection between both postures. In many ways it is true that inside every invitation there is a challenge, and within every challenge there is an invitation. For instance, when we look at our first example, Jesus changing the name of Simon son of Jonah to Peter, he offers Peter the keys of the kingdom. I think most people would find this very exciting and very challenging at the same time. But when we look at Jesus talking about taking up our cross—a very challenging statement —he includes the promise that we will find life—a beautiful invitation hidden within the challenge!

Invitation is about being invited into a relationship where you have access to a person's life and all the vibrancy, safety, love, and encouragement that resides there. You learn from the places you clearly see Jesus at work in a person's life, which you can see only by having access to them. But by accepting that invitation, you also accept the challenge that comes with it: The challenge to live into your identity as a son or daughter of the King.

Jesus created a highly inviting but highly challenging culture for his disciples to function and grow within. If we are going to build a culture of discipleship, we will have to learn to calibrate invitation and challenge. Jesus horse-whispered his disciples all the time, leading them around what we call the Leadership Square.[19]

Fundamentally, effective leadership is based upon an invitation to relationship and a challenge to change. A gifted discipler is someone who invites people into a covenantal relationship with him or her, but challenges that person to live into his or her true identity in very direct yet graceful ways. Without both dynamics working together, you will not see people grow into the people God has created them to be.

I use the following matrix to help leaders understand the reality of the types of cultures we create in our churches:

---

19 More on this in the second part of this book.

3. Jesus' Way of Connecting

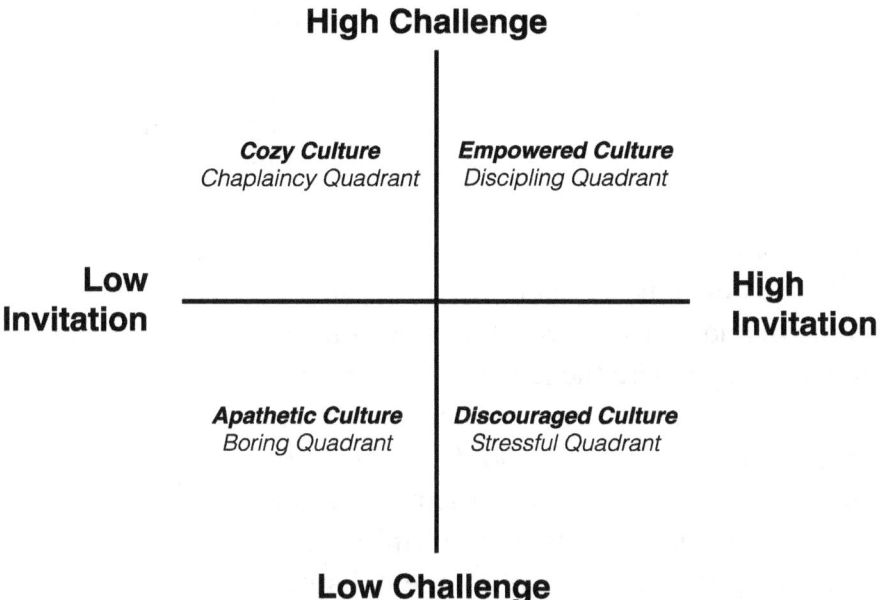

When looking at this matrix, we begin to understand why we've had such a difficult time discipling people in our churches. Many churches, as they seek to create comfortable environments in the form of worship services or small groups, have lost their ability to challenge people in meaningful ways.

Challenge may be given from the pulpit or stage on Sunday mornings, but challenge is always given best in the context of personal relationships.

We have the ability to hear a difficult sermon and decide not to do anything about it. Just because someone preached or taught on forgiveness doesn't mean anyone is holding us accountable to forgive people in the next week. If I don't want to do it, no one will know or say anything. The space is comfortable, inviting, and by-and-large anonymous. We can take what is said or leave it. In other words church worship services cannot be our only discipleship strategy!

The same thing is true of most small groups. While small groups are excellent at creating community and a warm, comfortable environment, they are not usually built to also offer challenge. Small group leaders are supposed to be facilitators of discussion and conversation, creating a culture where people who are new (and perhaps not Christians yet) can immediately come in and feel safe. What new person would feel safe coming into a group where the leader challenges them all the time? The new person didn't agree to that kind of relationship. So while many churches say, "We do discipleship in our small groups," the fact of the matter is that their small groups are missing one of the main ingredients of a discipling culture: Challenge. I'm not saying that having environmental spaces like small groups aren't important; I'm simply saying discipleship as Scripture defines it doesn't necessarily happen there. If the pandemic taught us anything, it is that many people were poorly discipled by their churches because so many left the church as soon as the regular Sunday and weekday offerings were removed. Many, many people were simply unprepared to stand without the support structures of Sunday church.

Now here's the thing.

If we have churches with warm, cozy, comfortable, inviting environments, someone is paying the price to make sure that happens. That means for all of the invitation that is offered to a large portion of the church, another group is shouldering all of the expectations and challenge of producing that kind of atmosphere. Church leaders. Pastors. Staff. Elders. Deacons. Board members. Volunteers. Whatever your church has. Usually 15–20% of the people are doing almost all of the work. Because

3. Jesus' Way of Connecting

of that, the experience of these people is extremely high on the challenge side of things but very low on invitation. What space is there for these people to receive encouragement, rest, downtime, and investment? Every week has to be bigger and better than the last! So these people are constantly discouraged, frustrated, and stressed. Burnout is normal, as is a high degree of turnover.

I'm sure that, if you're reading this book, you're above average as far as spiritual commitment is concerned. And my guess is that you can place yourself in this scenario and agree quite readily that you are often very busy, maybe even at times overextended while the majority of believers around you seem to put in very little effort compared to you! Of course it's easy to get bitter and judgmental about the situation, but that's not going to solve it either. For me discovering a way to see myself as a follower and partner with Jesus has been the key to finding a solution. Hearing the call to be followers who become partners is a process all of us will go through as we follow him.[20]

It doesn't really matter in which of these two quadrants you are currently functioning. Neither is the ideal way in which Jesus wants you to lead others. From working with thousands of church leaders from all over the world, I have observed one certainty—no one creates a discipling culture, modeled on the life and ministry of Jesus, by accident.

No one accidentally creates disciples. Discipleship is an intentional pursuit.

Learning how to balance invitation and challenge appropriately in the lives of those we are actively discipling will

---

20 Chapter 12 on The Square will show us one way to do this.

be a difficult task, but it will also be extremely rewarding. If you want to free people from the captivity of the client/provider relationship we've seen emerge in the church and create an empowered/discipling culture, it must be viewed as a must-win battle. We should expect and appropriately plan for some degree of failure, aim for "low control, high accountability," and invest all we have in creating empowered leaders who can function as producers rather than consumers. In general, organizations and institutions like churches work with a high control/low accountability culture. This is because it's easier to control the delivery of programs than invest in the development of people.

Of course, Jesus continues to use the same methods of invitation and challenge to develop his disciples. He made it clear that the Holy Spirit would function as our discipler after his ascension,[21] and so we can expect the Holy Spirit to continue this working in our lives. I know it's certainly been true with me; on a daily basis I'm aware of Jesus speaking to me by his Spirit through the Scriptures and in prayer. He continues to calibrate both invitation and challenge so that my relationship with him deepens and my capacity to imitate him increases. Of course, like everyone else. I'm particularly conscious of him doing that at crucial moments in my journey of faith. I can still hear him saying "let me do it" when as a young man I was recovering from third-degree burns in a hospital bed. In the midst of my frustration and embarrassment at causing such injuries to myself, I found myself also deeply depressed at my apparently fruitless ministry. His words communicated through the testimony of John Wimber transformed my life. The words "let me do it" meant that the challenge of seeing so little fruit from my life of mission became the invitation to come closer

---

21   John 14:16

3. Jesus' Way of Connecting

to him and allow him to produce the fruit I longed to see. And that changed everything! Within weeks I saw revival in every area of my life!

It has rarely been so dramatic, but very few weeks go by without me sensing the gentle challenge, and gracious invitation of Jesus as I worship, pray and read his word.

When Jesus committed to developing his team of disciples he understood—often with real frustration—how long it would take to produce people who could do what he did.

> *"O unbelieving and perverse generation," Jesus replied, "How long shall I stay with you and put up with you?"*
>
> *Luke 9:41*

Surely we can expect to have at least the same level of frustration as Jesus experienced, but in the long run being able to develop people who will be able to imitate us as we imitate Christ will be an enormous win![22]

As G.K. Chesterton once said, "If a thing is worth doing, it is worth doing badly."[23] No one was born as a great disciple maker. It takes time and practice. You are, right from the start, going to be better at either invitation or challenge and will need to learn how to do the other well. But because discipleship is worth it, it's worth not being great at it from the start so we can learn to do it well over the long haul. Of course, maintaining

---

22   1 Corinthians 11:1
23   G.K. Chesterton, *What's Wrong with the World Part 4, Education: Or the Mistake about the Child–14, Folly and the Female Education* (Dodd, Mean and Company, 1910).

this kind of humility will also demonstrate that we are committed to the same posture those that we disciple will need to adopt. Everyone in a discipling culture—those that lead and those that follow—will need to adopt Chesterton's axiom that if it's worth doing, it's worth doing badly.

Put simply, building a culture of discipleship is the only way you will produce the kind of community that Jesus and the New Testament writers would recognize as church—a dynamic, living organism with sufficient organization to enable it to function effectively, yet remaining an authentic community that is full of the life of God. A community where hearts are open to the Lord, to one another and to a world in need.

During his time on earth, Jesus epitomized the church he wanted. Jesus demonstrated in a flesh and blood way how his followers should be a community that reflected his life:

Jesus went out to a mountainside to pray, and spent the night praying to God. When morning came, he called his disciples to him and chose twelve of them…He went down with them… A large crowd of his disciples was there and a great number of people…who had come to hear him and to be healed of their diseases.[24]

His church was to be like this—a community of disciples living in a constant dynamic relationship with his Father with other disciples and a lost world. He made this explicit when he said:

---

24   Luke 6:12-19

3. Jesus' Way of Connecting

"I tell you the truth, anyone who has faith in me will do what I have been doing. He will do even greater things than these, because I am going to the Father.

John 14:12

4. Community

Jesus was an amazing teacher. He was able to shape ordinary people into followers who would represent his message and his way of life to the world. To do this he used all of the methods of great teaching—methods that until recently had not been fully explained. For instance, Jesus used all of the spaces of human interaction—the contexts of relational engagement that anthropologists might call the intimate, personal, social, and public spaces.[25] Jesus was an expert in sharing his life in all of these spaces. With the three disciples in the inner circle, he shared intimate spiritual experiences. With the 12 and the group of women who walked with him, he constantly shared words of nurturing faith. Among the larger group of disciples described as the 72, he shared his life of mission. Then of course, beyond these circles of followers he taught the crowds of followers who would hang on his every word, Jesus was a master practitioner in all of these spaces of human interaction and learning.

The Greek word for "disciple" is *mathetes*. When directly translated, it means learner. Scripture really seems to be getting at something here, something about orienting our lives around

---

[25] The science of this, called Proxemics, was initiated by anthropologist Edward Hall. wikipedia.org/wiki/Proxemics

becoming lifelong learners of Jesus. It is liberating to think that, with God's Spirit, over time, we can learn the ways of Jesus, doing the things that he did, while becoming the kind of person who more fully reflects his character in our daily experience. It doesn't happen overnight, and the expectation of Scripture is that it's a process that we need to hold onto and live into.

> *To the Jews who had believed him, Jesus said, "If you hold to my teaching, you are really my disciples."*
>
> *John 8:31*

As Dallas Willard so aptly put it: "Discipleship is the process of becoming who Jesus would be if he were you."

Now what's fascinating is that, when you really start to dig into the subject of learning theory, you discover that we as humans are hard-wired to learn things. Imitation is central to the process, but it is supported by information and an immersive experience that allows us to innovate as we learn. What's of particular interest to me is how we see these things play out in the Gospels over and over again.

There seem to be at least three different environments in which we learn, environments that Jesus was a master in curating and integrating. He seemed to understand that we learn best when there is a dynamic interplay between each learning environment. These environments are:

- Classroom/Lecture (passing on of information on what to think about)

- Apprenticeship (revealing how to do things)

- Immersion (an environment where the what and the how

4. Community

are lived out)

Classroom learning is when information, processes, and facts are taught from teacher to student in the classic classroom setting. Apprenticeship is when someone learns a certain set of skills by imitating someone who has already learned the skills. Immersion is when someone is put into an environment, setting, or culture and learns by intuitively picking up what he or she sees and experiences there. Immersion is, of course, another form of imitation; it's just not as one-on-one an experience as an apprenticeship.

The classroom experience is based on passing on facts, thoughts, processes and information.

A teacher in a university English literature class wants people to understand James Joyce when they read Ulysses, so the instructor teaches on Joyce's standard kind of writing: Stream of Consciousness. A biology teacher wants his or her students to understand how energy is manufactured on a cellular level, so the instructor teaches the different parts of the cell, spending a special amount of time on the mitochondria.

We get this. We know this. We grew up in this. Information is passed on in a rather didactic manner, from the teacher to the students.

However, most of us recognize the limitations of this way of learning.

For instance, if you are learning to become a plumber, you can take hours upon hours of classes, with scads of information on how plumbing systems work, how to deal with leaky sinks and blocked pipes. But there is a huge difference between knowing about how to fix a pipe and actually fixing a pipe. At a certain point, the head knowledge from the classroom isn't enough.

This is why apprenticeship is so important for the process of learning.

You don't simply learn to fix a sink by reading about it; you actually have to go out and do it. Inevitably, however, you probably won't be able to fix everything on your own or figure everything else out. That is why many professions have apprenticeship programs as part of their process for accreditation and employment. Essentially, an apprenticeship is stating, "If you want to learn how to do this, you're going to need someone to show you how to do it. Information is good, abstract theory and concepts are incredibly helpful, but this actually has to work in the real world."

So we have Master Plumbers. Master Electricians. We have developed a whole medical learning experience where students don't simply go to medical school and learn about surgery; they have residencies during which they apprentice themselves to someone to learn to do what they do. I don't know about you, but I don't want someone operating on me who has only head knowledge.

In life, when we want to learn how to do something, we find someone with real flesh and blood and have that person teach us how to do what they do.

In many ways, the practice of apprenticeship is about investment. Someone invests their time, energy, skills, and life into ours, teaching us to do what they do.

The last way educators and sociologists say we learn is

4. Community

through immersion.

If you want to understand this, just watch toddlers learn to talk. Exactly how did they go from babbling nonsensical phrases to stringing together words and sentences, asking questions and conveying thoughts and feelings?

There wasn't a class.

They really didn't apprentice themselves to anyone.

Over time… it just… happened.

Suddenly they can talk!

This process is called immersion, and it is the subtlest way of learning. This is obviously where our learning environments and personalities are powerfully shaped. If you're a foreign exchange student, it is perfectly normal to tell hilarious stories when you are back at the dorm with the other students.

"You'll never believe what I accidentally said today."

"Are you serious? You really called them that?!"

"Yeah, well at least it wasn't as bad as that thing that happened a month ago. I had no idea what that woman was saying, but she looked like she wanted to kill me."

We are learning by immersion.

But slowly, over time, those students become fluent in the language. This is the power of immersion.

When we gather together a group of people who are competent at their craft or skill and introduce people into the culture who are learning those skills they will slowly learn simply by being immersed in the environment. It happens slowly, subtly, almost under the radar. But it is happening. You learn things, pick up tricks of the trade, and learn the language of that culture simply by being in the middle of it. Immersion teaches and shapes in powerful ways that are sometimes hard to even see.

The key to immersion is having access to the culture you are hoping to shape you.

Dietrich Bonhoeffer has probably written more to help us understand the nature of discipleship than anyone in the past few hundred years, particularly in his book The Cost of Discipleship and his short, but brilliant, book Life Together. However, it is in studying Bonhoeffer's actual life that much of his writings come alive. Recently, Eric Metaxas released a biography on Bonhoeffer. Consider this quote by Otto Dudzus, one of the men Bonhoeffer was discipling:

> *Whatever he had and whatever he was, he made that accessible to others. The great treasure he possessed was the cultivated, elegant, highly educated, open-minded home of his parents, to which he introduced us. The open evenings [his house was open for his disciples and family to come, eat, play music and sing together, discuss, laugh, tell stories on Friday nights] which took place every week had such an atmosphere that they became a piece of home for us, as well.*[26]

---

26 Eric Metaxas, *Bonhoeffer: Pastor*, Martyr, Prophet, Spy (Nashville, TN: Thomas Nelson, 2010).

4. Community

Then, Metaxas notes:

> *Even when Bonhoeffer went to London in 1944, his parents continued to treat these students like family, including them in the larger circle of their society and home. Bonhoeffer did not separate his Christian life from his family life. His parents were exposed to other bright students of theology, and his students were exposed to the extraordinary Bonhoeffer family.*[27]

This is what access looks like. This is how people learn, through immersion, the nuances of being a disciple. People are given access to a discipling culture.

Sociologists agree that learning best happens when there is interplay between all spaces of learning. You have to learn the cold, hard facts because they actually mean something and have practical implications. By apprenticing yourself to someone, he or she teaches you how to take things that are only in your head and put them into practice in a way that produces something. You can go from poorly skilled to quite skilled fairly quickly by having an excellent apprenticeship. And if you are able to combine those two things with an immersion experience where the language, the nuances and the everyday uses are learned intuitively... Well, that is a powerful combination.

What's the best way to learn a foreign language? More than likely, it's going to be a combination of all three. You'll want to learn the basics in a classroom setting before moving to Madrid. Take Spanish 101, 102, and 201. Hire a tutor who is fluent and can work with you on the nuance of the language. Finally, move to a culture where the language is fluently spoken, and over

---
27 Ibid.

time, probably over a two-year period, you will become fluent. It takes all three methods of learning.

Any parent who had a child try to learn from home when COVID quarantines forcibly closed schools knows the limits of merely transmitting information. Students lagged in test scores around the world because, while they mostly heard curriculum information from virtual school, they had no chance to imitate teachers and peers through apprentice-type learning, nor were they able to immerse themselves in subjects. Clearly information was not enough.

It is probably fairly obvious to see where all of this is leading, right?

As we know it today, discipleship is mostly about that first kind of learning: the classroom experience. And really, that's about it.

We learn from the pastor's teaching on Sunday. We learn from Bible studies. We go to Sunday School. We learn from small group discussion guides, online coaching and YouTube. We learn from reading books. We learn from taking classes at church.

Notice that all of this is completely information driven, in some sort of classroom-esque experience. There is virtually no apprenticing happening in our churches.

But shouldn't there at least be immersion happening? After all, we have millions of Christians in the United States regularly gathering together. They come to a worship service on Sundays. They gather as small groups, hopefully they are actually friends outside the small group, and maybe they take a class every once in a while. How is that not immersion in a community? We tell

4. Community

people to join a small group because that's where discipleship happens and where they can find community. We're at least expecting some immersion to happen, right?

The hard reality is that immersion works only when people are actually fluent in something.

For instance, a toddler is never going to learn English if she's hanging out only with people who don't know English themselves or if she hangs out only with other toddlers. Likewise, because most churches have so few actual disciples running around, there simply aren't enough disciples at churches to create a quality immersion experience.

The way most churches have structured the discipleship process is as if we are saying, "If I can just get the right information into their heads, if they can just think about it the right way, then they will become more like Jesus."

Right Information + Right Behavior = Discipleship

But think about it practically: How successful has that actually been for us?

Or think about it like this: Would you trust a doctor to perform open-heart surgery on you who has had only classroom experience and no residency? Yet that is how we have structured our discipleship processes!

Most church leaders I know, after hearing this, usually say the following: "Well, we can't be responsible for feeding them. They need to learn to be self-feeders. They have to be responsible for being disciples. I can't do it for them." There's a little truth in that, but I think it fails to acknowledge the complexity of the problem.

Getting people to a place where they can nourish themselves with the Bible, through prayer, community, and other spiritual disciplines doesn't happen just because we tell people that's how they can nourish themselves spiritually. That's like telling third graders that, in order to function in school, they need to learn to write in cursive, but offer no in-depth way of teaching them to do this. And to be clear, kids don't learn to write in cursive because the teacher gives a 30-minute lecture on how to do it.

One of the problems that occurs when people become Christians is that we either explicitly or implicitly give them a list of things to do that we think will help them become "self-feeders" (admittedly, I believe "self-feeders" is a terribly unhelpful term):

- Read your Bible
- Pray
- Tithe
- Go to church services each week
- Find a small group (or whatever your church does)
- Tell your friends about Jesus

Think about it. Aren't we making some pretty gross assumptions here?

Why do we assume, when telling people to read their Bibles, that they will know how to read Scriptures well? Why do we think they know what in the world to do with this gigantic book

4. Community

that somehow introduces us to the "Living Word"? Jesus often quoted and taught from the scriptures, but the most important thing for the disciples was experiencing how he lived out his teaching. He could have taught a lot about reinterpreting the law of Moses, but until his disciples saw him healing on the Sabbath (and by so doing disagreeing with the rabbinic view of what should be done on the Sabbath), it would have been difficult for them to get it.

We tell people to pray. We teach sermon series on prayer. Maybe we teach classes on prayer. But we forget that Jesus' own disciples had no clue how to pray like Jesus and they grew up in an incredibly immersive culture that was focused on prayer. Something about the way Jesus prayed was so profound, so connective, visceral, and life-giving, that they said, "Please, please teach us to pray like you!" Prayer should be the easiest example of this disconnect for us to understand.[28] We are asking people to talk to an invisible person as if he were observably right there! People really need help with this, and more than just a sermon, class, or book.

Why are we assuming that simply by giving people information (pray, read the Bible, read doctrinal statements, be a part of a small group), they will actually know how to do it or can figure it out by themselves? I can read a book on how to run an emergency room in a hospital, but if you turn up with a gun wound, do you want me to operate on you?

We have become so enculturated in our Cartesian, Western worldview that we believe knowing about something and knowing something are the same thing. What we have managed to do is teach people about God. Teach them about prayer. Teach

---

28   Luke 11:1-2

them about mission. But the point isn't that they should just know about discipleship but to know the discipler. Just listening is not going to get the job done.

We don't want to just know about God; we want to know God. In the same way that we don't want to collect random facts and nuances about our spouses, we want to know them through and through. That's why Paul seems to give this guttural cry:

> *I want to know Christ and the power of his resurrection and fellowship of sharing in his sufferings.*
>
> *Philippians 3:10*

Discipleship isn't a random assortment of facts and propositions and behaviors; discipleship is something that is you to the core and is completely incarnated in you. If it is information, it is information that has worked its way into you and is now part of you, in the same way that John talks about the logos being wrapped up in the person of Jesus:

> *The Word became flesh.*
>
> *John 1:14*

It goes from being information to being knowledge that is experienced as we put it into practice. This is how Jesus puts as he concludes the Sermon on the Mount—his big statement of how discipleship should work:

4. Community

Therefore everyone who hears these words of mine and puts them into practice is like a wise man who built his house on the rock.

Matthew 7:24

Yet almost all churches have built a whole discipleship process on that first style: classroom teaching. Hear the sermon. Join the small group. Go to the membership class. Read your Bible (hopefully you figure out how to do it). Go to class 201 or 301, and "yes, we have classes for that."

Of course our churches aren't seeing the life, vibrancy, and power we read about in the Gospels and Acts. No one has a clue how to do the things that Jesus taught his disciples to do! Most people know they should be doing these things. Most people know these things are important. We would even guess that most want to know how. But knowing I have a broken carburetor in my car's engine that needs replacing isn't the same as knowing how to put a new one in! In the same way, there's a big difference between knowing forgiveness is central to Jesus' message and actually going out and forgiving your dad for what he did to you when you were a kid. Knowing something in your head alone is never what Jesus was after. The truth of Scripture is meant to be worked out in us, not something that we hold as an abstract reality.

We don't want people to understand forgiveness or prayer or mission or justice only intellectually. We want people who can forgive, who can hear and respond to God, who actually know him. We want people who have hearts that break for our world and the people in it and do something about it. We want the kind of people in our communities who resemble the people we see in Scripture.

How Jesus Taught His Disciples

Clearly Jesus was a master discipler, he fully understood what was needed in each context for his disciples to be fully formed. In this he demonstrates a knowledge of the spaces of human interaction and learning that the behavioral sciences have only recently come to understand.

I can remember as a young theological student being told that the report from the parish that I was training in was that I was good at communicating in a public setting, and to some extent with groups, but as yet had not learned the skills of one to one discipleship. I can remember being really quite challenged and chastened by that thought but from that day committed myself to trying to become competent in all areas of discipleship and learning.

Perhaps there's one particular context that you are strong in and another that you're weak in. Perhaps like me you need to concentrate your efforts to become more competent in certain contexts. The great thing for us as disciple makers is that we have the 'greatest of all time' who we can readily observe in the gospels, and he's even sent his Spirit to help us learn what we need to learn to become the expert disciplers we desire to be.

Jesus really was the GOAT (greatest of all time). Seriously, just look at what he did!

He called twelve guys and a group of women to follow him and be his *mathetes*... his disciples... to be learners of him. People who would learn to do all of the things he does and

4. Community

somehow learn to carry his very essence through the ongoing work of the Holy Spirit.[29] And by this change the world forever!

Now many of our sources for rabbinical practices don't really start to appear until the end of the first century, but it seems fairly reasonable to assume many of these things were happening among other groups of disciples at the same time Jesus was leading his disciples.

Disciples at this time learned to do every last thing that their Rabbi (teacher) did.

How many steps did he take on the Sabbath? That's how many they would take.

How many hours did they memorize, ponder, and meditate on Scripture each day? That's how many hours they would, and it's how they would interact with the sacred text.

How did they treat their wives? That's how they would treat their wives.

How did they raise their kids? That's how they would raise their kids.

You get the picture. They were very detail-oriented and quite precise, right down to the length of their hair, prayer shawls, eating, sleeping, and bathroom habits. In almost every way that we can imagine, the life of the Rabbi was transferred into their lives. Obviously, these disciples had their own personalities that shone through, but this was the way it was done.

So when Jesus was asked by his disciples in Luke 11 to teach them how to pray as he prays, this is not a strange request.

---

29 John 14:12

In fact, their comment was,

> *Teach us to pray like you do; after all, John taught his disciples to pray like he did.*
>
> *Luke 11:1*

Jesus didn't give them another sermon on prayer. He taught them to pray like he did. By their behavior, the disciples seemed to say: "If I do the things that he does, I can feel fairly certain I'm going to have a good outcome, and my life may actually look more and more like his." This kind of thing probably happened quite a lot. Obviously, apprenticeship is happening here.

You want to learn to be a mechanic? Find a Master Mechanic and do what he does. You want to learn to be a disciple? Find someone with a life that resembles the life of Jesus and do what he or she does.

This is what the disciples were doing, and I think Jesus understood what was going on and intentionally initiated this process. What Jesus says in Matthew 11 indicates this:

> *Come to me, all you who are weary and burdened and I will give you rest. Take my yoke upon you and learn from me, for I am gentle and humble in heart, and you will find rest for your souls. For my yoke is easy and my burden is light.*
>
> *Matthew 11:28-30*

If you know first-century Roman Palestine at all, you know

4. Community

that at least 80% of the people were involved in farming. This was an agrarian-based economy, and Jesus regularly used stories and metaphors drawn from this culture. This passage is no different as he references a yoke in a way that people would easily understand, as it was their normal experience.

When it was time to plant the crops, you needed to be able to plow. The massive, wooden plows were quite heavy, and usually only a team of oxen was able to drag the plow through the field, tilling and preparing the soil for the seed that would come next. Obviously, the team of oxen pulled the plow together and was held together by a yoke that bridled them.

What these farmers did was partner a young, very energetic ox with a much older, seasoned ox that had plowed the fields for many seasons. The farmers found that the younger ox would push quite hard at the beginning of the day, using up all of his energy, and would have nothing left for the second half of the day. Remember, we're talking eleven-to-twelve-hour workdays. However, when bridled with an older, more experienced ox, the younger ox would be forced to learn the rhythm and pace of the day. He couldn't run ahead because he was bridled to the older ox. And so eventually the young ox learned the best rhythm from the older ox so he could last for the whole day and keep an even, sustained pace. The rhythms of life were passed from one to the other.

Eventually, the younger ox would grow older, have more seasons under the metaphorical belt, and would then be paired with a new, younger ox. The cycle would continue.

Eugene Peterson's translation really lifts off the page, as it taps into this word picture:

> *Are you tired? Worn out? Burned out on religion? Come to me. Get away with me and you'll recover your life. I'll show you how to take a real rest. Walk with me and work with me—watch how I do it. Learn the unforced rhythms of grace. I won't lay anything heavy or ill-fitting on you. Keep company with me and you'll learn to live freely and lightly.*
>
> *Matthew 11:28-30, MSG*

When you see this picture that Jesus is referencing and then see how Jesus was constantly teaching and showing his disciples how he lived, very clearly a high level of apprenticing was going on.

Jesus preaches the Good News, heals the sick, cleanses the lepers, and drives out demons. In Luke 9, he sends out the twelve to do the same. They've seen him do this for months now. In Luke 10, he then sends out the seventy-two. The disciples almost seem astounded that his stuff is working in them!

> *The seventy-two returned with joy and said, "Lord, even the demons submit to us in your name."*
>
> *Luke 10:17*

It's as though they had been thinking, "We know Jesus can do this, but seriously… us too?"

On one occasion the disciples reported back to Jesus that they were having issues with one spirit that just wouldn't leave.[30] You can almost see Jesus casually shrug his shoulders and say,

---

30 Mark 9:17-29

4. Community

"Oh yeah, that one... well, with that one you need fasting and prayer before you deal with it."

This is what apprenticeship looks and feels like.

And of course there is classroom learning as well. Remember, the Sermon on the Mount (which is basically Jesus' Teaching 101 on the Kingdom of God) is directed to his disciples.

> *Now when he saw the crowds, he went up on a mountainside and sat down. His disciples came to him (some translations actually say, "those apprenticed to him came to him") and he began to teach them.*
>
> *Matthew 5:1*

Jesus is constantly teaching his disciples. Always giving penetrating insights from Scripture, thoughts on reality and the world we live in, and speaking to the character of his Father.

Teaching is incredibly important. Theology is incredibly important. Doctrine is incredibly important.

But Jesus didn't compartmentalize teaching, theology, and doctrine into ethereal, cognitive realities. Teaching and theology were ways of describing reality, and then he showed his disciples how to live in that reality. "What is reality? The Kingdom of God! And if you do what I do, you can live fully in that reality."

So how was immersion happening?

The better question might be to ask when wasn't it happening. The disciples were almost always with Jesus.

But even the way in which Jesus allocated his time gives us an important insight. Jesus had what many scholars call his Retirement Ministry, a period of time that was dedicated completely to the disciples, when he retreated to places the crowds would never follow, when the disciples could be immersed in relationship and have complete access to him. Here's the interesting thing: Most people think that at least eighteen months of Jesus' public ministry was this time.[31]

That means at least half of his time was spent with these twelve guys.

They were a Family on Mission.

Jesus believed so powerfully in discipleship that he basically put all of his eggs into that basket. (It's worth noting that it paid off.)

Often, immersion is about learning the nuances and finer points of something. You learn big chunks of information in the classroom experience and you learn how to develop specific skills in an apprenticing relationship, but with immersion, you see how all of these things start to connect together in even the smallest things.

A good example would be when Jesus first met Andrew, the brother of Simon Peter. When he and "another disciple" (believed by many to be John), introduced themselves to Jesus, and showed interest in knowing what it meant to follow him, he simply invited them to spend the day with him. And this was at the very beginning of the journey of discipleship. Jesus understood that an immersive experience was a necessary component in the pattern and process of what it meant to be

---

31   Mark 6:31

4. Community

his follower.

The disciples saw a life in Jesus that they wanted for themselves (even if at first they didn't fully understand this).

We find an incredible example of immersion at work in the book of Mark[32] as Jesus enters into his first week of ministry. He drops by Capernaum and does things that seem normal to Jesus but extraordinary to everyone else: teaching with confidence and authority they hadn't witnessed before, healing everyone who asked, casting out evil spirits, and healing Peter's mother-in-law. Just an average day at the office for Jesus. And by the end of the day, word has gotten out into all of Galilee, and the house is flooded with every sick, battered, and broken person in the vicinity. And Scripture says, even as the sun was now down… he healed them all. Not a bad first day of ministry, to say the least. One might say revival had just broken out in Capernaum. Then something very interesting happens.

Before the sun has come up, before it's even dawn, Jesus gets up early and goes to a spot by himself to spend some time resting and talking with his Father. Apparently Peter and the rest of the guys get up, can't find Jesus (chances are pretty good more people have arrived at Peter's in-laws' place, waiting for Jesus to do more teaching and healing), so they go to find him. They finally find him, and Peter, probably pretty excited about his second day (what might Jesus do for an encore?) says, "So, ummm, yeah… everybody is looking for you. Probably might want to make our way back to the house now."

And amazingly, Jesus's response is, "Hmmm. Yeah, I don't think so. Let's leave. We've got other places to go."

---

32 Mark 1:21-38

Seriously?

Now let's be honest here. If we had started something and there were thousands of people who just showed up out of nowhere (on the first day!), if we had seen the things that Capernaum had seen the day before, it's safe to assume we'd start a building campaign. A podcast. A newsletter. A Twitter feed and an Instagram page. A blog. A new website.

And. Jesus. Leaves.

How did he know he was supposed to leave?

Well, early in the morning, before dawn, he got up and spent time with his Father, and then did something contrary to what seems like the reasonable course of action. When we think about it like this, it's kind of baffling that he does this. What we see from Jesus is that success isn't thousands of people and an ever-expanding church.

Success is obedience to what the Father asks.

Sometimes it comes with bigger churches, buildings and popularity. Often it doesn't. It's about obedience. We don't decide what the Father does.

Clearly, Jesus saw Capernaum differently than we probably would have.

Notice we don't have any indication that Jesus says he got the instructions from his Father; we can really only deduce this. My guess is, as the disciples were in an immersion experience with Jesus, they picked up on this, too. It was probably small at the time, very subtle, but I'm guessing they noticed. I'm guessing it further locked in their minds and their spirits what it meant to live in the Kingdom of God.

4. Community

Peter, in Acts 10, up on a rooftop resting and praying, receives very specific instructions about bringing the news of Jesus and his Kingdom to the Gentiles: a man named Cornelius. Since Peter was an orthodox Jew, this had to go against every rationale and cultural fiber of his being. And yet... he went.

This instance seems very similar to the one Jesus lived out. Peter had a plan for reaching the Jews, and yet, because Peter had learned from Jesus, he learned how to listen to and obey the voice of the Father. He had learned that the Kingdom of God operates differently from what we are used to, and he was able to respond.

He chose obedience over what was the most logical route.

John gives us insight into how Jesus lived in constant communion with the Father:

> *Jesus said, "I tell you the truth, the Son can do nothing by himself; he can do only what he sees his Father doing, because whatever the Father does the Son also does."*
>
> *John 5:19*

We may not be able find a passage that gives the details of how Jesus watched for how the Father was working, but when we take his whole life into account we begin to understand how Jesus operated and why Jesus told his disciples to open their eyes:

"Do you not say, 'Four months more and then the harvest'? I tell you, open your eyes and look at the fields! They are ripe for harvest."

John 4:35

Jesus was referring to the evidence of a whole Samaritan town coming out to listen to him after hearing the testimony of a Samaritan woman who had experienced a life-changing encounter with him. He could see what the Father was doing and he wanted his disciple to see what he saw.

This is what success looks like for us as well—seeing what the Father sees. We will learn to do this best by watching others who already know how to do it. And once we see what the Father sees, then we can begin to invest in others and help them do the same.

5. Investing Capital like Jesus

The feeding of the 5,000 is a fascinating example of how Jesus wants us to approach the task of discipleship. He takes what it is that we have to offer (in the case of the disciples, five loaves and two fishes "borrowed" from a young lad) and multiplies it to meet the need of the occasion. This miracle—the only one recorded in all four gospels—is clearly intended to be more than a demonstration of God's capacity to provide for our needs; even more, it is a picture of how he intends to work. In Luke's account, Jesus does something very interesting that might give us a clue to the deeper meaning:

> *Taking the five loaves and the two fish and looking up to heaven, he gave thanks and broke them. Then he gave them to the disciples to set before the people.*
>
> *Luke 9:16*

Christians from the liturgical traditions of the church would recognize this four-fold action as identical to what Jesus does in the Eucharist or Last Supper, which he initiated as he celebrated the Passover on the night before his death. Jesus takes the bread, blesses the bread (gives thanks for the bread), breaks the bread, and gives the bread.[33] This is a picture of his life being taken, blessed, broken, and given by his Father as an offering for the sin of the world. But it is also a picture of how Jesus takes what we offer, blesses it, breaks it, and gives it as we partner in his mission to make disciples.

We have seen how Jesus surrendered his life to be taken in use for the Father's mission. We've seen the incredible blessing his life was to those who encountered him. And of course we are familiar with the breaking, beginning in the Garden of Gethsemane concluding on the Cross of Calvary. Here the breaking of Jesus' body opens into the giving of his life—first through the forgiveness of sins and continuing as his resurrection life is released to all who have faith in him through the impartation of the Holy Spirit. This becomes our model as we offer ourselves in response to the great gift of Jesus so that we too can be taken, blessed, broken, and given to the task of the continuing mission of Jesus to the world.

Jesus wants to multiply what we offer in his mission, but it almost always involves a costly sacrifice. This will feel like a breaking in the midst of the blessing.

If you're anything like me and the many leaders I have worked with, the more you reflect and pray through this calling to make disciples, the more daunting the challenge feels. It's not like we can avoid the message—it's expressed in so many ways. For instance, when we read the parables of Jesus and the teaching that surrounds them, the challenge doesn't seem to diminish at all. Quite the opposite! Apparently if we want his kingdom life—pictured as a pearl of enormous value or as treasure buried in a field—we have to give everything we have.

---

33 1 Corinthians 11:23-25

5. Investing Capital like Jesus

This was demonstrated in the lives of his first disciples, who, when he called them, left everything to follow him.

This kind of investment does come with significant personal cost—a cost we will need to fully embrace if we are to see this work grow.

Much of my own work has been spent developing young women and men to become discipling leaders. This inevitably means that many of them have moved to other places and fresh pastures. It can be difficult at times to feel as though you are growing great leaders to benefit other people's ministries! Unless we are able to see our work of making disciples as a kingdom investment for a kingdom return, we will become reluctant to pay the price to pull it off.

It's perhaps for this reason that Jesus emphasized that the final and full return on our investment is seen in the consummation of the kingdom on his return.

In the parable of the talents, it's when the master returns that the servants receive their reward for investing the capital he had given them.

> *His master replied, "Well done, good and faithful servant! You have been faithful with a few things; I will put you in charge of many things. Come and share your master's happiness!"*
>
> *Matthew 25:23*

Jesus doesn't appear to be interested in limited investment. If we are to receive his greatest gifts, we have to give all of our resources to receive them.

Building a Discipling Culture

If it's going to require such a significant investment, then we need some kind of plan, some kind of framework, that will help us along the way. In this chapter I want to offer you a clear roadmap toward competent, effective discipleship that will help you develop a strategy for continuing the process into the future. By developing a concrete, step-by-step approach, I am not offering a plug-and-play program, but instead a broad framework that will give you pointers about how to take your first steps.

Let's look at it this way.

In Malcolm Gladwell's book Outliers, the central question is this: Why are some people successful? He examines many of the factors that seem to contribute to people being successful, but one thing he gets into, in particular, is of interest to us.[34]

Gladwell seeks to debunk the myth that some people are born geniuses, and because of this can't help but become successful. He shows, with wonderful stories and details, how this has played out in history. His equation for extraordinary people goes something like this: Someone with a certain threshold of competency (you don't have to be a genius) + the right set of circumstances + 10,000 hours of practice (which he guesstimates at about 10 years) = very high chance of success.

Mozart had a musically gifted father (right set of circumstances) and was himself a musical prodigy (threshold of competency). Mozart wrote his first symphony at the age of twelve. But it wasn't until he was twenty-two, ten years and 10,000 hours later, that he wrote his first symphony considered a masterpiece.

---

34 Malcolm Gladwell, *Outliers* (New York, NY: Little, Brown and Company, 2008).

5. Investing Capital like Jesus

Same with the Beatles.

Same with Michael Jordan.

Same with Bill Gates.

Even if you're lucky enough to be born a genius, you've still got to put in the time to learn and understand your craft, as well as walk into the right situation. What I want to do is help you learn the craft of discipleship and encourage you to put in the hours and perseverance necessary to become great at it. After all, that's what Jesus' last words were going after: Make disciples. If there's anything any of us should become great at, it's making disciples who can make disciples.

Investing Wisely

It's worth noting that, after Jesus completed his time in the wilderness being tempted by the Devil, his next step was discovering where the Father was indicating that he could best invest his time and energy. He went to his hometown, Nazareth—a natural starting point—and was immediately rejected. So he moved his operational base to Capernaum, where he knew there were people who were interested. John puts it this way:

> *He came to that which was his own, but his own did not receive him. Yet to all who received him, to those who believed in his name, he gave the right to become children of God.*
>
> *John 1:12*

Those who first received and believed in him were Andrew and another disciple who is often identified as John and Andrew immediately went and told his brother Simon Peter that he had found the Messiah![35] So understandably, Jesus went to their hometown of Capernaum and explored whether they would be his first followers.

As we take on our disciple-making journey, we of course want to understand the challenge of the three A's of Appetite, Approval, and Ambition that we discussed earlier. But as important as this is, making disciples is much more about making positive choices to invest our time and energy wisely. As we consider this, perhaps a good place to begin is by using the tool of the Five Capitals, which will help us identify and to some extent quantify our investment.[36]

Let's look at one example of how Jesus explained this strategy—the strategy that the disciples he was teaching first received. Jesus often used the contemporary language of financial investment to reveal his approach. One of his more challenging parables is an excellent place to start.

> Jesus told his disciples: "There was a rich man whose manager was accused of wasting his possessions. So he called him in and asked him, 'What is this I hear about you? Give an account of your management, because you cannot be manager any longer.'
>
> "The manager said to himself, 'What shall I do now? My master is taking away my job. I'm not strong enough

---

35 John 1:40-41

36 I break down the Five Capitals in much more detail in my book *Oikonomics*. What follows here is an overview of this strategy.

5. Investing Capital like Jesus

to dig, and I'm ashamed to beg—I know what I'll do so that when I lose my job here, people will welcome me into their houses.'

"So he called in each one of his master's debtors. He asked the first, 'How much do you owe my master?'

"'Nine hundred gallons of olive oil,' he replied.

"The manager told him, 'Take your bill, sit down quickly, and make it four hundred and fifty.'

"Then he asked the second, 'And how much do you owe?'

"'A thousand bushels of wheat,' he replied.

"He told him, 'Take your bill and make it eight hundred.'

"The master commended the dishonest manager because he had acted shrewdly. For the people of this world are more shrewd in dealing with their own kind than are the people of the light. I tell you, use worldly wealth to gain friends for yourselves, so that when it is gone, you will be welcomed into eternal dwellings.

"Whoever can be trusted with very little can also be trusted with much, and whoever is dishonest with very little will also be dishonest with much. So if you have not been trustworthy in handling worldly wealth, who will trust you with true riches? And if you have not been

> *trustworthy with someone else's property, who will give you property of your own?*
>
> *"No one can serve two masters. Either you will hate the one and love the other, or you will be devoted to the one and despise the other. You cannot serve both God and money."*
>
> Luke 16:1-13

The best way to tackle this parable is to go backward from the ending. In the very last sentence, Jesus seems to distill the parable into a single statement. When Jesus says, "You cannot serve both God and money," he is saying that we can have only one ultimate point of reference. Eventually, the thing we value highest will win out, whether that is God or money.

He was telling his hearers that their method of assigning value to the elements of the world around them was way off. In fact, this entire parable is about how to value various forms of capital in order to invest it wisely.

Two different kinds of capital are placed in apparent juxtaposition to one another—financial capital (money) and what might be called spiritual capital (God, or, more specifically, a relationship with God as a disciple of Jesus). Over and over, in this parable and in all his other teaching, Jesus shows us that spiritual capital is different from financial capital, and far more valuable and important. He has to repeatedly make this point because the world around him had it exactly the wrong way around. Like us, the people at the time of Jesus tended to value financial capital above spiritual capital. Sometimes they

5. Investing Capital like Jesus

actually equated financial capital with spiritual capital. The general assumption of the day was that if you were rich, it was a sure sign of God's favor on your life. This perspective caused them to make bad investments by choosing money above God.

We can quickly identify these two forms of capital in this parable. But there are other forms of capital in this parable and in the rest of the Scripture. What are they? How valuable are they? And how can we learn from Jesus how to invest them for a return? Let's look more deeply into this parable.

When the manager realizes he is going to be fired, he begins to think about what to do next. During his thought process, he admits, "I'm not strong enough to dig." Here he is contemplating one possible way of gaining financial capital after he loses his job: manual labor. I call this physical capital, the amount of time and energy we have available to invest. The shrewd manager realized that he had very little of this capital to invest and thus decided it wasn't a great option for him.

That makes three capitals: financial (the most tangible and highly valued by people), spiritual (actually the most valuable), and physical (apparently somewhere in the middle).

After contemplating his situation for a bit, the manager comes up with a brilliant idea, one for which he is later praised by his master (which is why this is the parable of the shrewd manager). The manager's shrewdness is actually another form of capital—intellectual capital. Intellectual capital refers to the ideas, knowledge, and creativity we have to invest. The manager used his capacity to think creatively (his intellectual capital) to come up with an idea for how to survive after he lost his job.

The final capital in this passage becomes evident in the

content of the idea the manager comes up with. He uses the last few hours of his authority over his master's financial capital to reduce the debt of several people who owed money to his master. The manager reasoned that this would allow him to be welcomed into their homes after he lost his job. In reducing their debt, he was gaining what can be called relational capital. He leveraged his intellectual capital to come up with the idea of investing financial capital in order to grow relational capital.

The master recognizes the wisdom in this move (even though the manager was scheming with his money) because the manager invests financial, intellectual, and physical capital to gain relational capital. Jesus says this is a great investment. Jesus says it quite bluntly: "Use worldly wealth to gain friends for yourselves."

Many of us wrestle with this verse. Was Jesus really counseling us to buy friends? In fact, I think he was! Jesus is saying it is worth investing your financial capital to grow your relational capital, because relational capital is worth far more than financial capital. That's the punchline of the parable! Jesus tells us to use our money to invest in people's lives so that we get friendship out of it. In other words, recognize the relative value of each kind of capital and make a good investment.

Jesus mentions at least five different forms of capital in this parable (spiritual, financial, physical, intellectual, and relational), and his point seems to be that part of following him and learning to live in the kingdom of God means valuing various forms of capital correctly and then making good investment decisions based on those values.

Think about another economic metaphor Jesus used. He said that a relationship with him, and with the Father through him,

5. Investing Capital like Jesus

is like finding a pearl of "great price,"[37] which far exceeds the value of anything else. It's like finding a treasure in a field. If you find a treasure of great worth in a field, the smart thing to do is liquidate everything so you can buy the field.[38] That's Jesus' message to us about the value of spiritual capital—it's far more valuable than your money and for that matter all other capital, so you will do well to sell everything to get it. Cash it all in for that one thing that is most valuable. It just makes good economic sense!

That is, it makes sense if you trust that spiritual capital really is more valuable than financial capital. The rich young ruler didn't take Jesus' investment advice because he valued financial capital more highly than spiritual capital. Jesus' offer didn't seem like a good deal because he was bringing his own value system into the equation. If we're honest, we have to admit we probably tend to look at things the same way. So Jesus' word applies to us also: spiritual capital is far more valuable than financial capital. Treat it as such if you want to experience authentic abundant life. The New Testament talks about our faith being of far greater worth than gold.[39] So investing my gold to grow my faith should be an easy decision for me.

Of course this doesn't mean that we are careless with our financial capital. In fact, in the passage above Jesus seems to indicate that our ability to invest financial capital wisely is a good indication of whether we can be trusted with spiritual capital. "So if you have not been trustworthy in handling worldly wealth, who will trust you with true riches?" When Jesus says, "You cannot serve both God and Money," he isn't

---

37 Matthew 13:45-46
38 Matthew 13:44
39 1 Peter 1:7

saying you can only have one or the other. He is saying we can only have one most important capital in our lives. Serving money means that financial capital is most important. Serving God means spiritual capital is most important, which allows our money to serve God.[40]

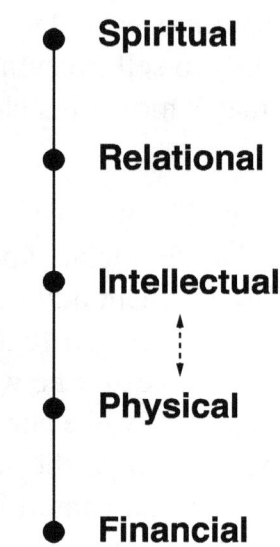

---

40 I have written and spoken about how physical capital is more valuable than intellectual capital, using the logic that if you have a migraine, you can't really think deeply about anything. But now I think that may be mis-ordered. Think about Stephen Hawking—a brilliant mind with absolutely no physical capital. His intellect has influenced the way the entire world thinks. Or think back before technology to Helen Keller—who could not speak or hear yet became an incredibly influential advocate by explaining the needs and desires of those with special needs. It may be that these two capitals—unlike the others—have values that are assigned differently according to circumstance. Perhaps at different stages of life or in different life circumstances these capitals move. In general when we are young, we need to build our intellectual capacity, and so perhaps intellectual capital is ahead of physical capital during this period of life for most of us. But as we get older and our bodies' natural frailty begins to affect our ability to function well, physical capital takes over. It is interesting to consider this as we think about investing all our capital in discipleship.

5. Investing Capital like Jesus

Investment in Action

John says, " We love because he first loved us."[41]

At the last supper, Jesus gave the most remarkable visual aid of his investment in our lives. He was about to offer himself completely—flesh and blood. In the most remarkable visual aid of his investment in our lives, he fully expressed the fourfold action of the Eucharist. He was taken. He was blessed. He was broken. He was given. And all this happened with his complete and willing cooperation. He was about to offer himself completely, flesh and blood, to rescue, redeem and renew the whole world.

As he described the bread and wine as a picture of his life—taken, blessed, broken, and given—he uses a particular word usually translated as "remembrance." In Greek, it's the word anamnesis, which means "don't forget who you are." Everyone's heard of amnesia, or forgetting who you are. Jesus uses the opposite word, anamnesia, telling us, "Don't forget who you are." I think this gives an incredible insight into what Jesus was going to do on the cross. He was about to give himself completely. In that great gift, we will discover the value God placed upon us, and then in that discovery begin to understand who we are in his eyes. When we invest all five capitals in those that we disciple, we express to them, in a way that perhaps nothing else can, the true value to us and to God. And when people know their true value, they can begin the journey of understanding the real identity.

To love is to invest, and when we invest, the call is to use everything we have—all five capitals! Making disciples is the great call—the great commission—and it requires the greatest

---

41   1 John 4:19

investment, an investment that Jesus demonstrated and revealed when he gave everything for us.

6. Finding a Way to Imitate

We ended the last chapter in the shadow of the cross, but of course, that's not where the story ends. There is also an empty grave and an open heaven. The Scriptures make it clear that the resurrection is the demonstration of the great victory won over the enemies that have been arrayed against humanity since the beginning: the enemies of sin, death and the Devil. Jesus rose to new life in a garden tomb, claiming back all that was lost to those enemies since our time in the first Garden.

The empty grave is a sign of victory, a victory heralded in the heavens as they opened to receive Jesus on the day of ascension. Paul tells us that in that journey to glory Jesus distributed the gifts of his grace to his people[42] so that now the whole body of Christ lives out the whole ministry of Jesus, which is the ministry that we will continue until his triumphant return at the completion of all things. The generosity of his grace poured out to us in his death, resurrection, and ascension means that Jesus has given us more than enough capital to invest in the next generation of disciples.

Such truths can be overwhelming, and so we need to find

---

42 Ephesians 4:7-11

ways to live them out in the practicalities of everyday life. To do this I think we need at least two things. The first is a desire to see other people blessed with all that we've been given. The second is an attempt to find ways of making that desire a reality through specific things that we do. Our hopes to see others blessed are one thing; it's another thing to do something about it.

When Sam, the youngest of our three children, was leaving home at 18 to go on a year of mission and adventure, I can remember praying for him at Phoenix Sky Harbor Airport, asking the Lord to multiply to him the many blessings that he had poured out on me. Sam tells me that was one of the most memorable moments of prayer in his life. But of course, such a prayer, however heartfelt, needs to be backed up by practical, concrete things

So at this point, we should get practical and look at some detailed ways we can invest in the lives of others.

In my experience, if you want to make disciples, if you want to build a discipling culture in your community, you are going to need three things:

- A discipleship vehicle (I call it a Huddle)
- An offer of access to your life (the texture of Family on Mission where imitation takes place)
- A discipling language (the discipling language I use is called LifeShapes)

Jesus' model of discipleship was life on life, but not everyone got equal access to him. He chose a team of twelve and a group

6. Finding a Way to Imitate

of women, but even within that team he offered a deeper level of intimacy to Peter, James and John and to others like Martha and Mary, the sisters of Lazarus and Mary Magdalene. Beyond the twelve were the seventy-two, and beyond them were the crowds. How did Jesus manage to balance his time and share his life with so many people looking to him for guidance? How can we possibly do the same?

Put simply, we invite only a few people into a discipling relationship with us. If Jesus invited a small group of people, we're going to assume right off the bat we can't manage as many as he did. And we invite these people into a HUDDLE.

A Huddle is the group of four to ten people you feel God has called you to specifically invest in. You will meet with them regularly (at least every other week) to intentionally disciple them in a group setting. The best discipling relationships always have an intentional, "organized" component to them, as well as a less formal, "organic" component. Having a regular Huddle meeting is the organized component.

Ultimately, I'm talking about creating a discipling movement in the place you live. Huddles do not grow by adding new members; Huddles grow when members of your Huddle start their own. Why do it this way? Because we all want to take seriously the principle that Jesus established: Every disciple disciples. You can't be a disciple if you aren't willing to invest in and disciple others. That's simply the call of the Great Commission.

Practically, I've seen it play out in what I call the 8:6:4 Principle.

In this picture, I gather eight leaders, and eventually those eight leaders Huddle six people each after an agreed period of time (often six to twelve months). The forty-eight leaders in the second generation then Huddle four leaders each once they are ready. If a third level of Huddles is established after twelve to eighteen months, there could be upward of 248 leaders being discipled.

I realize that theory like this often looks great on paper and doesn't often quite work out like this in reality. And while it doesn't work exactly like this in real life, even I am often surprised at how well it multiplies over time when we establish a discipling culture and a vehicle to transport an agreed-on discipling language. For instance, I have a friend who started two Huddles two years ago. One Huddle was part of his local church; the second was for pastors who were interested in learning to Huddle. Two years later, after that small investment in the lives of about ten people, more than seventy Huddles have been started, and they keep reproducing. That's the making of a movement.

Moses and Sarah Mukisa[43] are remarkable leaders of

---

43 Read Moses and Sarah's story at the end of Chapter 10 sharing how they built a movement of discipleship in Uganda.

6. Finding a Way to Imitate

Worship Harvest, a movement of Discipleship and Mission in Uganda that today is touching the world. It took seven years for the culture of discipleship to begin rapidly multiplying through huddles and missional communities. But what began invisibly first in Kampala, Uganda, is today seeing multiple thousands of people ushered into the kingdom by this amazing work of God.

Part 3 of this book is all about the details of what a Huddle is, how it works, how you disciple people in it, and how to multiply them, so more on that later.

While a Huddle is an important part of discipling people, it isn't enough. An organic part of discipling people happens outside a Huddle. That means you need to give these four to ten people much higher ACCESS to your life than other people get or than you are probably accustomed to giving the people you currently lead. You'll need to be strategic with your time if you are going to build a discipling culture that will bear long-term fruit. You will need to simplify your life so you have space for people to be invited into your life and home.

What might this look like?

Honestly, it's usually just inviting them to join what you're already doing. Invite them and their family to have dinner over at your house with your family. We often forget that while we may not consider it discipleship time, it doesn't mean we aren't teaching people what it means to follow Jesus. If we have people over at our house, they are going to be intuitively observing how we parent, how we love our spouses, how we order our lives. We are immersing them in our lives. For immersion to happen, we must give people access to our everyday lives.

Even when we have little time or opportunity to give access, we can find ways of inviting people into our lives. Often when I would visit a church in my years of international travel, I would ask whether there was someone who needed some counsel or coaching who could pick me up, or take me back to the airport. In this way, I was able to use what little time I had available to invest in the people I was trying to help and train

That's why it is crucial that we have a life worth imitating! We are inviting people into our lives and into our Families of Mission, and are asking them to imitate the parts of our lives that look like Jesus.

Giving people access to our lives doesn't necessarily mean we constantly schedule additional time for coffee or drop everything for them at a moment's notice (although depending on the situation, it could mean that). If someone is struggling spiritually, invite him or her to go to the grocery store with you and talk with you on the drive there and at the store as you shop. Fold the person into your normal comings and goings. It doesn't have to mean more work; it means we are more efficient and smart in how we use our time.[44]

This is exactly what we see Jesus doing.

He ate. He taught. He laughed. He healed. He prayed. He told jokes. He told stories. He visited friends. He fed thousands. He partied. He went to weddings. He went to the local synagogues. He went on retreat with his disciples. He cried. He went to funerals. He gave advice. He answered questions. And in all of his comings and goings, his disciples watched him doing this and observed. They were immersed in a life with

---

[44] The book *Family on Mission*, which I wrote with my wife Sally, provides much more detail on how to provide this kind of access while building a Family on Mission of your own.

6. Finding a Way to Imitate

Jesus. It should come as no surprise, then, that we see them doing the exact same things in the book of Acts.[45]

Discipleship didn't stop simply because it wasn't "intentional discipleship time." That kind of compartmentalizing is detrimental to the discipleship process. You are inviting someone into your life to learn how you follow Jesus in all aspects of your life. Giving people access to your life is a necessary component to making this happen.

To be honest, giving people access to our lives can be complicated. Everyone has baggage and personality complexities that makes much of this increased access potentially burdensome. I've often caught myself wondering what I've gotten myself into when yet another person shares their difficulties and problems! What this often comes down to is the tendency I have to try to fix people rather than disciple them. When I disciple others, I have to remember that my job is to help them answer the two big questions of discipleship: What is God saying to me? And, What am I going to do about it? I'm not a therapist, and although it helps me to be trauma-informed as I seek to relate to others, my task is to lovingly point others to Jesus as the solution to life's difficulties'.

The Gospel writers want their readers to understand this about Jesus—they want all who read the story of Jesus to see in his life the answer to our deepest needs the solution to our biggest problems and a pattern of life to follow. History suggests that this is what the earliest Christians believed and we can learn what they understood: that it's possible to learn to live like Jesus, and we do that by answering the two big questions of

---

45 The follow-up to this book, *Leading a Discipling Culture*, will break this down in far greater detail.

What is God saying? And What am I going to do about it?

Lastly, you will need an agreed-on DISCIPLING LANGUAGE that you will teach the people in your Huddle who will build this discipling culture. As we will explore in more detail in Part 2 of this book, language creates culture. We will share with you the language we have developed to create this culture and, in Part 3, explain how to best teach and use this language in a Huddle.

In conclusion, this is how discipleship works—in its simplest form.

As we have already discussed, most of Western culture lives in the Information part of this triangle, believing that Information without Imitation can lead to Innovation. However, Jesus taught his disciples, asked them to imitate his life, and then said, "You will do greater things than me." So when we read the book of Acts, we see the early church doing so many things exactly as we see Jesus doing them. But then we also see the early church taking those foundational things and innovating on them. Jesus' example showed that having the right information was important, and next came competency in using that information, seeing it in the life of another and imitating that person. Only when we achieve a base level of competence in using Information and Imitation can Innovation flourish.

I suspect that, given the current climate of the church, most Christian leaders are very leery of Imitation and apprenticing themselves. Why? There are probably many reasons, but one is because I've seen "cloning" happen within the church. Certain churches are particularly famous, and suddenly everyone is copying what they do, producing less effective, cloned versions of the same church. What inevitably happens for these churches

6. Finding a Way to Imitate

searching for the "as long as it works" answer is that eventually it stops working as well as it once did. However, because they lack the foundational Information for forming the original practices, the churches are unable to successfully innovate what they are doing.

What many have done is jump from ditch to ditch. Rather than taking a posture of learning through Information and Imitation and then Innovating in their own context, they've decided that unless they come up with it themselves, they are selling out. Instead of finding and learning the tried-and-true practices for discipleship and mission, they try to reinvent the wheel.

I want to suggest that if you want to be a disciple, and if you want the people you disciple to be able to disciple others who then disciple others, you will need to follow the path of Information to Imitation to Innovation. Information is incredibly important, but having it right in our heads isn't enough. We need to see how that Information becomes knowledge and is incarnated in the everyday life of another person. We then apprentice ourselves to that person, learning not only the Information but also how to do what he or she does. And finally, after becoming confident in knowledge and practice, we have the capacity to innovate new ways of discipleship and mission.

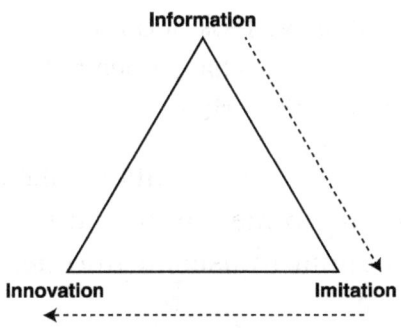

Practically speaking, what does this look like? Well, let's give an example. Most of us probably believe reading scripture and certainly having an intentional prayer time every day are fundamental components of becoming spiritually mature. But telling people to read and pray doesn't mean they can do those things well. So what would you do if someone asked you how to read the Bible in a meaningful way and how to pray? Well, more than likely you'll take the person to the places in scripture that deal with this and maybe give him or her a book or two that was helpful in shaping you (Information), but you'd also teach him or her how you do it! You would show the person the way you've learned to do it, and for someone who doesn't know how, chances are good he or she would start off doing it just like you do it (Imitation). Now that doesn't mean that a little ways down the road they won't branch out and discover ways of doing this that might be more suited to his or her personality (Innovation), but the person is starting with a foundation they can build on. That is the process of discipleship, and that is the path you can provide for people.

Above all else, know that good leaders always define their own reality. No one else can build a discipling culture for you—it must begin in your own life and then overflow into the lives of those you lead. You will not be the perfect example, but you can be a living example. It will more than likely be a difficult and challenging task, but as we look at our own lives and then to the stories from the leaders who have gone before us, we know that the prize is truly worth the price.

After his resurrection, Acts tells us that Jesus spent about six weeks continuing to meet with and teach his disciples.[46] Then, as he was about to ascend into heaven, he gave the

---

46   Acts 1:3

6. Finding a Way to Imitate

Great Commission for them to go and make disciples. But of course, making disciples required that the disciples themselves were empowered for the task, just as Jesus had been. Jesus made it clear to those first followers that they needed to wait upon the Holy Spirit to be filled with power—the power of the resurrection![47] The incredible training they had gotten wasn't enough—they also needed to be filled with the supernatural power of the Spirit.

The New Testament tells us that, even though the Holy Spirit comes to dwell within us, when we are born again into the kingdom of God,[48] we need to ask him to fill us over and over again every day.[49] The power of the Spirit, rather than the cleverness of our methodology or the strength of our will, is what enables us to make disciples who make disciples.[50]

So as we move from Part One to Part Two of *Building a Discipling Culture*, remember that the tools and methodologies here cannot be the whole story. Training and instruction never is—not even for the disciples. But when disciples make disciples using what they have learned by the resurrection power of the Holy Spirit, we will see incredible fruitfulness, as I have throughout my ministry. I hope that, by sharing some of the practical things I have learned in the pages to come, you will see the Spirit's mighty work in your discipling culture as well

* * *

This brings us to the end of Part One of *Building a Discipling Culture*. If you are a leader of a discipling process,

---

47 See Luke 24:49, Acts 1:4, Ephesians 1:18-21
48 John 3:3, 5
49 Ephesians 5:18
50 1 Corinthians 2:4-5

you might find it helpful to read Part One of *Leading a Discipling Culture* in which the narrative arc of first century discipleship extends from the story of Jesus to the account of the early church found in the Acts of the Apostles. After that I would of course recommend you continue with this book. If you are simply trying to learn more about a discipling culture, then read on!

Part II

Language Creates a Discipling Culture

Part II

Language Creates a Discipling Culture

7. A Language that Creates a Discipling Culture

Sociologists say that language creates culture. Now, language is the way that we communicate, verbally and nonverbally. In the book *Essentials of Sociology*, the authors write:

> *A common language is often the most obvious outward sign that people share a common culture... For this reason, groups seeking to mobilize their members often insist on their own distinct language... and according to some linguists, languages not only symbolize our culture but also help create a framework in which culture develops, arguing that grammar, structures and categories embodied in each language influence how its speakers see reality. For example, because Hopi grammar does not have past, present and future grammatical tenses, Hopi speakers think differently about time than do English speakers.*[51]

The idea that language creates culture may sound strange, but

---

51 David B. Brinkerhoff, Lynn K. White, Suzanne T. Ortega, *Essentials on Sociology* (Florence, KY: Wadsworth).

it's quite obvious when we start to see it all around us.

In all reality, it is not terribly difficult to create a corporate culture. We develop a whole system of language revolving around the central beliefs that we have. So because we want a polite, courteous, busy, productive, clean-cut, and respectful culture, we develop a language around that. There are ways that you address your superiors that are acceptable and ways that are not. There are ways that you treat your co-workers and ways you don't. Certain clothes are OK while others aren't. Certain work hours are required. There is an acceptable general physical appearance. Desks must have a certain kind of order to them. Corporate culture has "corporate speak": words, phrases, and reports that are a sort of agreed-on language. Everyone knows the language, and everyone uses the language.

When people share all these things and have them all in common, a culture is created. The language does not have to be completely verbal, for as we know, much of our communication is nonverbal.

Most of us know what it's like to create a religious culture. Most churches have a whole language that is particular to the church world that some people call "Christian-ese." Churchgoers use words that no one outside of church uses such as tithe, testimony, or "loving on people." We know religious spaces have certain rules, certain decorum, certain dress codes.

So as we consider the church, we must examine the agreed-on language we are using and how it is creating the culture we have.

We are creating a culture, even if it's unintentional. The question is, do we like the culture we are creating?

7. A Language that Creates a Discipling Culture

The reality of our church communities is that we simply do not have a shared language in which we can create a discipling culture. If we are to give our lives as living examples and create an environment for people where we can disciple them, we have to have an easily transferable language that we can pass on.

This language should be the DNA of Jesus' teachings, Scripture, leadership, mission, and discipleship. The language should be shared by you and the people you are discipling, and eventually, by everyone in your church community. If we want to create a culture of discipleship, we need a language to support it.

One of the reasons I have seen so much success discipling people is that this movement has an agreed-on language. The language I use, called LifeShapes, is a collection of shapes with each shape representing a foundational teaching of Jesus or principle from his life and is a series of tools that I started developing in the early 1980s. Over the past forty years these shapes have become fully formed into a language of discipleship. Of course, there's no suggestion that these or any other tools are prescriptive of a disciple-making process. Rather, they are descriptive of what we see in the life and teaching of Jesus. If one or some of the Lifeshapes don't work for you don't worry, move on and find one that does, or perhaps begin to develop your own.

Now if you are anything like most people, you may have just rolled your eyes a bit. Shapes? Seriously? Shapes?! You have got to be kidding. I know.

Your thoughts probably drift to what feels like yet another church program, fad or campaign. But I would humbly submit that when people learn this discipling language within the

Building a Discipling Culture

context of a discipling relationship something starts to happen: People's lives begin to look like the lives of people we see in Scripture. Because above all else it is life-on-life discipleship. Transformation actually happens. Perhaps the real question is this: Why are images so effective as a discipling language? So let's dive into this idea a bit. What is the following image?

For most of us, Mickey Mouse immediately comes to our mind. So how many questions about this shape can you answer: Who first drew Mickey Mouse?

- What is the name of his company?
- What is your favorite movie of this company?
- What about your favorite character?
- What is your favorite song from one of these movies?
- Sing the song.
- If you wanted to visit Mickey's home on the East Coast, where would you go?
- If you wanted to visit Mickey's home on the West Coast, where would you go?
- The company that created Mickey bought a computer

7. A Language that Creates a Discipling Culture

animation company a few years ago. What's the name of the company?

- What movies has the company animated?
- Which one was your favorite?
- What was your favorite character?

I could go on and on. I could do that for hours, and you could probably answer most if not all of the questions.

Here's what we all need to understand: When Jesus taught, he was living in an oral culture. Most people were illiterate and books were very expensive, so information was passed on from person to person and generation to generation through the oral tradition. People in Jesus' time had an unbelievable capacity to hear and remember.

Over time, the oral culture gave way to a written culture where large amounts of information were passed on through books. Because of this, people's brains were wired a certain way, and people were able to read and remember a large amount of information by reading it.

In the past hundred years, however, we have entered into an image-based culture, and we store large amounts of information, stories and data by attaching them to images. Our brains are literally wired differently than they were in previous generations. In his seminal book The Master and His Emissary, which discusses the brain and the development of culture, Iain McGilchrist suggests that our brains have become much more driven by content than context as the left hemisphere of our brains has usurped the right hemisphere as the leading feature of our neural experience. Our memories are stored and encoded in ways different from previous expressions of human culture. Perhaps this is the reason that we have become so dependent on images as our way of storing and communicating ideas.

Because of this, the idea of attaching the teachings of Jesus and Scripture to a few basic images is perfectly in line with how our brains appear to be already hardwired.

With the Mickey Mouse example, one image is a type of rabbit hole that goes deeper and deeper. Now you are probably more than capable of taking these principles and creating your own sticky, reproducible language for discipleship. However, we have spent more than forty years creating, tweaking, refining and putting this language in a post-Christian context, making the language as sticky and reproducible as possible. You see, for LifeShapes, it is as if each shape is a rabbit hole. You enter into it, and it seems small enough, easy to understand, but it takes you deeper and deeper into Scripture, the life of Jesus and the Gospel. Therefore, we can layer and add more and more information, adding depth to people's understanding of what it means to be a disciple and to live in the reality that is the Kingdom of God. The shapes serve as a beginning, as a kind of entrance to the rabbit hole, but certainly not the end. So what, you may ask, do these shapes encompass? Well, here's a first look at them. After a year in a discipling relationship—including in what we call a Huddle—this is what we'd want people to know, and this is what we'd want people to be able to do:

7. A Language that Creates a Discipling Culture

The Circle:
Learning from Life

Learn to be disciples by becoming life-long learners of Jesus. The key to this is learning to always listen to the voice of God and respond. We want people to know about God and the history of our faith, but we also want them to know God. As Paul says:"

I want to know Christ, and the power of his resurrection and the fellowship of sharing in his sufferings."

Philippians 3:10

This is the foundational shape and one every Huddle returns to as we continually ask, "What is God saying, and what am I going to do about it?"

The Semi-Circle: Rhythms of Life

Learning how to balance a greater intimacy and openness with God, a deeper understanding and appreciation of Christian community and a commitment to be on mission with God as we invite others to follow Jesus

The Semi-Circle: Deeper and Balanced Relationships

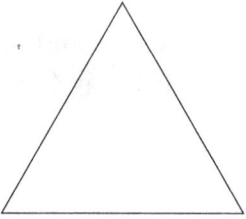

Learning a rhythm of rest and work in our days, weeks and years and how to apply the spiritual disciplines in healthy and sustainable ways.

7. A Language that Creates a Discipling Culture

The Square:
Multiplying Disciples

Learn the process Jesus used for discipling people, where you are in that process, and how to begin looking toward discipling people yourself.

The Pentagon:
Personal Calling

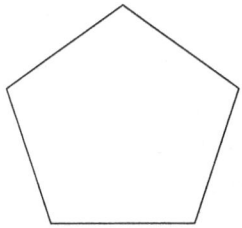

Learn the Fivefold Ministries found in Ephesians 4, understanding the unique way God has shaped you and what this means for your personal calling as a disciple.

The Hexagon: Personal Prayer

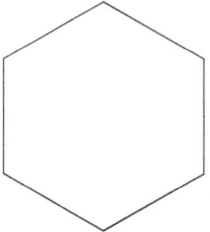

Learn to pray using the Lord's Prayer as the template that leads to a substantial relationship with the Father. In doing so, we also learn the importance of the Trinity and see the work of the Holy Spirit in our world, connecting us with the Father.

Using the Shapes

Each shape serves as a kind of portal, with an almost endless number of Scripture passages, stories or practices attached. Let's be clear: The biggest question about someone isn't whether he or she could teach for five hours on a silly shape. The question is, does his or her life actually embody and incarnate the shape and Scripture teaching, and can this person multiply that into someone else's life? That was Jesus' criterion and so it is ours as well.

Remember, you may be someone who has advanced training or theological education, but most of the people in our churches do not. These simple shapes that form a discipling language give people handles for their own life, as well as the ability to remember and teach them to the people Jesus is calling them to disciple. It's never just about us. Are we giving the people in our

7. A Language that Creates a Discipling Culture

communities the tools they need to make disciples and lead out into mission? Those are whom this language is for.

For each chapter in the rest of Part 2, I will go in depth on the first six shapes, beginning with the foundational shape of the Learning Circle.

Lastly, on a very practical note, if you are a pastor, I highly recommend you not teach LifeShapes in a sermon series. If you do this, you will be subtly telling your community that this is just another program, but more importantly, it'll come across as more information for them to engage or ignore. The best way to teach LifeShapes is in the context of a discipling relationship where you have all three types of learning functioning together. It's tremendously important that we recognize that what is offered here is not a program but an introduction to a process and it's not a prescription for discipleship content but a description of tools that are helpful to the process of developing disciples who can make disciples. I've learned this the hard way and seen other pastors make this mistake. Learn from our mistakes!

8. The Circle: Learning from Life

I went to college in Durham, England, at Cranmer Hall, which is the Seminary connected to Durham University. I had fortunately already completed most of the necessary courses to be ordained in the Church of England, which meant I could spend some time in research and do a Master's degree with the funding that the Church of England gave me. I was particularly interested in philosophical theology.

It was delightful, working in Durham University in the shadow of ancient Durham Cathedral and walking from one college on a multi-college university campus much like Oxford and Cambridge.

During my studies, certain things really drew my attention alongside the research that I was doing into human personhood. The professor of pastoral care, Mike Williams, specifically trained us on how to function as scholars and practitioners so that we could take our familiarity with theology and apply it to pastoral ministry.

Dr. Williams used to say, "You need to remember that no

one learns from experience. You only ever learn by reflecting on your experience." And he gave us a little tool that was a loop illustrating how you have an experience, analyze that experience, reflect on that experience, and then put what you're learning into practice. He drew this from educational theorists from different parts of the world.

He really wanted us as pastors and ministers to be those who were able to reflect on what we were doing, encountering, and experiencing. He said that by doing this, we would genuinely learn from our pastoral experience and grow and develop, unlike so many others who seem to have the same experience over and over again.

This got me thinking, and over the next few years I began to develop the idea of the Learning Circle as I thought through how Jesus called his disciples to engage with a moment and then reflect on it, and then put into practice what they were hearing from God. This process was the first stirrings of what it meant to answer the two questions of discipleship:

- What is God saying to me?
- What am I going to do about it?

How Jesus Led His Disciples To Learn

Jesus called people to follow him, calling those people disciples, or literally "learners." As you read and use this book, you will introduce your key leaders to the foundational vocabulary upon which you can build a discipling culture. The call to be a disciple involves a daily process of laying down our lives to follow Jesus. However, many leaders struggle to

8. The Circle: Learning from Life

confidently recognize the Lord's voice and often have no means of knowing when God is at work in their lives. The Circle will help you and the people you disciple learn from the situations and issues that arise in daily life.

Kairos Interrupted

There are several words in the Greek language that translate into the English word for time. Chronos is the one we would find most familiar, meaning successive or sequential time, the kind of time you find on your wristwatch.

Another is *kairos*, meaning an event, an opportunity—a moment in time when perhaps everything changes because it is the right time. A *kairos* moment is when the eternal God breaks into your circumstances with an event that gathers some loose ends of your life and knots them together in his hands. In *kairos* moments, the rules of chronos time seem to be suspended.

Kairos Events Can Be Positive or Negative

Do you remember the day you were married? How about the birth of your first child? Think about a favorite vacation you took with your family. These are all *kairos* moments where you cherished every minute. Some *kairos* events, however, leave an impact because of their tragic consequences—the death of a loved one, a divorce, an argument with a co-worker, the horrific events of September 11, 2001. *Kairos* events are rarely neutral.

Kairos Moments Can Be Recognized by the Impact They Leave on You

Perhaps you announce a new division at work or a building

project at your church. Instead of the expected enthusiastic response, you are greeted with silence and stares from others in the organization. Instead of asking for details, people shuffle out quickly. You notice the whispers and the fingers pointed back at you. You feel anxiety and fear. You are passing through a *kairos* moment. Your emotions are often a great indicator of *kairos* events, and often the negative events that produce negative emotions present the greatest potential for growth.

Kairos Events Signal Opportunities to Grow

This growth occurs on an individual level and on a corporate level. Perhaps you and your team are experiencing a *kairos* event even now: changes in your staff, loss of a facility, unexpected growth. Or perhaps there was a *kairos* event in your past—one that might serve as an entry point into the learning process. As you and the people you are discipling learn to recognize *kairos* moments as God's interventions, you will be able to enter the Learning Circle, and experience growth. You will be able to seize these opportunities and celebrate the kingdom life this process brings.

What does the Bible say about a lifestyle of learning? As a matter of fact, Jesus' very first teaching was on this subject:

> *The time has come. The kingdom of God is near. Repent and believe the good news.*
>
> Mark 1:15

These verses, which could be called a summary statement of the teaching of Jesus, say a lot more about learning than first meets the eye. In essence, Jesus is saying a great opportunity

8. The Circle: Learning from Life

is available: God's kingdom is within reach for all of us. The kingdom of God is near means that if you reach in the right direction, your hand will disappear through the curtain of this world and reappear in the reality of the next world. There is a portal in time that we can't see, and the in-breaking of God's presence is about to take place. The Learning Circle suggests a framework by which we can process what God is saying to us in the *kairos* event and learn how to respond in a way that enables us to grow in our discipleship.

The Circle shows us:

- What it means to live a lifestyle of learning as a disciple of Christ.
- How to recognize important events as opportunities for growth.
- How to process these events.

We leaders tend to be analytical. We tend to think of our journey of faith as linear; it has a starting point (salvation) and an ending point (heaven).

Salvation **Heaven**

Scripture would seem to indicate that a disciple's relationship with God is more dynamic. Let us suggest another picture. Here is a believer, walking what he considers to be a straight, linear path. Perhaps he has a purpose in mind; perhaps he is just walking in the direction he thinks is best. Then, seemingly out of the blue, a *kairos* moment (X) takes place.

He can react in many different ways. He can keep walking, ignoring the open door for growth. He can stop. He can go backward. Or he can enter the Learning Circle. Jesus extends a great opportunity to anyone who would seek to know him and follow him. God's kingdom is within reach—but to access it we need to go through the process of repentance and belief.

When a *kairos* moment occurs, we often want to study all the events that led up to it with the hope of preventing a similar thing from happening again. But we are looking through the wrong end of the telescope. Instead of looking back, we need to look forward to the growth we can experience because of what has happened. *Kairos* moments are God-given opportunities to enter into a process of learning kingdom living.

Keys to The Kingdom

The Circle represents our journey into the kingdom of God. To enter the kingdom, however, we must go through a process of repentance and belief. The process can be difficult and challenging and, more often than not, painful. It is through this process we learn how to lay down our lives and pick up

8. The Circle: Learning from Life

the cross.

What propels us into this learning process is a *kairos* event. As I discussed previously, it can be positive (a promotion at work) or negative (getting laid off from your job). It can be big (your wedding) or small (a date night with your spouse). Generally speaking, *kairos* moments are not neutral, as they leave an impression on us. But when a *kairos* moment occurs, we must decide to enter the Circle. From the moment we do so, we are in a learning mode.

Two key words in Mark 1:15 help define the learning process: repent and believe. You will remember that the word repent is from the Greek *metanoia*, meaning to change one's mind. As church leaders, we often encounter strong resistance when we say repent because of its unfortunate association with negative messages of condemnation without grace. Our people will respond differently when they realize that *metanoia* simply means a change of heart that shows up in a lifestyle or behavior change. Walking as a disciple of Jesus means constantly growing and changing inwardly as you take on more of the character of the Teacher. Change is not an option: it is a vital part of the life of a follower of Jesus. Once we change on the inside, the new attitude will affect our outward actions.

Where *kairos* is an event word—something that has a beginning and ending—repentance (*metanoia*) is a process word, as is believe (*pistis*). The Circle is a process—a way of living that does not have a specific beginning and ending. One does not become a disciple of Jesus and stand still; discipleship is a lifestyle of learning. And this learning begins with a change of heart.

Entering the Learning Circle

Having experienced a *kairos* event in our lives, we then begin the process of learning from it. The LifeShapes Circle has uniquely expanded this to six. There are three parts in the repent process (observe, reflect, and discuss) and three parts to the believe process (plan, account, and act).

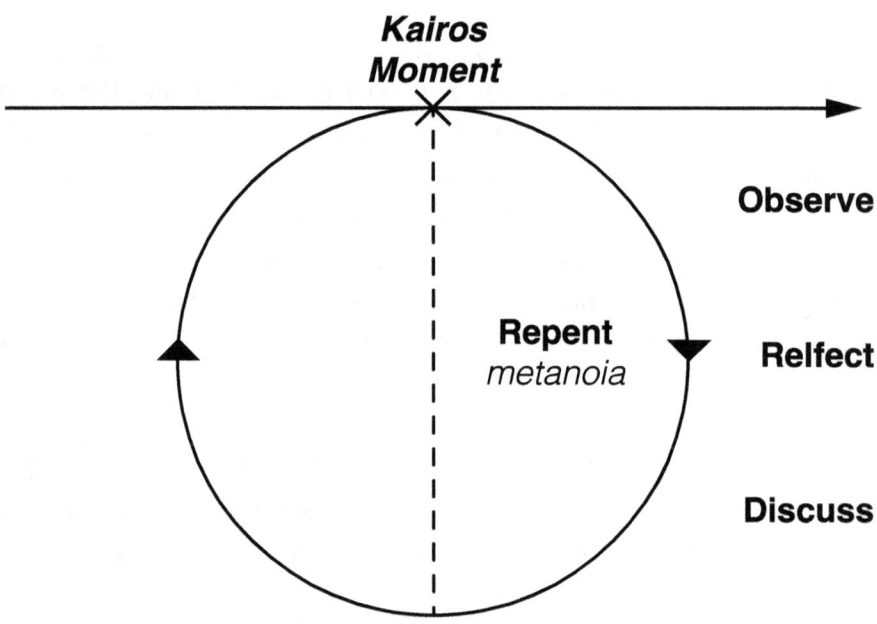

The first part of the repent process is observation. To change our lives, we need to observe where we are. When a *kairos* moment stops us in our tracks, this is the time to observe our reactions, our emotions, and our thoughts. We must be honest in our observations—see things as they are—if we are to change inwardly.

8. The Circle: Learning from Life

Once we observe our condition, we need to reflect. Reflect on what? Reflect on our observations. We need to ask ourselves why we reacted as we did, why we feel as we do, why a certain event brought these emotions to the surface. Asking questions is a great way to reflect. Again, our answers must be honest if real change is to take place.

If observing and reflecting are to lead to lasting change, we must invite others into the process with us. For repentance to take hold, we've got to share it with someone else. It is important that we have others in our lives we can discuss our observations and reflections with, and who will be honest in their response to us. Using the Learning Circle with the people you are discipling creates a space that is the context for confession, a place of honesty where we are able to challenge each other, share our struggles, and experience God's grace and forgiveness. These are trustworthy friends, who will stand with us, pray with us, and fight alongside us, but will not flatter us with empty words.

> *Therefore confess your sins to each other and pray for each other so that you may be healed."*
>
> *James 5:15*

Repentance is necessary if we are to grow as disciples, but it is not always easy.[52] Facing our failings, our pain, and our fears is something we want to put off, like a trip to the dentist or bathing the cat. As we step into the process of observing, reflecting on, and discussing our sins and shortcomings with

---

52 For my story of repentance, I encourage you to read the section "Letters to the Reader" at the end of this book.

others, we are not only opening up the ugliness of our lives for others to see, we are opening it up for us to see.

In a culture where our disciples look to our example and where our own pride often gets the best of us, we find ourselves running away from the sins and faults of our lives and toward the goal of fixing the problems in the lives of others. This is the picture that many of us paint rather than simply becoming authentic in our relationship with God.

The image of a leader who is constantly trying to flee from his anguish and fear, hoping that if he runs far enough or flies fast enough, he can somehow make it all go away is not the image of repentance that we are called to embrace. Dr. Larry Crabb writes, "A spiritual community consists of people who have the integrity to come clean. It is comprised of those who own their shortcomings and failures because they hate them more than they hate the shortcomings and failures of others, who therefore discover that a well of pure water flows beneath their most fetid corruption."[53]

What a great picture of discipleship: abandoning ourselves to the forgiveness of God, walking in his grace, and creating a safe place within our church communities for others to do the same. This only comes, however, if we are willing to walk first in the footsteps of repentance. Leaders define culture. If you want the people you're discipling to be honest and vulnerable about their lives, it will invariably start with you.

---

53 Larry Crabb, Becoming a True Spiritual Community: A Profound Vision of What the Church Can Be (Nashville, TN: Thomas Nelson, 2007).

8. The Circle: Learning from Life

Finding Your Way Around

What good is it, my brothers, if a man claims to have faith but has no deeds? Faith by itself, if it is not accompanied by action, is dead. But someone will say, "You have faith; I have deeds." Show me your faith without deeds, and I will show you my faith by what I do.
—James 2:14; 17–18

Just because we experience something—in other words, just because we go through a *kairos* moment—does not mean we learn anything. And repenting will not by itself bring about change. Repentance is only the first part of the Circle. Stopping after we repent only invites the experience to return and makes it harder to repent the next time.

After recognizing the issue, assessing why it happened, and discussing it with someone else, in the process of rethinking and repenting before God, we must move to the left side of the Circle and begin believing change is possible. Faith is the second half of our Circle, the next process in the lifestyle of discipleship.

"Faith," says the writer of Hebrews, "is the substance of things believed."[54] It is not simply a nice belief, but a substantive display of belief. Faith that cannot be seen, writes James, is no faith at all. Faith is action, and right action will take us into the kingdom. There are some who say that faith is spelled R-I-S-K. I disagree. If you are acting in faith, you are simply doing what you know God wills to be done. There is no risk in doing God's will. (There is, however, great risk in ignoring God and doing what we want to do.) If you need an alternative spelling for

---

54 Hebrews 11:1

faith, you can use these four letters: S-U-R-E.

Just as there are three spokes in the wheel of repentance (observe, reflect, discuss), there are three spokes for faith. The first is to plan. On the basis of our observation, reflection, and discussion, we need to make a plan to lead our inner change.

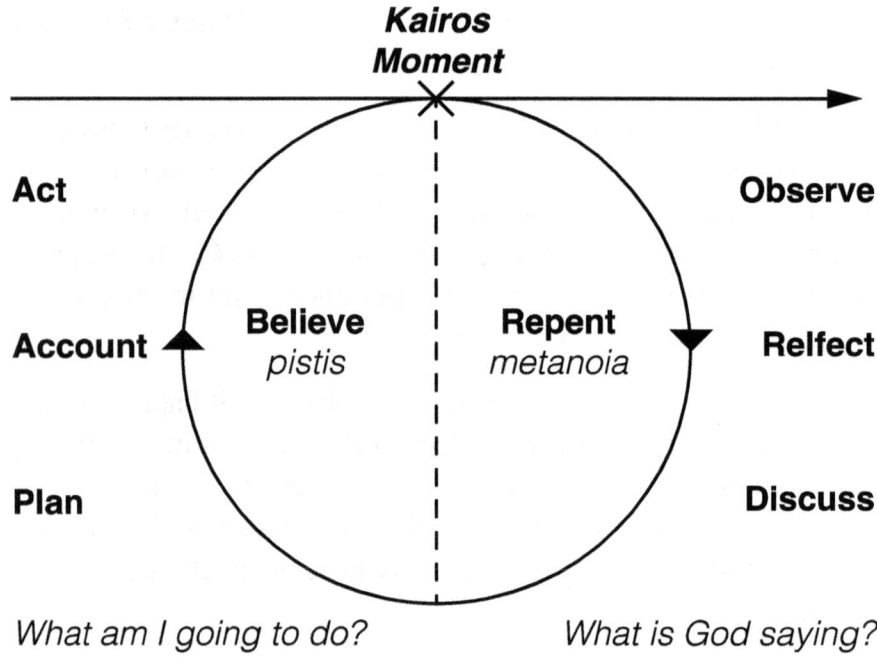

For example, if your growing credit card debt has finally escalated to the point of crisis and, in reflecting on the cause, the Lord reveals an emptiness or void you are trying to fill through shopping, have a strategy for recognizing the feelings that lead to binge shopping and for reacting in the proper way. Or if God has shown you that you need to respond with more encouragement to a staff member, develop concrete plans of when and how. Planning nearly always involves seeking the kingdom of God first, no matter what the issue. Most of us find

8. The Circle: Learning from Life

that ultimately our *kairos* events lead us to discover we have used someone or something as a substitute for God. If shopping is your substitute, make a plan to buy only necessities, to pay only cash, and then to let the Lord fill the emptiness within.

If a plan is to succeed, it is important to have at least one person hold us accountable to it. We need to externalize the things that have been going on internally. Change doesn't happen in private. Being afraid to share with someone else because you think your thoughts or feelings are too private will keep you from growing and changing. All the mistakes the heroes in the Bible made are eternally public. Just think how Peter feels today seeing people read and discuss how he denied Jesus. Accountability is important to Jesus, shown by his sending out the disciples in groups of two. Sharing your inner thoughts and outward failings with another person may be hard at first, but it is ultimately necessary if we are to grow. The Circle will not turn correctly if one spoke is left out or broken off. We cannot skip accountability and still say we are disciples of Christ. It is that simple.

Once a plan is made and a relationship of accountability established, the natural reaction is for action to take place.

Faith always comes to the surface and always produces action. It cannot be contained. Thoughts and intents that are held within and not acted upon are not faith, no matter what we like to say. ("My faith is personal" is a favorite. But that is a self-contradicting statement. Faith is always acted out, never kept bottled up within.)

The Circle on the Mount

Here is a biblical example of the Circle. Jesus and his followers are just wrapping up a long day. He goes up on a hillside and teaches what we now call the Sermon on the Mount. In this day-long teaching, Jesus outlines the radical lifestyle that he calls his followers to adopt. He talks about such things as murder, adultery, divorce, lying, revenge, loving your enemy, giving to the needy, prayer and fasting, and the love of money. As the people listen, they probably begin experiencing the kind of internal pressure that leads to a *kairos* event. (When this occurs, it can lead to anxiety and worry.) So Jesus addresses the situation.

> *"Do not worry about your life, what you will eat or drink; or about your body, what you will wear. Is not life more important than food, and the body more important than clothes?"*
>
> Matthew 6:25

An event has taken place. It causes worry, anxiety, and stress. The disciples need to learn about the problem of worrying from this event, so Jesus begins with observation.

> *"Look at the birds of the air; they do not sow or reap or store away in barns, and yet your heavenly Father feeds them."*
>
> Matthew 6:26

Having revealed what is happening in his followers' hearts,

8. The Circle: Learning from Life

Jesus takes them through the process that will set them free. First he tells them to look at the birds. No doubt this makes them wonder. Jesus is leading his disciples to observe their own lives by having them look at something else they can understand. The birds of the air do not sow or reap or store away in barns, and yet their heavenly Father feeds them. This is a simple, straightforward observation, and it helps the disciples recognize their own fears and lack of faith. Likewise, observing our *kairos* event leads to examining ourselves.

Reflection begins when Jesus asks:

> *"Are you not much more valuable than they?"*
>
> *Matthew 6:26*

This, of course, is a rhetorical question to which the answer is yes. (Asking questions is the best way to facilitate reflection.) Birds are valuable, but we are more valuable. Jesus is helping the disciples put things into perspective.

Reflection leads to conversation and discussion:

> *"Who of you by worrying can add a single hour to his life? And why do you worry about clothes?"*
>
> *Matthew 6:27-28*

There is no record of a discussion between Jesus and his disciples at this point, but the usual method for teaching in that day was question and answer. Discussion was a basic part of the learning experience; therefore, it is safe to assume this teaching included discussion that Matthew chose not to record. People need to talk things over with others in order to find clarity. We try to change the things we worry about, but Jesus says the person who worries is the one who needs to change. Change happens to us when we try to answer searching questions such as "Why am I worrying about this when I know God is in control?"

> *But seek first his kingdom and his righteousness, and all these things will be given to you as well.*
>
> Matthew 6:33

How do we build a life that is not based on worry but founded on faith? This verse illustrates the importance of planning.

Planning is built around a vision. We plan to attain something. Jesus tells us to make plans to seek his kingdom and his righteousness. Righteousness means right relationship.

Making plans on the basis of the kingdom, in right relationship with God, means the worries of tomorrow need not dominate us. God will take care of everything—including us! This is the essence of our vision: to make Jesus the true Lord of our lives.

To conclude this message, Jesus tells us we should be accountable for the way we live, speak, and think:

> *Do not judge, or you too will be judged.*
>
> Matthew 7:1

8. The Circle: Learning from Life

Don't live your life continuously calling other people to account for their actions. Instead, live your life in the recognition that you will be called to account. Hypocrites look for faults in others and miss their own faults. Jesus calls us to be accountable to one another.

He then tells a story of two men building houses—one on sand, the other on rock. We often place the emphasis of this story on building our own houses, or lives, on Jesus our Rock. But what Jesus emphasizes is hearing his words and acting on them. The wise man listens to what Jesus says—and then acts upon it.[55]

Living Like A Slinky

Once you are aware of the Circle—and put it into practice—your life can look like a Slinky, a series of loops held together by time, as Dr. Williams taught me back in seminary. Each time round the Circle means you have grown a little more and taken on a little more of the character of Christ. Our lives are really about events connected together over time and our response to these events. The correct response—repent and believe—leads us more fully into the kingdom. Skipping one or more of the steps in the Circle means you will more than likely continue to struggle over and over again with the same issue.

---

55 See Matthew 7:24-29.

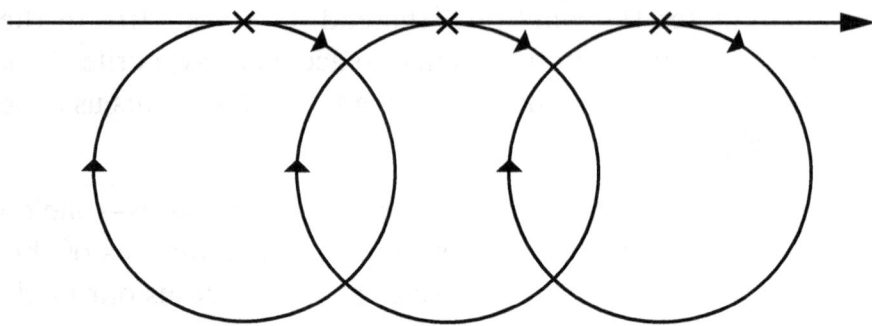

How do we take up the cross and become wholly devoted students following Jesus? Surrender to the process of change. Embrace the fruit of the Spirit he wants to grow in our lives. And when it gets hard to face the issues of sin that will ultimately surface in your life, push through. Don't turn back and look for relief from the internal struggle. The rewards will be great if you and your Huddle persevere. In fact, once you have tasted of the goodness of the Lord, like the man who found the pearl of great price, you will sell everything you have to keep it and know it more fully.

How I Learned the Power of the Circle

The particular event in my early ministry that really ingrained the importance of the Circle for me was when Sally and I moved from my first position in the Church of England as an assistant and then the team leader of a youth center in Cambridge to the inner city to a very under-resourced area of London called Brixton Hill, in the shadow of Brixton prison, which had been there since Victorian times. Brixton Hill was very disadvantaged and struggled a great deal. The churches in

8. The Circle: Learning from Life

the community were very small and often teetering on the brink of closure.

The church that I went to had a certain vitality about it, but was very tiny. Maybe 30 or 40 people gathered in a new building that had been purpose-built to enable the church to function in a community-conscious way. The Church of England had knocked down the old Victorian buildings that looked like a huge ecclesial barn and sold off some of the land for homes for the elderly and various other things. But despite this building, the church did not have deep ties to the community.

When I arrived in Brixton, it was very clear to me that I needed to really understand the community. And so I told the congregation that we needed to ask the parish what they thought the church should be doing. (The parish is the geographic area that surrounds a parish church.)

This was quite a novel idea at the time, one that arose from my reading in the publications of people like David Shepherd and Ray Bakke.

We decided to put a questionnaire together and to ask a few simple questions by knocking on people's doors. Our goal was to find out what people thought we should be doing so we could respond based on the actual experience of the people who lived in Brixton.

So we got a team of people together. We went and knocked on lots and lots of doors—I think hundreds of doors. Aside from asking a person's name and how long they had lived in Brixton, we asked a few basic questions.

What do you think the church should be doing? Where do you think the church should focus its attention?

Building a Discipling Culture

What are the best things about the community? And what do you think are the worst things about the community?

It was interesting that almost everybody said we should do youth work and children's work to attend to the concerns of teenagers and children. That was just fine with me, because up until that time those had been my main areas of expertise, and I had brought a team of youth workers with me from Cambridge to Brixton to do exactly that. It was a bit of a relief, since we were very much flying by the seat of our pants. So when youth and children's work was endorsed, we said, "Sure, we'll do that."

But nobody really agreed on what the best thing in the community was. Some people said racial harmony; others said access to the shops or public transportation. But while people mentioned many things as the best thing about the community, everybody agreed on what the worst thing was: litter on the streets.

Rubbish was everywhere. Trash blew around the streets and between the apartment blocks. It really did look a mess.

As we thought about this response, our reflection was that this made people feel like they were rubbish–like they were at the bottom of the trash can (or, as we would say in England, the dustbin). It made people feel like they were unimportant, unseen, and unvalued.

We reflected on this and discussed it quite a bit. Together, we decided we would come up with a plan to do something quite unusual. We would have a praise and litter march.

Praise marches were quite common at that time, getting going with Graham Kendrick and beginning to move around the world as a movement. But we felt that our praise march needed

8. The Circle: Learning from Life

to be something that was a practical expression of our care and concern for the neighborhood and a reflection of what we had heard from the neighborhood were its principal concerns.

So we decided that one Sunday after church, we would get together in a group. We strapped a large cassette tape player to a baby buggy and decorated it with balloons. And everyone carried a large bin liner and a rubber glove. We played praise music that we had recorded with me on my 12-string guitar and the other youth worker playing the church's old upright piano.

So off we went. And as we went around the community, you could see the curtains twitching in the houses as people looked inquisitively through their windows. Some people opened their doors. Eventually, someone called out to me in their Cockney accent, "Why vicar? What you doing?"

I went over and explained that the questionnaire had told us that litter was the principal problem, and that we wanted to show that we didn't want to just leave that problem untouched. We didn't believe that we could change the whole thing, but hopefully we could influence a little bit of the litter.

The community responded incredibly. The first person was so excited. This person called her husband, and they called their neighbors. Everybody began to open their doors and turn the kettles on and bring us cups of tea and cookies.

We had a wonderful time as a community of people picked up the bin liner with us and joined us as we collected trash, learning the songs as we went. Interestingly, that became a statement of intent for us as a church. Many people joined the church simply because of the way that we sought to identify with some of the needs of the area and do something about them.

The members of the area pretty much became community activists to deal with what was going on in the community itself, and the local council eventually responded by sending teams of workers to clean up the area.

But what was confirmed to me in this experience was that, as we engaged with this *Kairos* moment of arriving in this under-resourced and deeply disadvantaged community by making careful observations of the community through the questionnaire, and then reflecting on the answers that we got and discussing with one another and with the wider community what it really meant, we could begin a plan. We were publicly accountable to that plan, and we acted on it right in the community itself. We saw a demonstration of the Kingdom as people came together, as people's hearts were softened, and eventually as people joined the local community of believers and came to know Jesus for themselves.

That perhaps was the first demonstration of the Learning Circle in action in a way that was really easily measurable. From that point on, there was no going back for me. Every chance I got, we used the Circle to identify and process the *Kairos*. As the Circle has led to continuous breakthrough for me, I have taught it to others, and now it is a tool that helps discipling cultures around the world.

Read this story of the Circle's impact on Rogerio O.:

My experience with learning how to process kairos came after I had just journeyed through an extremely painful season of my life. Often we get to learn in the moment through the guidance of the Holy Spirit, but the most impactful kairos

8. The Circle: Learning from Life

process was when I asked God to help me make sense of the desert season in my past.

When Estela and I got married, we moved to a small town in the interior of São Paulo, Brasil after a few months. This was a season of abundance. We had our daughter Nicole, and soon she was starting to walk. I worked for a technology company with a good salary and working conditions. Estela worked with physiotherapy in a medical clinic and a hospital. We lived in a beautiful, comfortable farmhouse in the countryside, a reasonable distance from the city. We served a local church in every way we could, looking for ways to be helpful in the Kingdom.

One day a friend visited and gave us a prophetic word and said he saw a desert before us.

A short time later, we were suddenly out of work without income and health insurance. We tried all kinds of jobs, and nothing worked. With our free time, we dedicated ourselves even more to church activities, which supplied us with fuel. My parents helped with basic food, and Estela practiced gardening to provide some vegetables. There came a point when even the water well dried up. During this period, we have countless stories of small deliverances and punctual supplies from God. Toward the end of this period, Estela was pregnant with Artur, who was born in the desert. We spent almost three years in this desert season.

During that time we went to a biblical conference in another state, and a girl who had never seen us and whom we never saw again called Estela and me and told us that she had a message from God to us. She said, "The desert was over, and we had been approved because it squeezed us like toothpaste and found adoration instead of murmuring." A few days later, I was employed, and a few weeks later, Estela was also working. Two years later, we lived in an all-expense-paid water-park in the country's capital, and we have many other stories of abundance in the time that followed.

After some time, we learned about the Learning Circle and the inflection point of kairos through Mike's material during a trip abroad. I am naturally a logical person. Reasoning structures and tools like Lifeshapes are handy for me. However, in the case of kairos, when the inflection point is pointed out by the Holy Spirit, the lesson can be marked in the soul forever.

We submitted our desert experience from the past to the framework of the Learning Circle to identify what we learned in that season. It was a Spirit-led experience to be confronted with the questions of what God is telling us through this situation and what we will do about it.

It was clear that it was not a person teaching us but God himself.

There is beauty in adversity when we are sure that God is with us, that he has not lost control, and that he will use everything to teach us.

Today, looking at that situation is a beautiful testimony of what God did and how he did it.

The days of the desert and the trial we went through were tough, but after that period, we were more robust as a couple, a family, and God's servants.

9. Rhythm of Life: The Semi-Circle

The Semi-Circle that teaches the rhythm of life didn't emerge until later on in my work of ministry. By then I had gotten perilously close on a couple of occasions to complete burnout and breakdown—as you saw in the story of driving into the median at the beginning of this book.

Before I completed my training as a minister in the Church of England, I worked as a city youth worker in the East End of London. There, I really burned the candle at both ends and found myself desperately exhausted and feeling very depressed. Only the help and support of Sally, who I went to visit as she completed her college studies in Sheffield, brought me back from the brink of complete burnout.

Later on after Brixton, the community where we did our praise and litter marches, I got to a very similar place. I was emotionally strung out. I had been beaten and bruised along with Sally and our young family by all of the difficulties and struggles and challenges of inner-city ministry.

We took the opportunity to leave for a period of rest and

recovery and a new experience in America. We went there for a few years, and then came back to England to continue our work in Sheffield. While there, I met with a consultant, an older gentleman who came to visit the church on one occasion. He said to me, "It looks like you're doing very good things here. Do you know how to rest?"

I said I thought so and told him I had learned to play golf and often went off by myself to decompress by playing golf. Then he asked if rest was a lifestyle for my family, and again I said I thought so. I told him that we took a proper day off when we turned the phone off and didn't talk to people on those days and really focused on our family and enjoyed the company of our kids.

Then he asked if rest was a lifestyle that everybody in church agreed to and embraced. And I thought about it, and had to respond that I didn't think so. I realized in that moment that I had never taught anybody about rest because I hadn't ever learned the principles that support it, other than simple survival instincts.

So with that challenge in mind, I began to study the Scriptures, beginning in John 15 and also in the early chapters of Genesis. I began to understand what it meant for God to create us in the way that he did. And that understanding of rest and work transformed the way we did work and ministry and mission together.

The First Commandment

The very first commandment given to us by God was to

9. Rhythm of Life: The Semi-Circle

"be fruitful and multiply."[56] We were not created just simply to exist. Our Creator expects us to produce an increase. Jesus told a story about three servants, each given an amount of money from their master.[57] Two of the servants worked with the money to create a good return on their investments, while the third—called wicked and lazy when his master heard his story—sat on the money and did not produce an increase. The two who returned more than they started with were rewarded, while the one who gave back only what he was given was punished. Clearly we are not to be lazy and wicked servants; we were made to bear fruit.

But does this mean we are to be workaholics? Apparently many Christian leaders think so. Statistics bear the results of the work round-the-clock attitude many pastors have adopted. Studies suggest that more than a thousand pastors quit their churches every month. If this is not evidence of an epidemic of vocational burnout, we don't know what is.

Productivity, Stress, and Memory Foam

We all have stress in our lives, but it is not always bad stress. Stress, as we recall from our high school physics class, is simply force applied to an object to change its shape or course. Stress fractures occur when the object is unmoving or unbending. The right amount of stress on a violin string creates a beautiful note. Too little stress results in a maddening buzz; too much stress produces a shrill off-key sound. We can't—and shouldn't—try to avoid stress. It is part of life. But we are not made to bear too much stress. Studies estimate that forty-three percent

---

56   Genesis 1:28
57   See Matthew 25:14-30.

of adults suffer adverse health effects from stress, and stress-related ailments account for seventy-five to ninety percent of all doctor's visits.[58] It is estimated that the number of stress-related deaths in the UK to be 180,000 each year.[59] Why do we stand for this level of stress in our lives?

This pressure-filled lifestyle is just as prevalent among Christians. We may proclaim, "Cast your cares on him, for he cares for you,"[60] but we don't live it ourselves. We quote from Matthew, "My yoke is easy and my burden is light,"[61] but we continue to pack heavy burdens on our backs. Something has gone very wrong.

God designed us to be productive. But we build our identities around our activities. We are not living in the truth of who God created us to be. We have become human "doings" rather than human "beings." We need a biblical framework for a rhythm of life that allows us to be fruitful in balance with being at rest. We need to be secure in who we are, based on what Christ did for us on the cross and the very great promises we have that we are loved and accepted by him. We must stop striving to gain the acceptance of others by what we do, leading to a driven lifestyle.

Scripture reveals a pattern of life we are destined to live from the time of our birth. We can see it in the lives of Adam and Eve before the fall, and we see it lived out on a daily basis by Jesus. This is the pattern of life we call the Semi-

---

58   Danny Wallace, *The Joy of Sects: The Join Me Story,* Join Me, join-me.co.uk.story.html
59   Found in "Life Event, Stress and Illness" at the National Library of Medicine, https://www.ncbi.nlm.nih.gov/.
60   1 Peter 5:7
61   Matthew 11:30

9. Rhythm of Life: The Semi-Circle

Circle, so called from a picture of a pendulum swinging in a natural rhythm.

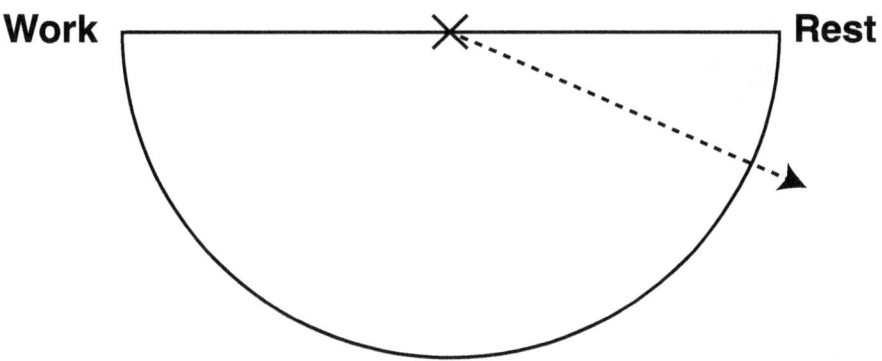

> *Then God said, "Let us make man in our image, in our likeness, and let them rule over the fish of the sea and the birds of the air, over the livestock, over all the earth, and over all the creatures that move along the ground." So God created man in his own image, in the image of God he created him; male and female he created them. God blessed them and said to them, "Be fruitful and increase in number; fill the earth and subdue it. Rule over the fish of the sea and the birds of the air and over every living creature that moves on the ground." Then God said, "I give you every seed-bearing plant on the face of the whole earth and every tree that has fruit with seed in it. They will be yours for food. And to all the beasts of the earth and all the birds of the air and all the creatures that move on the ground—everything that has the breath of life in it—I give every green plant for food." And it was so. God saw all that he had made, and it was very good. And there*

> *was evening, and there was morning—the sixth day. Thus the heavens and the earth were completed in all their vast array. By the seventh day God had finished the work he had been doing; so on the seventh day he rested from all his work. And God blessed the seventh day and made it holy, because on it he rested from all the work of creating that he had done.*
>
> *Genesis 1:26–2:3*
>
> *The LORD God took the man and put him in the Garden of Eden to work it and take care of it.*
>
> *Genesis 2:15*
>
> *Then the man and his wife heard the sound of the LORD God as he was walking in the garden in the cool of the day, and they hid from the LORD God among the trees of the garden. But the LORD God called to the man, "Where are you?"*
>
> *Genesis 3:8–9*

We see in Genesis that on the sixth day, God created man in his image. We need to stop here and consider the word image—it is very important in our understanding of the Semi-Circle. To us, image brings the idea of a reflection in a mirror or a portrait reflecting the likeness of someone. If a picture taken by a photographer shows a person's face, we say it is a good image of that person. But these thoughts would not have been in the mind of those who first heard these words. When Moses first composed these words, there were no mirrors, no portrait

9. Rhythm of Life: The Semi-Circle

painters, and no selfies. In those days, a person would get a reference point for how he or she looked by looking at others. So it makes sense that this is not the meaning of the image spoken of in Genesis 1. A better word would be imprint or impression. It is the picture of God leaving his hand-print on us when he fashioned us from clay. There is an indentation on us that can only be filled by the hand of God. Yet from the fall of man onward, we have been pulling away from the touch of our Creator, trying to fill the imprints with all sorts of insufficient fixes. This was seen from the very beginning with the first man and woman—our ancestors.

Have you seen memory foam mattresses? You can place your hand on the top of the mattress, and the imprint made stays there for some time. This is an impression that can only be totally filled with the hand that made it. This is the same with us. We have an impression in our lives that can only be filled by the hand that made it. (But the impression God puts on us never fades away.)

Working To Be Human

God is walking in the garden he created in the cool of the evening. He desired the company of those he made, Adam and Eve. The indication from the text is that this was a regular event, a routine in their daily lives. At the end of the day the Lord would turn up and expect his beloved ones to be there to go on a stroll with him. God made himself visible each evening so Adam and Eve could feel connected to their Father. It was a daily reminder that God's hand filled the imprint on each of them. This was how it was meant to be between the Creator and the created since the beginning of our time. This time of retreat and rest following a day of labor was not an optional "if you have time but if not don't worry about it" event. It was built into us. It is how God created us to live.

But on this evening our fore-parents failed to show up. They were hiding from the hand that alone could fill them and make them feel complete. After a confrontation with God, they were cursed to work among thorns and thistles, sweating in the heat from backbreaking labor. But this is not how it was supposed to be.

Work itself is not a curse. Before the fall, before Adam and Eve decided to go it alone without the hand of God in their lives (this phrase takes on a whole new meaning when you picture the imprint of God on us, doesn't it?), God had given them instructions on how to care for the garden. Work was assigned before the fall. We were designed for intentional activity to produce a sense of fruitfulness in our lives. This leads us to several conclusions.

Unemployment causes our lives to fall below what is standard. When people become unemployed, it's as though they have fallen from their God-given call to lead productive lives. That's why people struggle so much when they lose their jobs. The focus of productivity and fruitfulness in their lives is lost; it's as though they stop being fully human. No wonder depression often accompanies unemployment.

There is no such thing as retirement. If you leave your job voluntarily, it will not be long before you begin feeling the onset of depression. No amount of golf or fishing can take the place of being fruitful. And don't even get me started on sitting all day in front of the television. If you stop all productive activity in your life, you are pulling away from your God-designed

9. Rhythm of Life: The Semi-Circle

calling. You cannot live a successful life as a human. In fact, many people die within a year or two of retirement because they cease to be fruitful.

In the movie Secondhand Lions, Hub and Garth (played brilliantly by Michael Caine and Robert Duvall)—brothers and former fighters in the French Foreign Legion—have retired to Texas. When fiery, hot-tempered Hub overexerts himself he suffers a blackout spell that lands him briefly in the hospital. After checking Hub out, the brothers stop at a diner and order barbecue. Garth begins probing to see what is bothering Hub.

Garth: "What's the matter, brother? Are you afraid of dying?"

Hub: "Hell, no, I'm not afraid of dying."

Garth: "Then what is it?"

Hub: "I'm afraid of being useless."[62]

It is not until Hub finds a new purpose—raising his great-nephew, Walter—that he recovers his will to live.

There must be work in heaven. If you were counting on sitting in an endless church service, sorry. There was work before the fall; therefore, there must be work after the redemption. This life is a foreshadowing of the real life yet to come.

Work is a strategic part of human existence. We are to live productive lives or we will fall away from our God-given calling and the standard of basic humanity. We were created on the sixth day of creation in order to work. But even more important is what happened on the seventh day.

---

[62] *Secondhand Lions*, Screenplay by Tim McCanlies. Dir. Tim McCanlies. Perf. Michael Caine and Robert Duvall. New Line Cinema, 2003.

God created man and woman on the sixth day, setting them in a garden full of wild, wonderful creatures and delicious foods. He gave them instruction on caring for the animals and plants in the garden. He told them to be fruitful. But on the first full day of existence for Adam and Eve, God rested. All of creation took a well-deserved break in activity. This was our first full day, a day of rest. Then the work began. From this we see an important principle of life: we are to work from our rest, not rest from our work.

Murder, Adultery, Workaholic

Rest is God's healthy starting point for us. We are human beings, not human doings. This is the order God has established for us: rest, then work. But we have it backward. We pride ourselves on our strong work ethic, even using it as a sign of godliness. The true sign of godliness—imitating God—is to pattern our lives after him. And for God, rest is vitally important. As a matter of fact, rest from our activities is listed in God's Top Ten. The commandment to keep the Sabbath is right up there with "don't kill," "don't steal," and "don't commit adultery." In other words, being a workaholic is, to God, just as bad as being a murderer or adulterer. Rest is not an option if we are to walk in the lifestyle of a disciple.

Since our first experience as created beings with our Creator was a day of rest, we see that in order to fulfill our calling to be fruitful, we must start from a place of rest. Resting in God— abiding in his presence—is the only way we can be successful in what he has called us to do. Yet how many of us schedule days of rest and relaxation on the calendar before we schedule meetings, conventions, and other days of work? Is this

9. Rhythm of Life: The Semi-Circle

challenging to you?

You are facing pressure to be successful in your life. You are searching for ways to grow your church, build your business, or to be fruitful on whatever your mission is. This is good—you are meant to be fruitful. God wants your mission to thrive more than you do. Growth is a sign of life. But in order to be productive, as God wants you to be, you must live in the rhythm of the Semi-Circle.

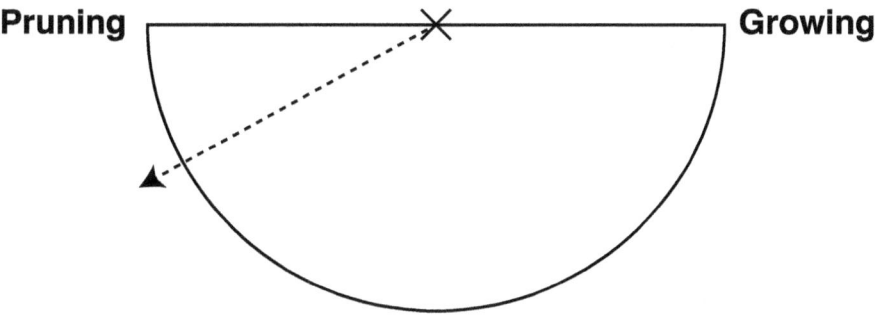

Imagine a pendulum swinging in rhythm—back and forth, to and fro. The shape created by this swinging pendulum is a Semi-Circle. At one end of the pendulum's arc is fruitfulness. At the other end is abiding. We can't have one without the other. We abide in Christ, then go forth to bear fruit. We bear fruit; then we are pruned back and enter a time of abiding. Rest, work, work, rest. It is a rhythm we see in nature as well.

> *"I am the true vine, and my Father is the gardener. He cuts off every branch in me that bears no fruit, while*

every branch that does bear fruit he prunes so that it will be even more fruitful. You are already clean because of the word I have spoken to you. Remain in me, and I will remain in you. No branch can bear fruit by itself; it must remain in the vine. Neither can you bear fruit unless you remain in me. I am the vine; you are the branches. If a man remains in me and I in him, he will bear much fruit; apart from me you can do nothing. If anyone does not remain in me, he is like a branch that is thrown away and withers; such branches are picked up, thrown into the fire and burned. If you remain in me and my words remain in you, ask whatever you wish, and it will be given you. This is to my Father's glory, that you bear much fruit, showing yourselves to be my disciples."

John 15:1–8

Fruitfulness happens in stages and seasons: abide, grow, bear fruit, prune, abide. This is the rhythm of the swinging pendulum, the Semi-Circle. It's really all about timing. We cannot bear fruit if we do not spend time abiding. But we cannot simply stay put in the abide mode, for a branch that does not eventually bear fruit will be cut off and cast into the fire.

It's interesting that nowhere in this text is growth mentioned. Growth seems to be a result of the right rhythm being established. Growth is not the same as bearing fruit. Sometimes we mistake spiritual growth for the fruit itself. This is not the case. We must grow before we can see fruit. An apple tree, for instance, does not bear fruit for three years. Grape vines are pruned back and forced not to bear fruit for two to three years so that their root systems can be established. Growth must happen before fruit is produced. And growth comes from

9. Rhythm of Life: The Semi-Circle

knowing how to abide.

Permission To Be Unproductive

Let's take a closer look at the first-century process of growing grapes. At the time of Jesus' incarnation, a vine would be cultivated, planted, and left to grow for three years before being allowed to bear fruit. Every time it tried to bring forth a bunch of grapes, it would be cut back. After the third year, the grapes would be allowed to grow on their own. By then the branches were strong enough to support the weight of the grapes without breaking. After the harvest, the branches were pruned back for a time of nourishment and rest before the fruit-growing season began again.

Bearing fruit is the most natural thing in the world for a branch. It doesn't do it by straining to push out a grape. Looking at our lives, however, it would seem producing fruit-making disciples is strenuous. If fruit bearing is not coming naturally in our lives, could it be that we have not spent the proper season abiding? Could it be that we are overgrown branches, too weak to support a single grape, let alone a bunch?

Pruning is not the fun part of life. We seldom see churches displaying banners advertising "40 Days of Pruning," or small groups practicing "pruning yourself to a better life." But if a grapevine is not pruned regularly, the branches grow spindly and weak. There is no abiding time when they gain their strength for the growing season.

We need to learn when it is our pruning time. This seems unproductive at first glance. After all, aren't we supposed to be pressing forth with all of our energy to do the work of the

Kingdom? In a word, no. We are supposed to pattern our lives after that of Jesus. It is not our energy and determination that impresses God, it is our living in the manner he made us that will produce the fruit he intends for us to bear. Pruning is not automatic for the branch. Left to its own plans, it would continue to grow, increasing in size but decreasing in strength, endurance, and health until it would be unable to hold the fruit it is intended to bear.

We need to have times of pruning in our churches, times when most, if not all, activity ceases. Times of rest and abiding. This runs contrary to principles taught in most church growth courses and seminars. How can one grow a church larger by shutting it down for a season? Yet that is exactly what happens at many of the churches where I have discipled the leaders and introduced them to the principles of the Semi-Circle. I encourage them to stop all small groups and to drastically scale back the worship service. Often there is just a simple time of singing and a brief word of encouragement shared. Many of the members go away on holiday or spend more time with friends and family. It looks to many like nothing is happening. But in this time of abiding, great strength is given to those who do the teaching, singing, and serving throughout the rest of the year. Without a time for their spiritual ground to lie fallow, there would be a very poor harvest in the year to come.

From abiding we grow, from growing we bear fruit, from bearing fruit we are cut back. This is the pattern of the Semi-Circle. When the Lord is moving you into a time of pruning and abiding, surrender to him. There is much grace to be found in the place of abiding.

9. Rhythm of Life: The Semi-Circle

Your Personal Style of Rest

Before you and the people you disciple begin to practice the rhythm of the Semi-Circle, it is important to discover how you rest. We don't all rest in the same way. Recognizing whether you are an introvert or extrovert is the first step in learning how you rest. Introverts and extroverts are refreshed and energized by different types of rest.

Extroverts prefer to direct and receive energy from the external world of people and activity. Introverts, on the other hand, prefer to direct and receive energy from the internal world of thought, reflection, and ideas. The following analogy may be helpful: Extroverts are by nature, solar powered, with their preferred energy source being external to themselves. Introverts are more battery powered; they prefer to recreate internally and away from external stimulation.

Introverts and extroverts process information in their preferred worlds.

Extroverts love to think out loud—it is often only when all the words are out there that they can begin to formulate what they really think. Most extroverts know moments in their lives when they have thought out loud and really wished they could rewind history! Extroverts give breadth to life, they tend to know a lot of people and delight in trying a wide variety of hobbies. An extrovert's idea of a relaxing weekend would often include entertaining friends and lots of social interaction.

On the other hand, introverts like to process information in their preferred internal world. If you are going to get the best out of an introvert you often have to give him or her time to process away from the crowd. They tend to prefer written communication as it allows them to craft their response and only to press the send button when they are sure it reflects their considered response. Introverts give depth to life, usually preferring a small number of significant friendships. When they are among people they know well and feel comfortable around, they often become gregarious and sociable. Attending social events where they don't know people well is invariably hard work for introverts, since there is little chance of them establishing deep friendships in such a short period of time. When they discover a hobby that fascinates them, introverts will often devote the time required to master it, spending their lives becoming more and more expert in their chosen interest. Introverts recreate on their own or with a small number of people they know well. They often enjoy reading and watching a good movie.

When it comes to knowing how to rest, understanding how God has created us makes all the difference. If you are an extrovert, don't expect to come away from a quiet evening spent by yourself all refreshed. You will be pining for interaction with others and may actually feel more worn out from being without human contact. Of course, we are to set aside time to spend with the Lord alone. And as we get to know him more intimately, these times will be the most refreshing of all. But there is grace in being who God made us to be. If a cookout with friends is your way to relax, by all means fire up the grill. If you are an introvert needing to recharge, don't feel guilty saying no to the cookout invite from people you don't know well.

9. Rhythm of Life: The Semi-Circle

Rhythm in Action

God's intention is for us to have rhythm at every level in our lives.

Days

Each day should have structure to enable rest and work, relationships and recreation. We need to work out a healthy pattern that prioritizes our life's circumstances. This framework is the order of our day, our personal disciplines. I often encourage people to break the day down into eight hours of sleep, eight hours of work, four hours engaging, and four hours disengaging.

Weeks

The seven days of the week give the next level to work out our rhythm. This will involve at least one day for rest and others for work. Our weekly routines should make way for special family members, church, and neighbors God calls us to love as ourselves.

Months

These longer periods give another level to develop variety and contrast—the Semi-Circle in action. Again, a conscious effort is necessary to plan and establish biblical patterns of work and rest so that a dull routine does not take over. Regular times of celebration and retreat should be scheduled so they are not forgotten.

Seasons

These are the phases of a year that enable us to rest for a longer time. Seasons are built into God's creation. We need to build similar seasons into our lives. Seasons include adolescence and adulthood; singleness and marriage; parenthood to empty nest. Working at a new career may require more of your time than a job you have been doing for a number of years. In each of these seasons, you must find time to abide and work.

How Jesus Rested

We can find biblical examples of the Semi-Circle in the lives of many in both the Old and New Testaments. Jesus lived the principles of the Semi-Circle in his life. If we are to be his disciples, we would do well to follow his example of abiding and fruit bearing. Jesus practiced a rhythm of life. He knew how to order his time in terms of being with his Father and doing the work of the kingdom.

Resting Through Extended Times of Retreat in Mark 1:12–13

Before Jesus began his ministry, he went out into the desert for forty days where he was tempted by Satan but made strong in the Spirit. He was alone, away from people, spending time with God. He knew exactly what he needed to do. He knew where he needed to start. He spent time retreating with his Father. The very first thing he did before he could begin his ministry was retreat. Jesus came out of the desert full of the Holy Spirit.

What does this say to us? We all need times of extended retreat, resting in the presence of God, focusing on him. Like Jesus, at the start of a new ministry or task or phase in our lives, we need to spend concentrated time receiving power and strength from the Father and sifting our motives.

9. Rhythm of Life: The Semi-Circle

Regular Daily Times of Quiet Resting with the Lord in Mark 1:35–39

In this passage we read that Jesus got up early in the morning to go to a solitary place to pray. He was about to begin his second day of ministry and crowds had already gathered, but Jesus got up early to slip away. Before doing anything else, before starting his day, he rested in the presence of his Father and talked with him. A leader's demand for our time and energy will always exceed our capacity, but working harder and longer is not the answer. Jesus said, "I only do the things I see my Father doing." He didn't get a three-year download to his Outlook calendar at his baptism; rather, each morning he had to retreat and establish the priorities for that day.

Teaching the Disciples to Rest in Mark 6:30–32

When you look at the pattern of life the disciples began to develop, it's clear that Jesus was trying to teach them the same thing. In this passage, the disciples gathered around Jesus, reporting back to him all that they had done after returning from being sent out in Mark 6:7. So many people were coming and going that they didn't have a chance to eat. Jesus told them to follow him to a quiet place where they could rest and eat. All this happened in the midst of what we would call revival. Jesus made rest a priority, and we are to follow his lifestyle.

How Deep it Goes

When we were in England, a young American who had joined the staff as a youth worker came into my office. I sat him down and reminded him that the last time we had talked, we discussed how he really needed to engage the teaching on the rhythm of life. He and his wife were newly married, but I had noticed he was overextending himself and not really spending a great deal of time with his new wife.

He admitted that this was a weak point for him, but he said that the Lord was doing great things and that there were so many demands made by the ministry that the sacrifice seemed to be justified.

So I asked him where he found that in the Bible.

He couldn't give me an answer to that.

I told him, "Here's the thing. If you continue in this obsessive and compulsive way of working, it won't be possible for you to continue as a member of the team here because we have a very high value on the rhythm of life and on being fruitful out of abiding. And however fruitful you are now, we don't believe that you're going to be fruitful in the long run. In fact, your collapse will be a great loss to you and a loss to the work in general.

"And so, if the next time we sit down, you haven't adjusted your lifestyle, I'm afraid you're going to have to leave the team."

He looked at me with shock and said, "You can't be serious! You're going to fire me for working too hard?"

I responded, "Well, yeah. Because if you work too hard and begin to demonstrate that the success you're seeing in ministry is because you're overworking, of course that will set a culture of overwork within the ministry—and that doesn't seem to be supported by scripture. The scriptures say that fruitfulness comes from abiding. So you have to learn how to abide."

9. Rhythm of Life: The Semi-Circle

It was a difficult path for him, and he got very close to the prospect of losing his job. But he was a sweet-hearted, humble individual, and in time he learned–just as I had many years before.

It was interesting that it was an American who had to get that close to being fired for overwork. After I got to the States in the early 2000s, it seemed to me that the rhythm of life–the semicircle and the pattern of rest and work so clearly demonstrated in the scriptures–was so important that in the early months and years I was here, I called it the gospel to the American Church. Honestly, based on some of the people that I've seen through the years that those who have learned it and those who haven't, I'd still have to say that the rhythm of life still is good news that needs to be embraced by the church and its leaders, especially in America.

To put the flesh on the bones of the Semi-Circle, listen to the story of my daughter, Beccy, and her husband:

This past year has been one of the hardest that we have walked through together. We've faced transitions, uncertainties, and the kind of exhaustion that seeps into your bones. Between my job, launching new projects, and trying to settle into a rhythm as a blended family, it felt like we were always running, always striving—until we hit a breaking point.

The concept of the semi-circle came to us as a quiet invitation: a different way of living, a rhythm rather than a relentless push forward. The semi-circle life shape is built on Jesus' own pattern of abiding and fruitfulness—of intentional rest leading to meaningful work. We had been stuck in an unhealthy loop of constant doing, neglecting the rest that allows renewal.

So we stepped back and gave ourselves permission to rest.

And something shifted.

Instead of seeing rest as a luxury, we started to see it as a necessity. We built in space for walks, for laughter, for unhurried conversations at the dinner table. We let go of the pressure to have everything figured out. And in that place of abiding—of simply being—we found that fruitfulness followed naturally. The work still mattered, but it came from a place of renewal rather than depletion.

The semi-circle reminds us that pruning is part of the process. There were things we had to cut away, things we had to release. But that pruning wasn't punishment—it was preparation for new growth. Now, as we move into a new season, we're choosing to carry this rhythm forward.

We don't want to live in burnout. We want to live in the fullness of a life that ebbs and flows as it was meant to. And if you're feeling exhausted, if you're wondering how much longer you can keep up the pace, maybe it's time to step back, to abide, to trust that rest is not the absence of work—it's the foundation of it.

10. Deeper Relationships: The Triangle

Let's go back to when I was working at Brixton. At times when I was there, it seemed as though the world was against us.

The people who were running the for-profit nursery in our building needed to move on and find other premises because our work had expanded. We wanted to help them find other premises, and everything seemed to be going great until one day I found the newspaper headline that said, "Vicar kicks out kids."

I had just been away for a couple of days of retreat with the family in the countryside. We drove back across London Bridge into South London and saw the news agents, or what Americans would call a newsstand. These news agents had hand-drawn banners proclaiming the day's headlines.

At one of the news agents just on the other side of Tower Bridge was the banner headline "Vicar kicks out kids."

I thought, "Wow, that guy must be really in trouble." Of course that guy really was in trouble, and that guy was me.

The folks in the for-profit nursery had decided they didn't want to leave the building after all, and they were going to cause a media stir to change our minds about the use of our buildings.

On Mother's Day, a news crew from the national news television station was outside the church, to cover the nursery workers picketing us to prevent people going to the Mother's Day church service on Mother's Day. It was a very, very hard time.

I remember walking around the community complaining to God, saying to him, "Really? What have you brought me here to do? Have you just brought me here to crush me?" I felt very much like Jeremiah saying that God had fooled him and that he was his fool.[63]

And it's not a very common thing for me, but I heard the voice of the Lord say something: "What did the early church do?"

Of course, the Lord knows how my brain works, because he made my brain. So I began to think through early church history and how the church had been so terribly persecuted. Yet all evidence shows that during those times of persecution, the church continued to grow.

Of course, that meant the early church couldn't have operated with an attractional model of ministry, because it's very hard to make persecution attractive. I thought about it a lot, and thought that there must be a strategy of evangelism that Jesus taught his first disciples that didn't require an attractional ministry.

---

63   Jeremiah 20:7ff

10. Deeper Relationships: The Triangle

That's when I plunged headlong into the New Testament (this was around 1989) and began to see the person of peace strategy and began teaching it in the local church.[64] We began trying it out doing the very thing that we'd been learning through the *Kairos* Circle. We were hearing what God was saying and then putting it into practice.

Some people whom I had gotten to know quite well, Bob and Mary Hopkins, were fascinated by this teaching, and they opened doors for me to share at other locations and venues, including the national Vineyard Conference in 1990.

During that time, they also shared the strategy with a good friend of theirs called Alf Patterson who was a missionary in Central America.

The Hopkinses came back from sharing that person of peace strategy with Alf to share with me some of the things Alf was doing that seemed to really articulate the person of peace strategy. They also showed me a triangle he used when he was beginning to define a thing that he called DNA.

I looked at that and thought, "Gosh, that's very similar to the things we would call Up In Out." And so the Up In Out Triangle was born.

We'd been using Up In Out for six or seven years, maybe more, until that point. Up In Out had become part of the language of our mission and Ministry, and now we had a triangle that made it very memorable (or now we would say mimetic). It was amazing how the triangle became so central for our team and our church.

---

64 More on this in the chapter 11.

So the triangle was born into the same environment as the learning circle—a very under-resourced, underprivileged, disadvantaged community. It's fascinating to me how, starting in that context, so many churches today have these three dimensions so clearly articulated in their vision statements when you read their websites.

The Three Dimensions of Jesus' Life

When Jesus came to the region of Caesarea Philippi, he asked his disciples, "Who do people say the Son of Man is?" They replied, "Some say John the Baptist; others say Elijah; and still others, Jeremiah or one of the prophets." "But what about you?" he asked. "Who do you say I am?"

Matthew 16:13–15

Who is Jesus to you? How you answer that question has more to do with the growth of your church than any strategy or plan. Living out the answer in front of the people you're discipling and the wider community is equally important. The lifestyle of Jesus was thoroughly consistent. His followers could see it operating on a daily basis. As we take up the challenge to become disciples of Jesus—and to train those we are discipling to do the same—we need to model our lives after the Master.

Jesus lived out his life in three relationships:

Up—with his Father

In—with his chosen followers

Out—with the hurting world around him.

10. Deeper Relationships: The Triangle

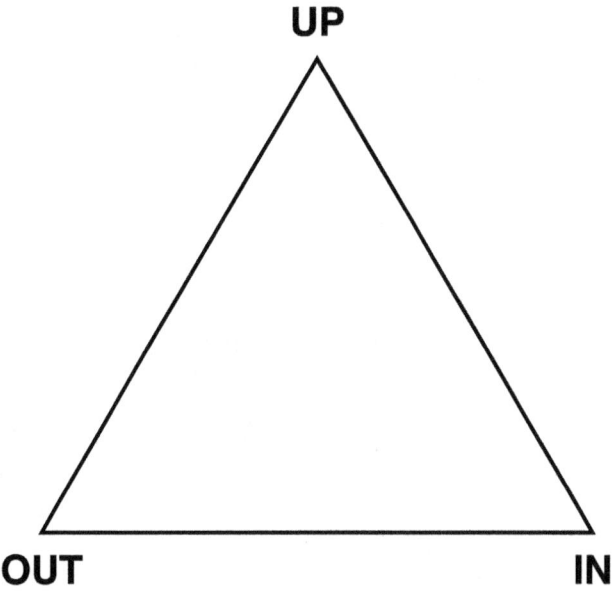

This three-dimensional pattern for living a balanced life is evident throughout Scripture. It can inform us on how to experience fruitfulness in our ministry, our relationships, and our personal spiritual walk. We see these three dimensions in Jesus' lifestyle throughout the Gospels. Let's take a look at one passage in Luke 6.

Jesus Got Up

One of those days Jesus went out to a mountainside to pray, and spent the night praying to God.

Luke 6:12

Jesus prayed regularly. On this occasion he went up the mountain to pray and spent the whole night praying. Mark tells us that when the disciples got up in the early morning, Jesus had already gone out to pray. Luke tells us that he could often be found in lonely places praying. Prayer was as fundamental an element in the life of Jesus as breathing. He inhaled his Father's presence so he could exhale his Father's will.

Jesus was in constant contact with his Father, whom he spoke of in a very personal, intimate, and familiar way. The source of Jesus' fruitfulness was in his Up relationship with the Father. Jesus did what he saw the Father doing. Jesus also introduced his disciples to this very personal relationship with God, calling us into the same kind of intimacy with the Father that he himself has always known. We are to live out the reality of that relationship always.

Our Up relationship with Jesus is how we abide in him. As his disciples, we are to model our lives after our Master. We (the branches) must abide in him (the Vine) if we are to produce fruit. Our efforts are worthless if we do not have the Up in our lives. We will be fruitless without it—there is no other way.

Jesus Invited Others In

When morning came, he called his disciples to him and chose twelve of them, whom he also designated apostles: Simon (whom he named Peter), his brother Andrew, James, John, Philip, Bartholomew, Matthew, Thomas, James son of Alphaeus, Simon who was called the Zealot, Judas son of James, and Judas Iscariot, who became a traitor.

Luke 6:13–16

10. Deeper Relationships: The Triangle

Jesus came back from his time of prayer described in Luke 6 and he called twelve of his followers into his first "Huddle." Mark gives us a clearer picture of this group's purpose.

He appointed twelve—designating them apostles—that they might be with him and that he might send them out to preach.

Mark 3:14

Jesus selected these twelve specifically so he might be with them, spend time with them, and build strong relationships with each of them over the three years he had his public ministry. But this was not just a "seminary setting." Jesus came as a human being and showed us the way human beings are to live out their lives in society with others. From the crowds who followed him, he had seventy-two followers he sent out on kingdom business.[65] From that wider circle, he chose the Twelve, and within that inner circle, he had three close friends—Peter, James, and John. Jesus shared food with these friends, laughed with them, and met their families—in other words, he "did life" with his chosen circle. This was the "In"-ward dimension of his relational life.

Jesus Reached Out

He went down with them and stood on a level place. A large crowd of his disciples was there and a great number of people from all over Judea, from Jerusalem, and from the coast of Tyre and Sidon, who had come to hear him and to be healed of their diseases. Those troubled by

---

65   See Luke 10.

> *evil spirits were cured, and the people all tried to touch him, because power was coming from him and healing them all.*
>
> *—Luke 6:17–19*

Jesus never lost sight of his Father's vision—to reach out to a dark and dying world. Jesus prayed to his Father before calling a team of people to share in the kingdom work. Jesus chose from the larger crowd of disciples a group who would become his friends, and he lived out his life in their presence. But he also walked among the crowds—teaching, feeding, healing, comforting. Jesus did not wait for the spiritually dead to come to him. He went to them and ministered to them at their point of need—and his critics hated him for it.

We were created to be three-dimensional beings. When one dimension is missing or is suppressed, the other two do not work as they should. If we do not have all three elements of the Triangle—the Up, the In, and the Out—we are out of balance, and we will wobble through life. If you've ever driven a car with tires out of balance, you know what we mean. It's not only a bumpy ride, but eventually there will be a blowout—it can be downright dangerous. Jesus' model of a balanced life for leaders is also the model needed for a healthy church.

Two-Dimensional Churches

Most churches are strong in only two of the three elements—Up, In, and Out. Every church experiences seasons when one or two dimensions receive more emphasis than the others. It is more likely, however, that a church reflects the dimensional

10. Deeper Relationships: The Triangle

strengths of its leadership. So if, as a church leader, you lack balance or you attend to one discipline more than another, it is likely your church will be out of balance as well. But Jesus does not want us to settle for two out of three when his perfect plan is for us to live in balance, with all three dimensions fully functioning. Jesus showed us how and calls us to live in the fullness of three dimensions. Let's take a look at some common two-dimensional types of churches.

Up and Inners

Churches that have traditionally emphasized gifts and the ministry of the Holy Spirit have been very strong torchbearers in the areas of Up and In. These churches have helped to usher in modern worship, with emotionally charged music and introspective lyrics. They have also encouraged conversations with God, talking directly with him as well as listening to his responses. Receiving a "word from God" emphasizes the Up.

These churches also do a good job building community. Small groups based on common interests come naturally in this setting. Bible study (Up) and fellowship (In) go hand-in-hand in such places. Those on the outside, however, often express how hard it is to be accepted by an established small group. As for the worship itself, people can come and go and remain anonymous. The more exciting and elaborate the worship, the larger the crowd that gathers. And the larger the crowd, the easier it is to attend without commitment. Thus, churches that traditionally stress an emphasis on the gifts and ministries of the Holy Spirit can be said to have strong Up and In relationships, but often are weak in the area of Out.

Up and Outers

There is another group of churches that is very committed to the Upward aspect of the Triangle. Churches that have traditionally emphasized the importance and inerrancy of the Scriptures have helped to make the Bible available to the widest audience possible through readable translations and practical, expository teaching. From these churches we have also learned much about prayer, as they emphasize the verse "Ask and it will be given to you; seek and you will find."[66] While the expression looks different than our first group, they have a strong Up dimension.

This group of churches also is concerned about reaching outside the church walls to the surrounding community. Outreach campaigns and witnessing seminars are held regularly in these churches, enabling us to take the Gospel to the lost. You also will find strong global support of mission work, both through significant financial contributions and by supplying missionary workers. People in these churches often spend their vacation time participating in short-term mission trips. Out is a real strength for them.

The Inward area of relationship, though, is not so strong in these churches. It may seem that attendance at a small group Bible study is more duty than desire. Self-sacrifice is rightly emphasized, but it somehow seems to also apply to self as it relates to those who belong to the church. "We" is not as important as "they," so the In is out of balance.

---

66   Matthew 7:7

10. Deeper Relationships: The Triangle

In and Outers

Then there are the churches, many of which are part of older, mainstream denominations that stress the importance of incarnational ministry. These churches often are found in the heart of our cities, perhaps even the only church within the city limits. They do a wonderful job caring for the hurting and lost, providing levels of help that community agencies cannot. Many people are attracted to these churches as safe havens from the dangerous environment that surrounds them. These churches are very strong in both In and Out relationships.

Like our first two groups of churches, these brothers and sisters also are out of balance in their ministry. The emphasis on our revelatory God is not a strength. Prayer is often rote rather than a personal petition. Scripture reading is part of the service format, but is not often expounded. For these churches, Up is the weak link.

Evaluating Your Church

Take a moment to consider your church. Are you strong in proclaiming the Word, in prayer, in worship? This is your Up relationship. How are you in building community, listening, and responding to the needs of those committed to your church? This is In. Do you take the Gospel outside the walls of your church to the community? This is Out. Using this diagnostic, in which of these three areas is your church the strongest? The weakest? Acknowledging where you are out of balance is the first step toward Alignment.

You can do the same when evaluating ministries within your church. Let's say one of your Huddle comes to you questioning why his or her small group is not growing. Use the Triangle as a diagnostic tool to discern where there may be a weakness in the small group. Ask the leader to evaluate for you, on a scale of 1–10, how their group is doing in Up. Do they have a regular time of worship? Do they spend time studying Scripture together? Do the same with In. How are they doing listening to one another's needs, and then setting about to meet those needs? Then comes Out. On a 1–10 scale, how are they in reaching those outside of their small group? Do they have a way of intentionally sharing the Gospel? If the group is healthy, they will be above 7 in all three areas. If they come in at 6 or less in any area, time and effort may be required to bring the group into proper balance.

There is no secret formula to church growth. All healthy churches, small groups, and ministries grow. To be healthy, you must be in relational balance as pictured in the Triangle: Up-In-Out. It really is that simple.

What's Up?

Now, let's do a deeper dive into some key aspects of the three dimensions. We'll start with Up.

> *With what shall I come before the LORD and bow down before the exalted God? . . . He has showed you, O man, what is good. And what does the LORD require of you? To act justly and to love mercy and to walk humbly with your God.*
>
> *—Micah 6:6, 8*

10. Deeper Relationships: The Triangle

When Jesus calls his disciples, he invites them to walk with him. "Come, follow me" (Mark 1:17). The indication is that Jesus is walking, and we are to walk with him. Here we have, in one verse, the summation of what is expected of us as followers of Jesus. It is a lifestyle of balance in our relationships: Up, In, and Out.

"Act justly"—Out

"Love mercy"—In

"Walk humbly with your God"—Up

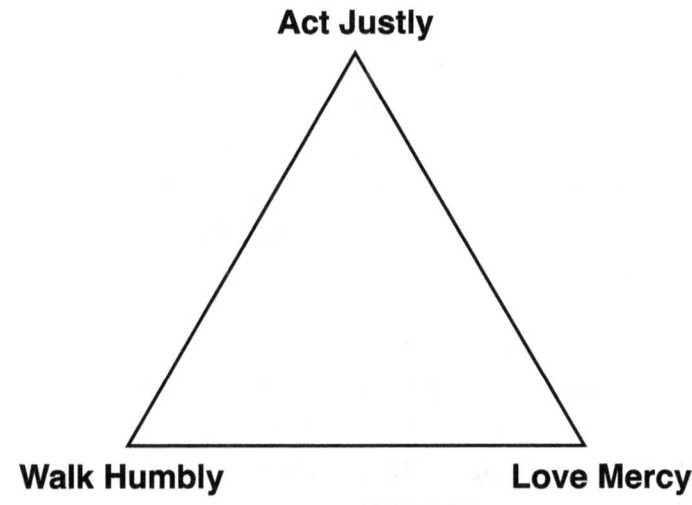

Start Walking

Jesus has invited us to walk with him. This is not just about talking with God. Micah does not read, "talk humbly with your God." We have somehow boiled down the Upward dimension of relationship to only talking and listening to God. If our relationships with others, especially those most significant in our lives, were defined only by talking with them, those relationships would be rather limited. The same holds true in our Upward relationship with God. We can't just talk it out—we need to really walk it out with him. Walking with Jesus should be a joy, not a duty.

Frank Laubach, a missionary to the Moslems of the southern Philippines in the early twentieth century, resolved to pursue the kind of daily intimacy Jesus modeled for his followers. As an ordained minister, he confessed to being ashamed that he had often overlooked the joy of sharing God's presence. His writings encourage us to get to know "the invisible Companion inside you." "God," he wrote, "is infinitely more important than His advice or His gifts; indeed, He, Himself, is the great gift. The most precious privilege in talking with Christ is this intimacy [that] we can have with Him. We may have a glorious succession of heavenly minutes. How foolish we are to lose life's most poignant joy, seeing it may be had while taking a walk alone!"[67]

Walk with Jesus. Invite him to be a part of your everyday life. Let him accompany you as you drive, as you work, as you play. If we are to really be in relationship with him, wouldn't that include our "regular" life as well as those times we set aside as spiritual? Teach your people to be full participants in their own faith journeys as well as the journey you are on together.

---

[67] Brother Lawrence and Frank Laubach, *Practicing His Presence* (Goleta, CA: Christian Books, 1973).

10. Deeper Relationships: The Triangle

The Look of Up

We were created to be actively engaged in the Upward dimension of a balanced life. A.W. Tozer expressed it this way: "God formed us for His pleasure, and so formed us that we as well as He can in divine communion enjoy the sweet and mysterious mingling of kindred personalities. He meant us to see Him and live with Him and draw our life from His smile."[68] Can you remember God's smile? If we have not experienced it recently, we may be at a loss to tell others how they can also experience it. How do we do this in our lives? How do you model this with those you are discipling? It would seem that, if the chief end of man is to glorify God and enjoy him forever, today's church is spending a disproportionate amount of time on the first half of that statement and giving little attention to the second half.

Many Christian leaders fall into the trap of being so ministry-focused that they spend too little time enjoying God. Sermon preparation takes the place of delighting in his presence. Prayer is something done mainly for the benefit of others, and the familiarity of worship may not necessarily breed contempt but indifference.

We understand completely how that can happen. But we also know that a church without Up is a church lacking in vision and purpose. The good news is that this is not your responsibility alone. As you model this principle with the people you're discipling and encourage the wider community to also have a walking, talking connection with Christ, as well as balance in the other two dimensions (In and Out), you will find your

---

68   A.W. Tozer, *The Pursuit of God* (Harrisonburg, PA: Christian Publications Inc., 1948) 34.

leaders' unity of purpose and strength of vision increasing.

The Power of Up

Today's unchurched are not so much rejecting Christ as they are suspicious of Christians. Churches that practice the presence of God have great appeal to a generation that is hungrier than ever to know and be known by a God worthy of reverence. Donald Miller, in his book Blue Like Jazz, relates the following story illustrating the powerful influence that really knowing Jesus can have.

A guy we know named Alan went around the country asking ministry leaders questions. He went to successful churches and asked the pastors what they were doing, why what they were doing was working. It sounded very boring except for one visit he made to a man named Bill Bright, the president of a big ministry. Alan said he was a big man, full of life, who listened without shifting his eyes. Alan asked a few questions. I don't know what they were, but as a final question he asked Dr. Bright what Jesus meant to him. Alan said Dr. Bright could not answer the question. He said Dr. Bright just started to cry. He sat there in his big chair behind his big desk and wept.

When Alan told that story I wondered what it was like to love Jesus that way. I wondered, quite honestly, if that Bill Bright guy was just nuts or if he really knew Jesus in a personal way, so well that he would cry at the very mention of His name. I knew that I would like to know Jesus like that, with my heart, not just my head. I felt like that would be the key to something.[69]

Like so much of the life of discipleship, the principle of

---

69   Donald Miller, *Blue Like Jazz* (Nashville, TN: Nelson, 2003) 233.

10. Deeper Relationships: The Triangle

living in intimacy with Christ is simple yet hard. You can invite God into any part of your day. Truth is, he's there already, and it is rude to ignore his presence. He's never too busy to talk with you, he enjoys the same things you enjoy, he wants to be a part of your life—he really does.

Balancing our In Relationships

One of those days Jesus went out to a mountainside to pray, and spent the night praying to God. When morning came, he called his disciples to him and chose twelve of them.

—Luke 6:12–13

Jesus understood the need of every human being for relationship. We long to belong. The need for healthy relationships with other believers in the body, the Church, is another aspect of the Inward dimension of the balanced life. It is foundational to the building of a discipling culture, the training and sending out disciples who can make disciples. It is in the In relationship that Jesus modeled the skills his followers would need to grow the Church. As Jesus is our model, we are to follow his lead in the area of covenantal relationships with one another. Covenant is an underlying principle in Scripture. From the covenant with Abraham in Genesis 15 to the new covenant sealed with the blood of Christ, we are constantly reminded that God has a covenant, or contract, with us. But the idea of covenant is much more than just a contract. It is a gracious commitment, fully identifying with one another, sharing all possessions, loyal no matter the cost. This relationship is expressed in the very nature of God becoming incarnate.[70] This Inward relationship—living in love with one another—is the only identifying mark Jesus said Christians were to have. "By this all men will know that you are my disciples, if you love one another."[71]

A Culture of Disconnection

If Jesus, the most brilliant leader of all time, placed a priority on relationships, what can we learn from his example? A healthy, relational balance is essential to effective leadership. We were created to be in relationship, to live in society with others. The smallest indivisible unit in the kingdom of God is two. We do not function well when we are left to ourselves. Jesus practiced this principle in his own life, and he taught it to his disciples. He did not send the disciples out alone to do the work he taught them. Even when Jesus sent for a donkey, two disciples were dispatched to lead the animal back. Jesus' followers were not meant to operate independently - community is always at the core of discipleship.

In our world today, the 'In' relationships are breaking down at ever increasing rates. We are a nation of fractured families, disenfranchised friends, and increasingly independent individuals. Reality TV lets us experience living life together by proxy. Many faith communities have become little more than gatherings of isolated individuals, while the number of online communities continues to grow. Loneliness has been described as epidemic. We are a society of disconnected people longing for connections.

---

70 My book *Covenant and Kingdom* explains this in far more detail.
71 John 13:35

10. Deeper Relationships: The Triangle

You don't have to look far to know this is true. People in your community are in pain because they do not have a strong In aspect in their life. Our culture will continue to try to fill the void if we don't. "The affirming message of the gospel is that God wants to aid and guide us in the struggle to be human and invites us into a relationship with him. The Bible also teaches us that we find ourselves and true fulfillment not in isolation, not even as we engage with one another, but rather when we relate to God through one another. The challenge for the church is to emphasize the communal nature of the Christian faith and to commit to authentic expressions of that nature."[72]

Jesus Wasn't Worried About Being Fair

Let's increase the challenge: Fundamentally, you can't model for others what you personally are not experiencing. Do you have close friends you can be completely open with? Many of the pastors I work with have been burnt in the past and have concluded that the safest option is not to have close friendships with those they lead. This is not a solution—scar tissue, left unattended, creates complications that lead to great sickness and pain. We need to go to God for healing from wounded relationships, then move on. We cannot stay away from close friendships just because we have been hurt.

Pastors and ministry leaders are sometimes the loneliest people in the church. We have bought into the false idea that we must maintain a professional distance from those in the congregation. We also don't want to be accused of "playing favorites." Look once again at Jesus and his relationships. He

---

[72] Craig Derweiler and Barry Taylor, *A Matrix of Meanings: Finding God in Pop Culture* (Grand Rapids, MI, Baker Academic, 2003) 81.

had three very close friends—Peter, James, and John. What did the other nine think of this? Apparently, Jesus didn't care what they thought. And what did the seventy-two think of the twelve? Jesus had a closer relationship with the twelve than the seventy-two, but again, he doesn't try to be fair. He needed close friends in his life and did not shy away from inviting the three, then the twelve, into a tighter circle than others. As a Christian leader, you cannot escape the human need for close relationships just because others might be jealous. If you are going to preach the In aspect of life, you need to model it by inviting others into a discipling relationship with you.

'Join Me, The Karma Army'

In case you think I'm carrying this "life together" bit too far, let me tell you about what happened when a single Englishman got an idea.

Danny Wallace was between jobs—having recently left a position as a producer for BBC-TV in London—when he learned his great-uncle, Gallus Breitenmoser, had passed away at the age of ninety. Danny went to Switzerland for the funeral, and while there heard about the crazy idea his great-uncle had pursued.

Following World War II, Gallus had grown tired of living in his city, where there was much gossip and slandering, and wanted to do life with others who would work and live together out of respect for one another. He owned some land, so he decided to start a community farm, hoping to attract one hundred others to live with him.

He got only three.

10. Deeper Relationships: The Triangle

After a week, he gave it up. But for the rest of his life, his family talked about Gallus and his crazy idea. They were still laughing about it at his funeral. This was the first Danny had heard of his great-uncle's quest for community. And the more he thought about it, the more Danny wanted to see if he could collect people together today. In a tribute to Gallus, Danny placed a small ad in a small London newspaper. It read:

Join Me. Send one passport-sized photo to...

(and he gave his address)

A few days later, Danny received a letter from Christian Jones, who included a photo of himself as well as a menu from an Indian restaurant in his part of London. Danny had his first joinee. He put up a website, and in a short time had 101 joinees, surpassing his great-uncle's goal. Why had people joined? There were no meetings planned, no tasks to accomplish. So far, people had just been asked to send in a photo. That's it. Within weeks, more than one hundred people had done so. They signed up for a group for no other reason than to belong. This was social media long before Twitter existed or Facebook mattered—based on the simple platform of a newspaper classified ad.

Danny was astounded and a bit put out. His joinees now expected him to give meaning to this community. But it had no purpose... until Danny came up with one. He sent an email where he revealed the plans for the collective. They would be called the Karma Army, and their purpose was to undertake one random act of kindness every Friday, now to be known as Good Fridays. The Karma Army had its marching orders. A joinee would buy a sandwich and give it to a stranger on a bench. Others bought newspapers and gave them to those sitting in the park. Lunches were bought, groceries were carried, and lawns were mowed: all done freely because they were part of the Karma Army.

For more than a decade, people went online or even to Facebook to become part of the Karma Army. It grew worldwide in spite of the fact that there are no club dues, no regularly scheduled meetings, and no rules and regulations to follow. Or, perhaps it grew because there are none of these things.

The Karma Army shows us that people are starving for community. So hungry, in fact, that they will join others simply because they are asked to. Social media reminds us every day of this reality. And it's really not hard to uncover. Combine the viral nature of information and the connecting power of digital connections, and you get the atmosphere in which movements can blossom and spread incredibly quickly. The hunger for connection is there, just below the surface.

So where is the church with this hunger going on around us? Why do we not ask others to join us? Danny Wallace and his Karma Army get it—we must have the In as part of our lives to be balanced and whole. And if Christians are not going to lead the way, then the Karma Army will.

Balancing our Out Reach

Jesus lived a three-dimensional life. First, he did nothing apart from his Father. He called a team of people together to be his friends in the kingdom community he was building. Having communicated with the Father (Up) and gathered these friends (In), Jesus then moved (Out) into the crowd and

10. Deeper Relationships: The Triangle

did the work of the kingdom—proclaiming the Good News, challenging injustice, teaching the people, healing the sick, and revealing the love of the Father to the world. Most of the people you lead will eagerly practice the Upward dimension of the relationship triangle. They may even be willing to work harder on their relationships within their close circle—the Inward dimension. However, the thought of giving expression to their faith in relationships outside of their comfort zone may be a frightening idea.

One of the most obvious areas of seismic cultural change is in outreach. In the past, nonbelievers clearly identified the church as the place to go for answers to spiritual questions. Many of our current models of evangelism are still based on that premise. Unfortunately, many of these methods are still navigating by landmarks that are no longer there: a shared moral code, childhood exposure to church, a common spiritual language. We continue to offer answers to questions that most unchurched people are no longer asking. Today we have a generation of nonbelievers that might not ever enter the doors of a church unless they have already had a positive encounter with a Christian in the world. The idea of evangelism frightens many Christians. They rarely see outreach modeled in a way that they feel capable of doing. That is why their evangelistic efforts are usually confined to bringing a friend or colleague to church in the hope that a professional Christian will share the Gospel with them. But once Jesus' strategy of outward relationships is explained, that fear often vanishes. When they are encouraged to look for people they naturally connect with and build relationships with them, sharing the Gospel message seems much more possible. We don't have to force ourselves on the unsuspecting: we can make a connection with a person God has already prepared.

The Uncomfortable Balance

Jesus said he would make us fishers of men. In Jesus' day, fishing was done primarily with nets, unlike our recreational method of hook and bait. The men worked cooperatively to lower the nets into the waters, dragging them through the sea toward the boats, where they could be hauled on board. Dragnet fishing indiscriminately gathered in fish of all sizes, along with a good bit of sea debris. The keen eyes of the fishermen were then set to sort through the catch. It was grueling work, but the fishermen never expected the fish (or just the right fish) to jump into their nets. If we simply stay in our safe zones—our church, our small group, our Christian sub-culture—we will not be where the lost are. We have to leave our comfortable settings and get out where there are people who do not yet know that God loves them so much he cannot stop thinking about them. We must have an outward relational dimension in our lives that draws others in.

Living out of Purpose

Let's revisit Danny Wallace and his collective known as Join Me. Within a relatively short time, several thousand joinees sent their photos to Wallace to become part of this collection of diverse individuals from all over the world. Each joinee had an upward relationship with Danny, whether they met him at a pub in London or on his American book tour, or only communicated with Danny via email. In any case, there was an active Up element with the creator/vision-keeper. (Note: Individuals who don't know our transcendent God often default to another human to fill the need for the Up relationship.)

Of course, the In dimension was seen in their Join Me

10. Deeper Relationships: The Triangle

gatherings. Sometimes these were planned events, but most of the time it was just a spontaneous get-together at a pub or coffee shop. New friendships were made between former strangers.

But Join Me would not have lasted had the members not found a purpose, a cause, a way to reach out to those not in their collective. Danny realized this and created the Karma Army. Joinees are all encouraged to sign Good Friday agreements, promising to carry out at least one random act of kindness to a total stranger every Friday. Danny paints this picture of Good Fridays:

All over the country, little things were happening... little moments of joy in towns and cities across the land. Little events that were brightening up people's lives, even if it was for just a few seconds. Pints were being bought for strangers. Shopping was being carried. Cups of tea paid for. Boxes of chocolates handed out in the streets. Flowers deposited at old people's homes. Cakes left on doorsteps. Sure, none of these events was world-changing, but they were... well... life-affirming, somehow. Strangers being nice to strangers. For no reason whatsoever.

All over Britain, and, in fact, all over Europe now, thousands of people are sticking to their Good Friday agreements and carrying out their little acts of kindness, for no reward or personal gain other than the warm glow they get for having done one. The Karma Army is non-religious. It is non-political. It is about walking into a pub, buying a pint, putting it on a stranger's table with a nod, and walking away. It's about offering someone your [newspaper] on Sunday when you've finished with it. It's not about being thanked, or getting any credit, or going to heaven. It's not about changing humanity; it's about being human.[73]

Danny Wallace and his joinees get it. We do not encourage all the things they do. Yet it seems to us that they are doing what the body of Christ is supposed to be doing. They have seen that life only works when all three dimensions of relationship are present. They have Up, In, and Out all in place in their lives. We are all made to have a relational balance in our lives. Somehow, Join Me has stumbled onto this where many Christian communities today haven't.

Operating in all three dimensions may not come naturally, but it is how God made us to function. If it does not come naturally; it must be done intentionally. We have to make a commitment and effort to have Up, In, and Out in balance. When one dimension is missing or is suppressed, the other two do not work as they should. Up, In, and Out provide three-dimensional balance in the relationships that make up your life and the life of your community in the same way Jesus modeled for us while here on earth. Our intention should be to live all three dimensions in our lives. When we do, we will experience fruitfulness.

Check out this story of fruitfulness that my friend Moses M. shares:

Since the launch of Worship Harvest Ministries in 2006, we desired to understand and practice Biblical discipleship. This desire led us to try myriad practices of community. However, regardless of our creativity and change, something was just not working: the communities were too cozy and inward-focused and simply lacked what we were seeking.

---

73 Danny Wallace, *The Joy of Sects: The Join Me Story*, Join Me, join-me.co.uk/story.html

10. Deeper Relationships: The Triangle

Our answer to the discipleship quest came in 2012 when Tim and Rebecca Lindsay introduced us to the teachings of Lifeshapes. We immediately connected with the material, put it into practice, and hit discipleship gold. We launched with 17 Missional communities in late 2012, and by the grace of God, we have over 1,100 missional communities as of October 2022.

Through missional communities designed around the three dimensions of the Triangle, our core strategies for fulfilling our mandate came to life.

The discipleship triangle is not only the most known meme in the Worship Harvest movement, but our ethos, strategy and practices are also organized around it. Our very mission is drawn from the triangle: We are a movement of the Gospel (UP), Discipleship (IN) and Mission (OUT)

Our strategy is Celebration 3000 (UP), Connection 120 (IN) and Commission 111 (OUT). That is, to plant 3000 Locations by 2042, by every Location planting one every three years (Celebration 3000), have a Missional Community for every 20 members at a Location (Connection 120) and have each MC leading one person to Christ a week and serving one Frontier a month (Commission 111).

We organize our community practices around the teaching of the Triangle as well and found incredible fruit and clarity:

UP

Missional communities gather to pray every weekday on Zoom from 5am to 6am. On Wednesdays, we have Flow Prayer in person and online from 5am to 8am. Then on Sundays we gather to celebrate together what God is doing.

IN

Every Wednesday, we gather in our missional communities to pray together, play together, eat together and grow in the word. We currently have over 18,000 members in over 1100 MCs.

OUT

Every week, every MC is mandated to lead one person to Christ through evangelism. This has taken our salvations from about 500 a year as a movement to over 500 a week. Every month, each MC reaches out to a meaningful frontier within their community. We serve at least 700 frontiers every month, reaching tens of thousands of people.

- Moses Mukisa

Learn more about Worship Harvest here:

www.worshipharvest.org

11. Relational Mission: The Person of Peace Strategy

We've used LifeShapes for more than 30 years now, and they have been tremendously helpful to many people. This discipling language has been indispensable to discipling cultures around the world.

But we have found that the Heptagon and Octagon are not as widely helpful as the others. We believe it's because of the size and numbers of points they contain.

So we've moved these two shapes to the appendices. I encourage you to delve into them there.

However, at this point I feel it's important to share a new insight that has bubbled to the surface more recently. More recently, I have developed a new way of talking about the Person of Peace Strategy alongside or even instead of the Octagon.

The Person of Peace

The Triangle is one of our most used Lifeshapes, and I have discovered in my Huddles and interactions in recent years that it works well in discussing the Person of Peace as well. That's because the Triangle is all about living a balanced life that is UP toward God, IN toward other Christians, and OUT toward the world.

Very often, the third dimension, OUT, is the one we find most challenging, or is the one we are most fearful about pursuing. But we don't need to be fearful, and it doesn't have to be a monstrous challenge. We just need to understand and imitate the way Jesus described the process of reaching out through relationships. And that is the Person of Peace. So let's make sure we understand Jesus' strategy so we can put it to use as a key way of living OUT in a balanced life.

> *After this the Lord appointed seventy-two others and sent them two by two ahead of him to every town and place where he was about to go. He told them, "The harvest is plentiful, but the workers are few. Ask the Lord of the harvest, therefore, to send out workers into his harvest field. Go! I am sending you out like lambs among wolves. Do not take a purse or bag or sandals; and do not greet anyone on the road. When you enter a house, first say, 'Peace to this house.' If a man of peace is there, your peace will rest on him; if not, it will return to you."*
>
> *Luke 10:1–6*

The destiny of the Church is directly tied to how passionate she remains to her mission. In past decades, our zeal to fulfill the Great Commission has often led to the great omission[74]—we've made converts without making disciples fully trained

---

74   As Dallas Willard called it

11. Relational Mission: The Person of Peace Strategy

and equipped in all Jesus taught. As the Church, we are all to participate in God's command to go and make disciples according to the model that Jesus has given us.

How we approach outreach in today's culture has fallen under scrutiny in recent years, and rightly so. Many of the techniques that have worked in the past are obviously not working as well anymore.

We've already stated that Jesus was the wisest man that ever lived, as well as the best leader and teacher. It just makes sense that he would also be the best at evangelism. In his book Permission Evangelism, Michael Simpson looks at Jesus' interaction with the rich, young ruler (Mark 10) and sums it up this way:

"Christ was evangelizing, but it sure doesn't look like the way most people do it today. Even though it says Jesus loved him, he stood there and let the man walk away. Why did Christ not follow him when he walked away? Why didn't he try harder when this man seemed so eager? Why didn't Jesus 'get him saved' before addressing this difficult area of his life [his riches]?

Christ didn't run after the rich young ruler because he knew the young man's heart wasn't ready. Jesus knew and let him walk. Jesus never ran after anyone. Instead, he made himself available to those willing to wholeheartedly seek the Way to God, the Truth about God, and the Life found in God."[75]

---

75 Michael L. Simpson, *Permission Evangelism* (Colorado Springs, CO: Cook Communications Ministries, 2003) 51.

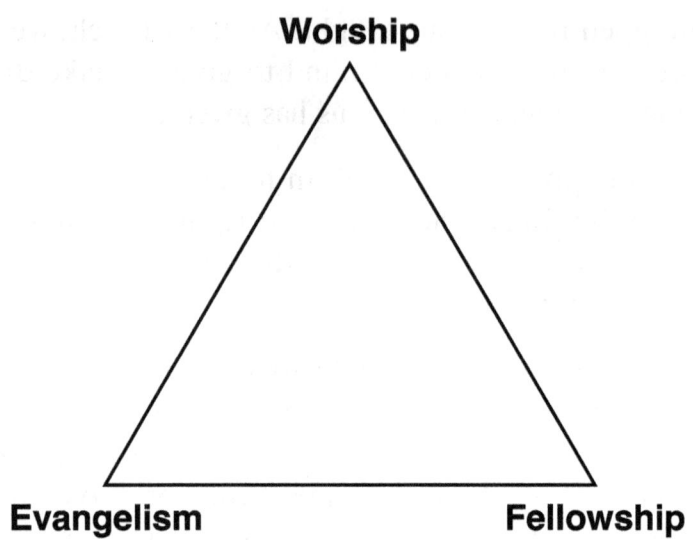

Person of Peace

As Jesus commissioned the seventy-two disciples to go ahead of him, proclaiming the coming of the kingdom of God, he gave them directions for how to proceed.

"When you enter a house, first say, 'Peace to this house.' If a man of peace is there, your peace will rest on him; if not, it will return to you"

—Luke 10:5–6

Jesus' message to his disciples then, and to us today, is that as we are walking in this world, we are to be on the lookout for a Person of Peace. Who is this Person of Peace, and how do we recognize him?

Very simply, a Person of Peace is one who is prepared to hear the message of the Kingdom and the King. He is ready to receive what God will give you to say at that moment. This

11. Relational Mission: The Person of Peace Strategy

should be our prayer as we venture forth each day. "Lord, bring into my path today a Person of Peace, and give me the grace to speak your words to this person." One who is not a Person of Peace will not receive what you have to say. We are not to belabor the issue. Jesus says to shake the dust off your feet and move on. No amount of coercion on our part can make someone become a Person of Peace. This is the job of the Holy Spirit; he alone can prepare a heart to hear the Gospel. Our job is to have our spiritual eyes open, looking for a Person of Peace to cross our paths. Perhaps this concept will make more sense as we see it modeled by Paul when he went out on his mission trips.

How Paul Found the Person of Peace

We read in Acts 16 that Paul, along with Silas, Timothy, and Luke, made plans where to go next, but were "kept by the Holy Spirit from preaching the word in the province of Asia."[76] They then turned toward Bithynia, but once again the Spirit kept them from going there. Then in the night Paul had a vision of a man in Macedonia crying out for help. Right away they packed up and set out for Macedonia.

Once they arrived in the Macedonian city of Philippi, Paul set forth to find a Person of Peace, someone prepared to receive the Word of God. It was the Sabbath, and Paul knew he would find devout Jews and "God-fearers" (Gentiles who worshiped God and adhered to the Jewish scriptures) by the river praying as the custom was. When they found a group of women there, Paul—a rabbi by training—assumed the role of a teacher and sat down.

---

76 Acts 16:6

As he proclaimed the Gospel, the Lord opened the heart of one woman, a dealer in purple cloth named Lydia. Paul recognized that she was a Person of Peace for that moment. We don't know what he said to her, or her exact words in response. We do know that she and her household were all baptized into the faith, and Paul and his friends stayed with Lydia while they continued to plant a church in Philippi.

They stayed in Philippi long enough that they became regulars at the riverside prayer meetings. One time as they were heading for the river, a slave girl possessed by a demon spirit followed them shouting, "These men are servants of the Most High God, who are telling you the way to be saved."[77] Surely this must be a Person of Peace! This was an open door for evangelism if ever there was one, right?

Paul did not see it that way. He commanded the evil spirit to leave the girl, which it did immediately. The problem was the girl, under the influence of the evil spirit, could tell the future and was being used by her masters to make large amounts of money. Now her masters were furious that their way to wealth had been torn out from underneath them. They dragged Paul and Silas before the magistrates, and the apostles were beaten and thrown in prison.

Once again, even in the confines of these circumstances, Paul was on the lookout for a Person of Peace. This time, it came in the form of the jailer who guarded them. You are familiar with the story: around midnight, as Paul and Silas were singing worship songs, an earthquake shook the prison so that all the chains were loosed and all the doors flung open. The jailer thought the prisoners must have escaped and, saving his

---

77   Acts 16:17

11. Relational Mission: The Person of Peace Strategy

commanding officer the trouble, set about to take his own life.

"Don't harm yourself!" shouted Paul. "We are all here!"

"Sirs, what must I do to be saved?" cried the jailer.

Acts 16:30

As Paul was present in the jail (not by his choice, but there he was), the person God had prepared presented himself, and Paul walked through the open door.

The Person of Peace is someone God has prepared for that specific time. It is no good trying to force open doors that God has not opened, and we must not be distracted so that we miss the doors he has opened. This really is exciting news. Even in the most important task we have been given, the assignment to go and make disciples, God does most of the work. Our main job is to walk through life with our eyes open and our ears listening to the Spirit as he reveals to us the Person of Peace he has prepared.

Empowering Evangelism

Our outward relationships are not just to be occasional outreach projects or evangelism programs. We are to live a lifestyle of mission, evangelism, and service. Jesus explained his mission imperative to his disciples as "the reason I have come."[78] He spoke of sending his followers as the Father had

---

78   Mark 1:38

sent him,[79] commissioned them as disciple-makers,[80] and described them as his witnesses in continually-expanding spheres until their message reached the ends of the earth.[81] In every account of Jesus addressing his disciples (the twelve and the seventy-two), he recounted their mission. This biblical strategy for evangelism is a key way for us to reach OUT.

So let's take a look at five things to keep in mind as you look for the Person of Peace.

Time

Jesus preceded his sending the disciples with an exhortation that there are specific times and places the harvest is ripe.[82] He links this discernment with an observation: lift up your eyes. Not every section of society, subculture, or individual is equally ready and open to the Gospel. In some contexts we need to sow, while in others we should be prepared to reap. Part of our mission task is to have God's perspective showing us where there is spiritual openness. Remember what we learned with the Triangle: before we can have an outward relationship, we must have the upward connection.

Every Christian community is to be involved in both sowing and reaping. Many of our current ways of doing church might make us uncomfortable with what Jesus is telling us here. Jesus says we should be glad to invest in a harvest even though the benefit of our labor might go to the church down the street. If our mission is the expansion of the kingdom, it shouldn't matter who reaps the benefit of our labor. As kingdom workers, our

---

79 John 20:21
80 Matthew 28:19
81 Acts 1:8
82 John 4:34-38

11. Relational Mission: The Person of Peace Strategy

job is to learn to discern the season of each person's soul. Is it sowing time or reaping time?

Team

Our inward relationships lead to our outward ministry. We are not called to go it alone, as we have seen in our discussions of the inward dimension of the Triangle and in our discussion of the contrast between organizations and living organism (which you find in the appendix about the Heptagon). The mission-minded church will develop a team model for evangelism.

There are good reasons for this even apart from the fact that it is the way Jesus did it. In our culture today, longing to belong makes authentic community a very powerful drawing force. Just as in the times of the early Church, unbelievers are compelled to check out the message of such groups. This principle can be seen in the ministry of Paul. He is constantly referring to his teammates—Barnabas, Silas, Timothy, Titus, and more. Jesus' presence is promised wherever two or three believers are together.[83]

Target

Jesus was very strategic in his outreach. He knew he could not be everywhere at once, and neither could his disciples. He focused their outreach on the lost sheep of the house of Israel[84] and warned them against being distracted by those not ready to receive their message.[85] In mission and evangelism we should look for people who are open to us and our message. We should concentrate on these receptive People of Peace, and not force

---

83 Matthew 18:20
84 Matthew 10:6
85 Luke 9:5, 10:4

dialogue or relationship where they do not naturally flow.

Task

The assignment for the disciple is to share the Good News of the Kingdom with the Person of Peace, whenever and wherever that person is found. How do we recognize the Person of Peace? According to the instructions Jesus gave his disciples in Matthew 10 and Luke 10, the Person of Peace will:

Like you. They will welcome you into their life if that doesn't happen then remember that you need to use your time and effort somewhere else and so you are to "shake the dust off your feet"(Matthew 10:14).

Listen to you. People will show their welcome by being interested in who we are and the message we carry. It's always good to remember that those who listen to you are listening to Jesus (Luke 10:16).

Serve or support you. We should step out conscious of our needs and how God wants to meet these needs through the people to whom we are sent. We must allow a Person of Peace to serve us and supply what we don't have (Matthew 10:10).

Many of those we lead feel very uncomfortable when they hear the word evangelism—perhaps guilty. However, Jesus simply said to look for people who want to listen to you—people you will encounter in your everyday walk. This is something they can do within their existing contacts and relationships. There is a great burden lifted from our people as we share with them God's part in the process.

Trouble

If the teacher is not received, said Jesus, the students should

11. Relational Mission: The Person of Peace Strategy

not expect a warm welcome either. As we go out into the world looking for the Person of Peace and sharing the Good News of the kingdom of God, we must expect trouble in our lives. There will be many who are not yet ready to hear the message, and they will react strongly against what they perceive as intolerance or insensitivity on your part. It is not an "if" but a "when" as to this happening.

Our mission to the world has not changed. What we need now is to express it in such a way that everyone you are discipling as well as the wider community feel empowered to participate. Many Christian leaders spend their entire lives within the confines of the church campus and wonder why they see little breakthrough in the area of evangelism. Leaders define culture and as such, your disciples and the Huddles they lead will imitate what you actually do, not necessarily what you teach.

For more information on the Person of Peace strategy, you may find the full explanation of the Octagon in the appendices helpful. We encourage you to delve more deeply there.

If you feel uneasy, take encouragement from my friend, Mike S.:

When I first encountered the Person of Peace (POP) strategy, which encourages you to look for someone who likes you, listens to you, and serves you, I was initially taken aback. After all, who serves me? That just sounds a little odd!

My immediate assumption was very one-sided placing all the burden on the other person, and my definition of 'serve' was a bit off. Serving isn't always about grand gestures. Sometimes, it's about small, everyday actions—listening attentively, offering help when needed, or simply being present. It's in these quiet acts that true connection is formed. I also realized that as much as they served me, I naturally responded reciprocally. After all, the POP strategy is rooted in relationship, not a form of evangelism that often catches people off guard and, more often than not, alienates them.

As I began to assess the relationships I had with people in my community, I began to see that there were a number of people who actually "qualified". My next-door neighbors and others that I had met in my neighborhood, my supervisor in a part-time secular job, people I encountered in my work with an international exchange agency I work with, parents I got to know through my kids' sports, people I worked out with at the gym, and of course, people I met at my local coffee shop, just to name a few.

As I counted these various relationships, I recognized that the real challenge—and the real beauty—lies in deepening these connections. I believe the key to any of these connections evolving from acquaintances to real relationships is making them feel "seen". Making people feel seen is what moves them from strangers to POP, from just workout partners sharing social banter to extended conversations in the parking lot, to one-on-one coffee shop conversations, deep conversations. Yes, it takes time, but that is the model Jesus espoused. Evangelism was never meant to be an encounter followed by a prayer, but a relationship followed by a healing of the heart and soul. That's why counseling involves sitting across from a therapist who sees you, sometimes deep inside of you, and helps you find healing mentally and emotionally. Our calling is to help people find healing at a much deeper and eternal level. Fortunately, the Holy Spirit is the catalyst we have that accelerates the

11. Relational Mission: The Person of Peace Strategy

process, but that doesn't mean it's simple work.

The greatest challenge I have found over time, is refreshing or adding to the list of POP. I often get caught up in my little community of friends that feels comfortable, and I am a natural extrovert. For those who have a more introverted personality, the challenge can feel even more daunting. But it doesn't have to be about large social circles. It's about making meaningful connections, even if it's just one person at a time.

The good news is we shouldn't feel like we have a quota to meet, nor should we feel like the measure of success is based on the performance of another. Our list of POP will certainly ebb and flow. However, if we are aware of humanity and engage humanity with empathy, our list will continually be filled with people we can invest in as POP. We just have to be like-able, good listeners, and humble. Shouldn't be a problem for a follower of Jesus!

12. Multiplying Life: The Square

The square came from a combination of insight I found in the work of Ken Blanchard and David Watson.

Watson's seminal book *Discipleship* described the four stages of discipleship as:

- I do it, you watch
- I do it, you help
- You do it, I help
- You do it, I watch

I'm not sure where Watson got that, but it certainly was writ large in his superb book that had such an influence on me, and many others including people like John Wimber here in America.

Blanchard's work presented a reflection on the work of Abraham Maslow, where Maslow said the way that people learn is by going from:

- Unconscious incompetence
- To conscious incompetence
- To conscious competence
- To unconscious competence

These two insights began to meld together for me, and I adjusted Blanchard's square so that it would work more easily with the things that I was thinking about and reflecting on. I also dove into the ministry of Jesus to look at the ways in which he developed his team of disciples.

It was clear from Watson's work that leadership happened in four stages, and it was clear from Blanchard's work that these four stages fully articulated the way Jesus called his disciples and then sent them out at the very end. And so the Leadership Square from the perspective of Jesus the discipling leader was born.[86]

How Jesus Led

> *Jesus called them together and said, "You know that those who are regarded as rulers of the Gentiles lord it over them, and their high officials exercise authority over them. Not so with you. Instead, whoever wants to become great among you must be your servant, and whoever*

---

[86] I had the privilege of sharing this material with Ken Blanchard later, after he had himself tracked it through the ministry of Jesus. Blanchard had become renewed in his faith and wanted to share his materials not simply with the many millions of people who had benefited from his work in management leadership, but with those who are engaged in ministry and mission. It was great fun for Sally and I to have those conversations. Blanchard was such an encouraging man.

12. Multiplying Life: The Square

wants to be first must be slave of all. For even the Son of Man did not come to be served, but to serve, and to give his life as a ransom for many."

—Mark 10:42–45

Jesus' leadership style provides us with powerful tools for leading our people through the current challenges of cultural change. The old adage that "as the leaders go, so goes the Church" is true. Leadership "Jesus style" is not about position, as we can see from the passage in Mark 10, but about how we relate to one another. Our priority as leaders should be to live out a transformed life in front of those we seek to lead. To do this, many of us will have to change our leadership style.

Managed To Death

Our culture, and as part of it the Church, has developed into a management-oriented society. We want to manage growth, manage productivity, and manage human resources. In times of crisis, however, people do not turn to managers for help. In those times, we need leaders. In times of war, soldiers do not follow a manager. In a hospital ER, it takes a leader to make split-second decisions that will save a life.

The Church is crying out for leaders who model a life worth imitating. Dan Kimball puts it this way: "Leadership in the emerging church is no longer about focusing on strategies, core values, mission statements, or church-growth principles. It is about leaders first becoming disciples of Jesus with prayerful, missional hearts that are broken for the emerging culture. All the rest will flow from this, not the other way around."[87]

We need leaders who will step out of "managing church" and make discipling others their primary objective. The time has come to humbly acknowledge before God that we have failed to train men and women to lead in the style of Jesus. Whether through ignorance or fear, we have taken the safe option, training pastors to be theologically sound and effective managers of institutions rather than equipping them with the tools they need to disciple others.

A Square Model For Leadership

There is a great need to restore and encourage leadership in our culture, including the Church. And the Church is the best place to offer a genuine model of leadership. We have Jesus' example to learn from and to share with the rest of the world. When we take on the lifestyle of Jesus as a leader, those outside the Church will see and respond. This is not just a message to senior pastors—Jesus calls us all to be leaders. The commission to go and make disciples is a call for leaders—you are leading when you are making a disciple.

Jesus was the best leader the world has ever seen. He was also the greatest leadership trainer or discipler. If we follow his example and his teachings, we can be the leaders God intends us to be. Jesus' leadership is seen in four stages or phases, thus I use a Square to help easily recall the following principles. Each phase of leadership (or side of the Square) naturally leads to the next.

---

[87] Dan Kimball, *The Emerging Church* (Grand Rapids, MI; Zondervan, 2003) 240.

12. Multiplying Life: The Square

Stage One

"The time has come," he said. "The kingdom of God is near. Repent and believe the good news!" As Jesus walked beside the Sea of Galilee, he saw Simon and his brother Andrew casting a net into the lake, for they were fishermen. "Come, follow me," Jesus said, "and I will make you fishers of men." At once they left their nets and followed him. When he had gone a little farther, he saw James son of Zebedee and his brother John in a boat, preparing their nets. Without delay he called them, and they left their father Zebedee in the boat with the hired men and followed him.

Mark 1:15–20

This passage describes Jesus' encounter with his first disciples. It does not appear that Jesus chooses these men on the basis of their resumes or their spiritual gift inventories. He simply offers them a relationship with himself and a vision to follow. Their enthusiasm fuels their confidence and immediately they step out, put down their nets, and follow him. They are confident but incompetent—they have no experience to base their confidence on. Are they scared? Probably. Had they known what awaited them on their journey, would any of them have started? Who can say? Yet into that situation, Jesus speaks clearly and directly, drawing them in. Jesus is directive and not particularly democratic. He doesn't begin with consensus-style leadership. He doesn't try to get any of these fishermen to agree with his strategy and tactics. He doesn't call for a vote on his teaching of the kingdom. He simply says, "Come, follow me, and I will make you fishers of men." This is very straightforward language. It is not the language he uses later on in his ministry; this is only used at the beginning. He leads by example, going about the land preaching, healing, casting out demons—while the disciples follow along, watching and observing it all.

Disciple Style: D1—Confident and Incompetent

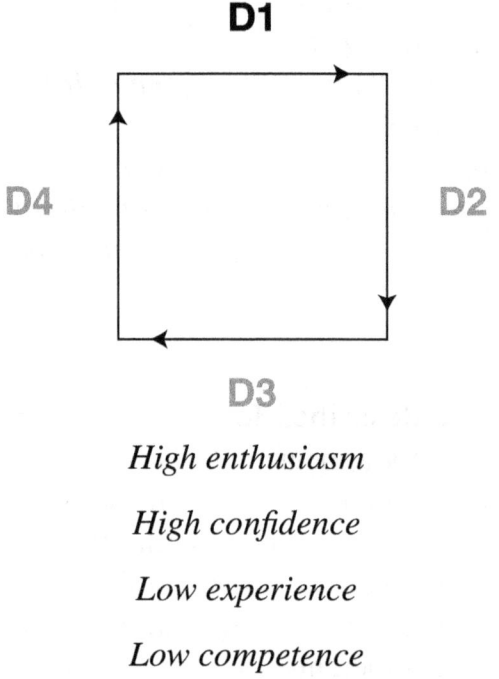

High enthusiasm

High confidence

Low experience

Low competence

At the outset, if you are a follower, there will be highs and lows. The first stage in development happens when you encounter a new idea, a new phase, or a new purpose in your life. It could be a new approach to work, a new team at work, a new small group, and so forth. Certain characteristics identify this particular stage. You feel confident and somewhat emboldened because of the new vision that has been shared. Yet you lack competence because you have never had this experience before. For example, do you remember your first day

12. Multiplying Life: The Square

in college or the first time you preached a sermon? No doubt you were excited—leading to confidence—and felt ready to take on the world. Soon, however, you began to feel the lack of experience and competence. Enthusiasm will only take you so far.

Leadership Style: L1—Directive

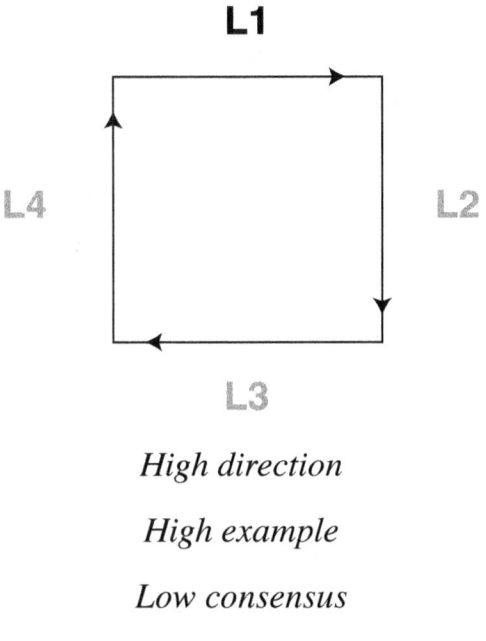

High direction

High example

Low consensus

Low explanation

The disciples followed Jesus at the beginning of his ministry as an answer to his call to them. He was directive in his leadership. At the outset of something new, be it a new Huddle, new team, new worship service, or new task, we should be directive in our leadership. This means announcing a clear direction and walking confidently, not being pushy or unpleasant. The followers are enthusiastic and wanting to do the right thing. Remember, managers do things right while leaders do the right thing. This is a time when an example needs to be set consistently.

This poses a problem for some people. Our system today sees directive leadership as suspect. We have a legacy within recent memory of directive leaders who have been tyrants and who have manipulated their followers' lives for evil intents. Also, our Western independent mindset automatically questions directive authority. We live in a democratic society and often think we need to carry this through in everything we do.

Yet when we start out on a new trail, we need a strong, confident leader to show us the way. There will be a time for consensus, for gathering and listening to opinions from those who follow you, but that time is not at the beginning. If you are to lead as Jesus did, you must do so with firmness and confidence. Jesus did not take a vote of his disciples as to where he should go next. He did not commission a survey of the people's felt needs. He started with the kind of confidence and directness we often lack.

It is imperative to recognize what the beginning of leadership requires. Jesus revealed this in his character and his style of leadership. Are we better leaders than he? Resist the urge to endlessly explain what you are doing or to get feedback from those following. Lay out your plan and stick with it. If people want to follow you, they will. If not, they can get on board somewhere else.

This is why Jesus said that leaders must be broken, humble servants. If you start out as a directive leader, but are not humble, you will soon find you are walking alone. There are times that a leader must take a stand and walk by himself, but not because of arrogance. Remember that as a leader you are

12. Multiplying Life: The Square

simply a representative of the Good Shepherd.

Stage Two

> *"Do not be afraid, little flock, for your Father has been pleased to give you the kingdom. Sell your possessions and give to the poor. Provide purses for yourselves that will not wear out, a treasure in heaven that will not be exhausted, where no thief comes near and no moth destroys. For where your treasure is, there your heart will be also."*
>
> *Luke 12:32–34*

Eventually the disciples become aware that they really have no idea what they are doing. The pressure begins to mount from outside as well as from within—the confidence of these previously successful entrepreneurs hits rock bottom. Worse yet, they suddenly realize they are following a man who is totally opposed by everybody in charge. This man they are following is seen as a curse to leaders of society and the disciples are guilty by association.

The disciples aren't having fun anymore! They start questioning and doubting their call and their decision to follow. We see this in Luke 9-12. At this point Jesus begins saying, "I'll do, but you help." He sends them out to do things he has been doing while they watched: preaching the Gospel, healing the sick, casting out demons. They are laboring in ministry while opposition from the Herodians and the Pharisees increases. The disciples feel overwhelmed; their early confidence is lost and they fall into despair. They fear for their very lives.

Notice that with Jesus' leadership style, experience comes before explanation. He tells the disciples,

> *Do not be afraid of those who kill the body and after that can do no more. But I will show you whom you should fear: Fear him who, after killing of the body, has power to throw you into hell.*
>
> *Luke 12:4-5*

They've just had a near-death experience at the hands of the Pharisees. Jesus comes in behind this experience with an explanation of why they do not need to fear these events. He gives them these instructions:

> *Do not be afraid, little flock, for your Father has been pleased to give you the kingdom. Sell your possessions and give them to the poor. Provide purses for yourselves that will not wear out, a treasure in heaven that will not be exhausted, where no thief comes near and no moth destroys. For where your treasure is, there your heart will be also.*
>
> *Luke 12:32-34*

In essence, Jesus is telling them to let go of their old securities. He wants them to find their security in him. To this point, they probably thought they were going to bring in this Kingdom of God. Now they're unsure whether anyone could bring it in. They're scared. Jesus reminds them it is all about grace. It's not what they can do for God; it's what God can do through them. They need to understand that the Kingdom of God is given, not earned; received, not taken. They can't do the

12. Multiplying Life: The Square

work of the Kingdom themselves. The Kingdom comes only by grace, not works. They begin to learn and believe this.

Jesus adapts his directive style of leadership to more of a coaching style, appropriate to this new situation. Key to this is the way he shares his vision and grace with the disciples. He also looks for ways to spend more time with them. He becomes their Shepherd, demonstrating the Father's grace and love. They begin going to faraway places just to get away from people. Jesus spends more time alone with his followers in order to relieve their fears and help them focus on what it means to live a kingdom life.

Disciple Style: D2—Unenthusiastic and Incompetent

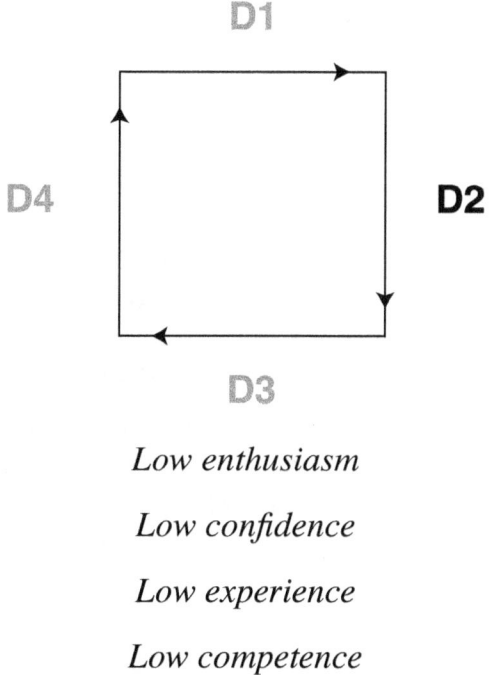

Low enthusiasm

Low confidence

Low experience

Low competence

Stage two is the most important in the development process for a disciple. This is when the excitement begins to die down and the feelings of incompetence and inexperience come to the forefront. Disappointments pile up; expectations are not fulfilled. It is hard to realize you really can't do what you are called to do. Opposition and difficulty begin to be overwhelming. You forget the vision and begin questioning how much you really understood it to begin with. There are no highs to balance the lows. You realize you aren't equipped for the mission and soon descend into the deep pit of despair.

What we tend to do at this point is try to regain the enthusiasm experienced in the D1 stage. Many of us go back and forth from D1 to D2, then D1 and D2 again and again. Instead of allowing God to take us completely through the vulnerability of D2, we choose to ignore it and go back to the feelings we had in the D1 phase. Soon we crash back into D2 again. If we do not have a leader to take us through D2, we will bounce back and forth between enthusiasm and despair, with the two coming at ever-closer intervals. We must receive the grace that comes only by fully experiencing the D2 phase.

Building a discipling culture is an incredibly attractive vision for leaders and not difficult to sell. However, D2 is inevitable, and you will be tempted to give up and return to your previous model of doing church. Without an L2 leader who is prepared to offer you time, vision, and grace, you will not make the turn into D3. It doesn't matter how gifted you are or how successful you have been in the past.

12. Multiplying Life: The Square

Leadership Style: L2—Visionary/Coach

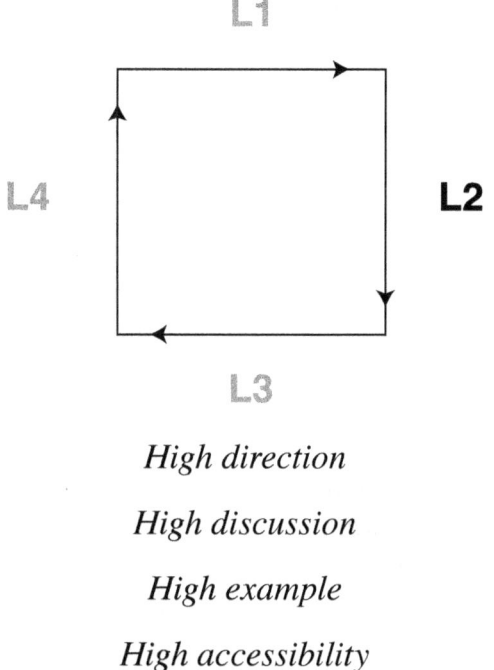

High direction

High discussion

High example

High accessibility

The second stage is the testing point of any leader. During this stage, the leader should clear his or her schedule and spend time down in the pit with the individual or team going through D2. Leaders need to be there to offer God's grace and encouragement. At this point, there is a ladder the leader can offer to bring his disciples out of the pit. The two rungs on this ladder are grace and vision.

It is when a disciple is in the time of discouragement and despair that vision is critical. Vision is needed when you don't know what you are looking at or looking for. Painting a vision for followers does not mean glossing over the hard truth. It simply allows the disciple to say, "OK—this is what I signed up for. It is about God's Kingdom, not my comfort. Let's go."

In this stage the leader needs to talk through the idea of grace and the concept that we can only continue on by God's grace, not by lifting ourselves up by our bootstraps. Grace is an incredibly difficult concept for us as humans to grasp. We all like to think that it's up to us to pull it off. It's not up to us—we are simply following God's directions to accomplish his purpose. He will always accomplish what he wants done. It is amazing what happens when a leader can take a person or group out of his own striving and into a place of resting in grace. Their confidence begins to grow because they are seeing it is God's work by grace, not their work by their own effort.

In addition to testing the competence of a true leader, these first two steps are critical to the growth of a disciple. However, the journey and relationship between leader and disciple does not end here; if it does, the leader has failed in his ability to disciple, and the disciple himself will suffer the consequences of being inadequately equipped. As leaders, we must learn to move our disciples, as Jesus did, into a new phase of confidence and experience.

The Language of Leadership

The goal of spiritual leadership," wrote John Piper, "is to muster people to join God in living for God's glory."[88] To meet this goal, we need to pattern our leadership after Jesus as he mustered his disciples in living for God's glory. Let's continue our look at how the four stages of discipleship match up with the stages of leadership modeled by Jesus.

---

88 John Piper, Brothers, *We Are Not Professionals: A Plea to Pastors for Radical Ministry* (Nashville, TN: Broadman and Holman, 2002) 11.

12. Multiplying Life: The Square

Stage Three

"My command is this: Love each other as I have loved you. Greater love has no one than this, that he lay down his life for his friends. You are my friends if you do what I command. I no longer call you servants, because a servant does not know his master's business. Instead, I have called you friends, for everything that I learned from my Father I have made known to you. You did not choose me, but I chose you and appointed you to go and bear fruit—fruit that will last. Then the Father will give you whatever you ask in my name. This is my command: Love each other."

John 15:12–17

Jesus begins to use their time away from the crowds to teach his disciples. This produces in them a renewed confidence based on experience. In this phase we see a period of growth. This is a time marked by "You do it, I'll help."

Jesus did not begin his ministry by calling the disciples with this kind of message, because it would not have motivated them to follow. They needed to go through the pressures, discouragements, and threats until they reached their low point. Once there, they would cleave to Jesus and to one another. There would be consensus.

Jesus now says to them, "You are my friends." Until now, the disciples had been like hired hands, doing what they were told without really seeing the big picture. But now they were called Jesus' friends. A friend is one who embraces a common objective and aim, one with whom life is shared. At this point, relationships begin to get warm. They have communion together. They laugh more. It feels very different from phases one and two. They love to hang out together, share the workload, and linger after teaching sessions to discuss what they have heard and what it means. During this phase, Jesus has all the time in the world for them.

Then he drops a bombshell. He tells the disciples he will be leaving them soon. He says he is going to prepare a place for them in the Father's house, and that they know how to get to where he is going. The disciples are confused. Thomas speaks for them all and says,

> *We don't know where you are going, so how could we know the way?*
>
> John 14:5

Jesus answers with perhaps the defining statement of all of mankind's existence:

> *I am the way, the truth and the life.*
>
> John 14:6

But they still don't get it. They are happy where they are and don't want this wonderful time to end. All that pain and suffering, and now this. The disciples thought they had endured the hard times and had arrived. It could even be said they were overconfident.

For instance, James and John, the sons of Zebedee, ask to sit to the right and left of Jesus in his glory.[89] They have a lot to

---

89   Mark 10:37

12. Multiplying Life: The Square

learn about servant leadership, hence Jesus' response:

Whoever wants to become great among you must be your servant, and whoever wants to be first, must be slave of all.

Mark 10:43-44

James and John are thinking of where they will sit in the Kingdom; they believe they have arrived. Jesus talking about going away doesn't fit this scenario. Jesus, though, is preparing them for the final phases.

Disciple Style: D3—Growing Confidence

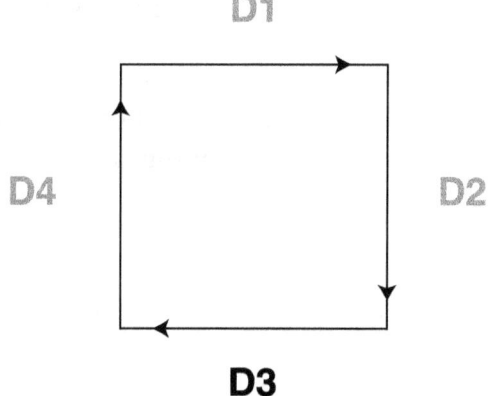

D3

Increasing enthusiasm

Growing experience

Intermittent confidence

Growing competence

When disciples are in stage three, the concept that sets them free is "God is in charge." They have to acknowledge grace and begin to work it into their lifestyle. This is not easy for most of us, but it is the one thing that will move us on to growth and maturity. It is the one thing that will move us out of the childish ways that blow us in every wind of doctrine, that lead us to grasp at any new thing that comes along. Going to this conference, buying that new book, listening to a new tape, jumping around from church to church—all can be substitutes for growing into the disciples God intends for us to be. We can escape out of that trap and move into a gradual growing process as the Lord works his grace into our hearts. As we walk out the lessons learned in stage two, we once again grow in confidence and find that our enthusiasm is increasing. Because we are beginning to act on what we have learned, we have more experience, and this also helps our confidence and enthusiasm.

At this stage the disciples were spending a lot of time with Jesus. Growth and development as a person is mirrored by a growth in intimacy. There is a growing intimacy between those being led as well as between the follower and the leader.

12. Multiplying Life: The Square

Leadership Style: L3—Pastoral/Consensus

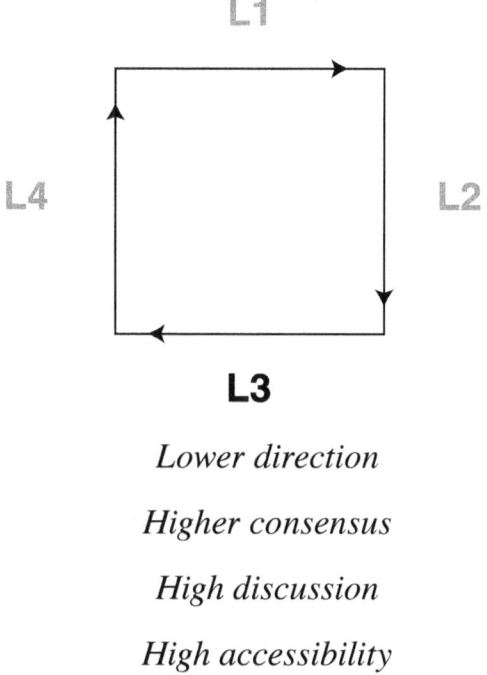

Lower direction

Higher consensus

High discussion

High accessibility

In stage three, strong friendships have been formed between the leader and those he or she is leading. Time spent with the disciples has helped create an intimacy they had not previously felt with Jesus. He calls them his friends at this stage. This is the Kingdom in action.

But as soon as this phase gets underway, and the disciples feel that all is well in the world, Jesus starts talking about leaving them. The disciples don't want this to happen. They begin flirting with D2 again. This will most likely happen with those you are leading. Yet you must now trust that your followers have the vision; they know the direction they are to be going. As leader, you have changed dramatically from a directive style to gathering consensus. Many leaders make the mistake of starting in this phase, trying to have a democratic style from the beginning. This will not work. The followers have to pass through stages one and two before they have the experience and vision to make their opinions worth considering. If you give decision-making ability to a disciple too soon, both the leader and the follower will soon be off track. Each phase must be allowed to run its full course.

Stage Four

> *Then Jesus came to them and said, "All authority in heaven and on earth has been given to me. Therefore go and make disciples of all nations, baptizing them in the name of the Father and of the Son and of the Holy Spirit, and teaching them to obey everything I have commanded you. And surely I am with you always, to the very end of the age."*
>
> *Matthew 28:18–20*

Sure enough, Jesus is taken away. He is arrested, tried, crucified. He comes back again, yes, but this time as the resurrected Lord. In his resurrected state, he doesn't hang around with them all the time like he did before. He just turns up every so often and in the most surprising ways. They have all the doors and windows locked and all of a sudden Jesus is there. They are scared and Jesus says, "The next time we meet will be in Galilee." So they all go off to Galilee. They search and look, but no Jesus. Not knowing what to do next, they go back to the only other thing they do know: fishing. In the morning, after a fruitless night of not catching fish, they see someone on the

12. Multiplying Life: The Square

beach. Guess who it is?

Jesus is preparing the disciples to spend less time with him. He is reducing their hours of contact with him because he is now delegating authority. He is giving them the job he had done; they are to become his representatives. In this last phase they are now empowered with confidence and competence as a result of their deeper relationship and ministry experience with Jesus.

So we have seen from the very first phase where Jesus says, "Come, follow me" to the last stage where he says, "Go out into all the world and do what I have taught you to do." As the disciples grow and change through each stage, so his leadership style adjusts accordingly. He has taken them through a process of development to equip them for their new task—taking the Gospel into the world.

Disciple Style: D4—The End Is in Sight

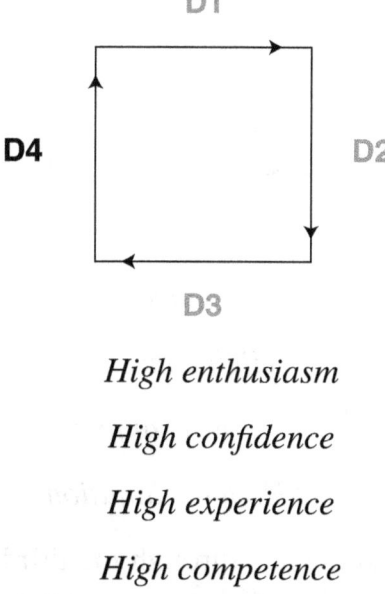

High enthusiasm

High confidence

High experience

High competence

When this stage is reached, the high enthusiasm is not just froth-and-bubble excitement. It has deep roots in confidence, brought about by a strong feeling of competence. There is knowledge of God's Word and his grace. The continual hearing of Jesus' teaching and putting it into practice sends roots down deep, strengthening the disciples against life's inevitable storms. Their confidence is in God, not themselves. They no longer rely on themselves; they trust God to complete what he starts. At this point, Jesus says, "Go and do what I have done—make disciples like I have."

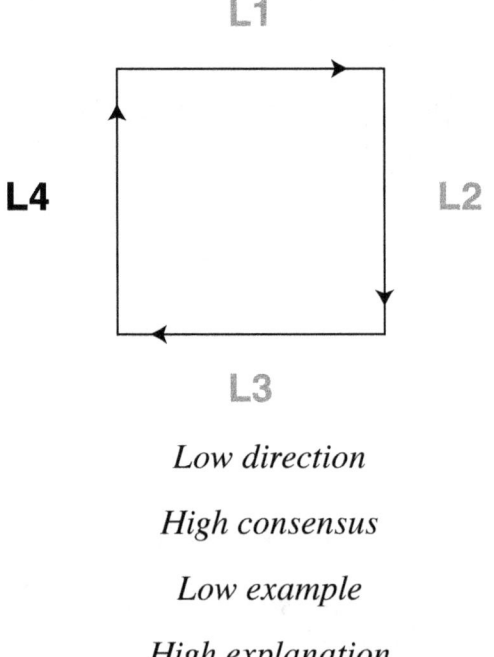

Leadership Style: L4—Delegation

Low direction

High consensus

Low example

High explanation

Growth has taken place through the third stage, experience has been gained, and confidence that once was lost now has

12. Multiplying Life: The Square

begun to return. The team now has competence. The leader takes into account what the team thinks and seeks to build consensus. The leader is also lower on example, because at this stage the disciples should be doing the work.

It is now time for delegating authority and responsibility. Good leaders always get people to the stage where they are ready to accept delegated responsibility. Delegating to disciples before this stage is a recipe for disaster. They may think they are ready, but until they have been completely through the first three stages, they are not.

Leaders must always be looking to give away their jobs to people who can do it as well or better than they. This calls for a level of intimacy between the leader and disciple that does not last. The leader begins to disengage; the disciple now becomes a leader. The closeness remains and is no longer defined by the amount of time spent together but by the openness with one another.

Stages of Delegating Responsibility

Stage One—I do, you watch

Stage Two—I do, you help

Stage Three—You do, I help

Stage Four—You do, I watch

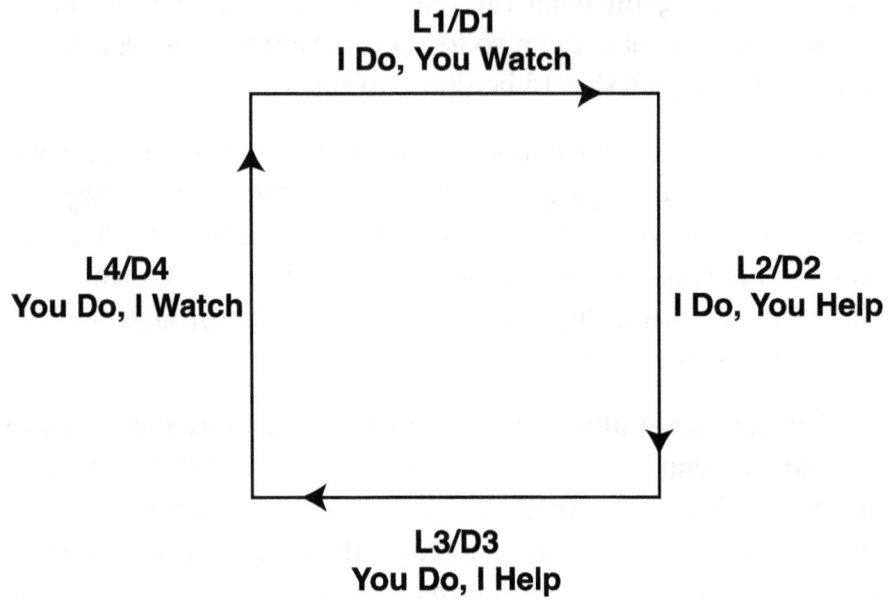

Look Deeper

Aside from the Scriptures we have looked at in our discussion of the Square, there are many other examples in the Bible of these principles of discipleship and leadership being lived out. For instance, look at the relationship between Mordecai and Esther. Esther grows in wisdom and maturity as the story unfolds, and by the end is able to make important decisions and take initiative, whereas at the beginning she was heavily dependent on Mordecai as her mentor.

As a leader, it is your responsibility to look inward on yourself and on your capacity to put these principles into practice. Take time to observe how Jesus and the great leaders

12. Multiplying Life: The Square

of the Bible illustrated the process of the Square and compare that to your own discipleship abilities. By making an honest assessment of yourself, you can begin taking the necessary steps toward building a Christ-like leadership character.

Read this reflection from Debra L. on her experience with the Square:

I used to approach discipleship as disseminating information, and you grab what you can and run with it. There was less coming alongside. Could some people pick up what I was lying down? Sure, but most people didn't.

So when I use the Square in my non-profit coffee food truck, it goes something like this:

1. *I make a specialty latte, you watch me make a specialty latte.*

2. *I make a specialty latte, you help me make a specialty latte by pumping the syrup.*

3. *You make a specialty latte, I help you make it by writing the name on the cup.*

4. *You make the specialty latte on your own! I watch you do it better than I could have imagined.*

For example, just yesterday I was training a young woman in her twenties on how to work the window, and by the end of the shift, she was greeting people with confidence and a smile in her unique way that I ended up learning from her. By the end of a five-hour shift in the food truck, the volunteer got it. We did it together. They got value and worth from it as they learned a new skill in serving others, and I got to see myself imprint onto someone else in a positive way. All this is because of a positive, grace-based, and highly relational approach to leadership development.

The Square is not a top-down authority structure, but a space in which life-on-life learning takes place. When I'm taking people through this process, we get to build a relationship in a God-space that only exists between this person and me—one that would not have existed otherwise if we had not entered that space with intentionality.

Now, I find myself using the Square everywhere—in my role as Executive Director of our coffee truck non-profit, and in the past as a Board President and café manager. I've used it in leading things like missional community, and I use it just as much at home: as a parent, as a wife, and as a grandparent. Because for me, it's all about relationships. The Square is a map of grace. And the reason it changes everything is because we enter into it willing to change — both the follower and the leader.

13. Personal Calling: The Pentagon

When I came to Sheffield in 1994, I wanted the church to begin functioning in a much more egalitarian fashion than it had. The Church of England, as an Episcopal church, is hierarchical like most churches of a liturgical tradition. Some people in the Church of England actually believe in the apostolic succession going back to Peter with a continuous line of Bishops that have been laid hands on by the previous generation of bishops. (I never believed in that and neither did most of my Evangelical friends.)

But what was the alternative to a hierarchical church? What was the alternative to understanding leadership as a largely directive and classically defined process where certain people are given responsibility and authority to lead the lives of others?

I still believe that God gives particular authority and particular responsibility to particular people on particular occasions to lead others in the task of ministry and mission. But I think that authority and responsibility is much more widely distributed in the body than previously believed. And I believe that God can raise up anyone: male or female, black or white, rich or poor, to a position of leadership for a time.

R.T. Kendall spoke about yesterday's anointing, today's anointing, and tomorrow's anointing, suggesting that there was a timestamp or a season for the authority and responsibility that a person carries. Kendall did a beautiful exposition of the lives of Saul and David, talking about yesterday's anointing with Saul and tomorrow's anointing with David, and how both of those would in some way or another be expressed in the work of today.[90]

This fascinating exposition fully underlined my belief that there would be people raised up at particular times for particular tasks. To support this belief, of course, requires an understanding of scripture that truly expresses the Reformation principle of the priesthood of all believers.

When I looked at Ephesians 4, my big struggle with the common interpretation of the passage was that there was no mention of leadership.

The common interpretation contended that the faithful ministries were given to particular individuals who then equipped the rest of the body who primarily did works of service, and that these works of service were not expressed in the fivefold ministry but in acts of ministry and mission and kindness and service of various types and descriptions. This was matched to teaching and studies that focused on the idea of people receiving a gift that enabled them to do a particular work of service. Maybe it was a gift of hospitality or a gift of giving or maybe in the more exotic circles a gift of healing or prophecy.

---

90   R.T. Kendall, *The Anointing* (Lake Mary, FL: Charisma House, 2003).

13. Personal Calling: The Pentagon

But the fivefold ministry appeared to be restricted, if it was believed at all, to an elite few who were at the top of the church.

The problem was that that's not what the text said. The text said the ministry of Jesus was expressed in the fact that he was the first apostle, the first prophet, the first evangelist, the first pastor, and the first teacher. He was the progenitor of all of those Ministries.

It also said the full ministry of Jesus was expressed by the whole body of Christ and that equipping was not something done for those higher up the hierarchy but for everyone, so they can use their gift of Grace to help others become more like Jesus.

And so if I'm an apostolic person, I help everyone understand that the call of Jesus is to be ready to be on mission with God. If I'm a prophet, then I help everyone listen to the voice of God. If I'm an evangelist, I help everyone witness.

Not everyone is an apostle, but everyone is called to go. Not everyone is a prophet, but everyone is called to listen. Not everyone is an evangelist, but everyone is called to witness. And so with pastoring and teaching.

Everyone is one of the five.

The story behind that is really fascinating. It caused great consternation among some of the people I taught, because it laid an ax to the sense of status, credibility, value, and affirmation that many church leaders believed that they had been given by God. Ordination itself seemed to be brought into question because it appears as though God had ordained everyone with a particular Grace to function in the fivefold ministry in particular ways–some in a great way, some in a small way.

Certainly the text seems to indicate that there is a degree of the amount of Grace given for a particular Ministry to some. So you could have people who were just as apostolic as everyone else but had perhaps a greater degree of capacity in that calling to help the body and other Apostles do the work of mission. So with the other fivefold ministries as well.

I struggled with that nuance a little, but kept returning to how the text said that the body as a whole needed to look like Jesus and that individuals in the body need to grow up to take on the full stature of Christ, which meant that they learned from all of the fivefold ministries so that they could function in all of them, even though it wasn't their base. So we described bases and phases of ministry, with the base being the particular apportionment of grace that God has given you, and the phase of ministry is the particular ways in which you're encouraged by the spirit to imitate the life of another and so grow more and more like Jesus in his works and ways.

This teaching caused quite a bit of angst, and you could hear the sharpening of pitchforks and the lighting of torches. It seemed at one point as though this issue really set me apart from others in my world of evangelicalism as something of a radical, if not a heretic.

On one particular occasion, I taught fivefold ministry to a group of interns in Sheffield, and a young guy from Australia called Alan came through with a team of people who were exploring different models of mission around Britain and Europe. Alan told me he thought the teaching on the fivefold ministry was revolutionary. That conversation marked the beginning of a long and fruitful relationship between myself and Alan Hirsch that is part of an enormously important

13. Personal Calling: The Pentagon

movement that I think has touched the entire world.

The cultural shifts of the past several decades have permeated the church, and consumerist demand from members upon their leaders is ever-increasing. Leading a church can become such a heavy burden that many pastors leave their churches and forsake their calling. While the Bible clearly defines roles within the church, the mission of the church was intended to be shared by the whole body. A healthy church builds a discipling culture and equips all members to participate in the missional work to which God has called them.

This next shape—the Pentagon—may at first feel threatening to some pastors and leaders because it will require a change in thinking about who your church really belongs to. Church leadership based on high control is not at all attractive to the millennial generation. For the next generation, the journey of faith in community will not be about doing church but about being the Church. One writer puts it this way: "If we can't live the sacred journey with Christ daily and are not actively drawing others into that journey—way outside the worship center or sanctuary and outside our stained-glass or silk-plant ghettos—we can't expect to do it in an hour on Sunday morning or Wednesday night."

The Pentagon can be great news to you and your ministry. It may feel a little strange at first, but give it a chance—it will soon feel very comfortable because the Pentagon is about unleashing the members of the body to function at their full potential. When we know what we have been designed for and called to do, we can save ourselves a lot of effort and striving in areas we were not built for. If we know who God has made us to be, we can stop trying to be someone we are not and let go of the stress that comes with living that kind of life. When we are walking the path God has called us to walk, we will discover grace beyond our expectations to succeed. God has buckets full of grace to pour out on us—but we have to be standing where the downpour is occurring. And that place is where he has designed us to fit.

Think of a person who struggles with math in school. He forces himself to pay attention to the teacher, and just doesn't get it when formulas are explained. He has to constantly rework his homework, and if he gets a correct answer on a quiz, it is most likely to have been a guess. Now, how would this person fare as an engineer? Would he do good work? Would he even enjoy the job? If you strive and struggle in a particular area of ministry and find it produces more stress than fruit, perhaps it's time to step back and examine your gifts. Discovering and acknowledging who God has made you to be will ensure you are standing directly under the bucket of grace, not beside it, and that you get a healthy soaking of grace, not just a little splash.

A Spiritual Gift Is Not Your Ministry

Several New Testament passages speak of gifts for the church, including 1 Corinthians 12, Romans 12, 1 Peter 4, and Ephesians 4. Most of us have been taught that God has given us one or several of the gifts listed in these passages, that these gifts are "ours." There is, however, an important distinction between spiritual gifts and roles as mentioned in Scripture. A spiritual gift is not a ministry in itself. Rather, it is a tool to use for the job at hand. The job is the role or function one is called to. To help in differentiating the gifts from a specific

13. Personal Calling: The Pentagon

role, it is important to look at the context in which each passage was written.

Both 1 Corinthians 12 and Romans 12 contain a list of gifts. What is often overlooked is that Paul wrote these letters to different churches facing different problems. He wrote to each of these bodies to teach them about grace and how to apply it to their particular situations.

Paul wrote 1 Corinthians to address problems and issues arising from this church's gatherings. Paul was teaching the Corinthians what their corporate worship should look like. In chapter 12, he explains that they should expect the Holy Spirit to be present in power, and to do certain things. The key word to understanding how the Holy Spirit works is "manifestation" in verse 7. In Greek, the word is phanerosis, meaning the revelation or enlightening that God brings. The English word we use for this has its roots in the Latin for "the dancing hand."

This is what I'm trying to get at: The dancing hand of the Holy Spirit falls on certain individuals during a gathering, causing them to exercise one or more of the gifts—wisdom, words of knowledge, tongues, prophecy, and so on. Anyone can receive any of the manifestations, or the dancing hand, of the Spirit mentioned in 1 Corinthians 12. Paul was saying that in corporate worship the Spirit will fall on certain individuals, giving them gifts for the moment. These are not permanent roles; we do not possess these gifts as our own "ministry." The key to the gifts is the Spirit moving as a dancing hand within our gathering, dispensing grace as it is needed.

Similarly, Romans 12 must be examined within the context that this passage was intended. Paul was trying to help the Church in Rome get past the growing rivalry and division that existed between Jews and Gentiles. The Church was struggling with ethnic division and, because of this, not functioning as a single, united church. Paul pleads with them, in view of everything he has shown them about God's mercy and grace, to live sacrificial lives. He wants them to stop arguing and start living their lives for one another. Sacrifice and service are the context of this passage. Paul gives some practical examples: If your gift is teaching, stick to teaching. If your gift is to give aid to those in need, keep your eyes peeled for opportunities. This is not meant to be an exhaustive list of roles within the Church, merely a few examples to make a point.

Both Romans and 1 Corinthians were written to specific churches facing specific problems and circumstances. The book of Ephesians, though, was not written to just one church for a special moment in time, but for all the churches in Asia Minor. Ephesians is a memo of sorts to many churches. It doesn't address specific problems but outlines foundational teachings for how a church should function. In this letter, Paul shares what the roles of all believers are to be within the Church.

The Fivefold Ministries Are For Everyone

But to each one of us grace has been given as Christ apportioned it... It was he who gave some to be apostles, some to be prophets, some to be evangelists, and some to be pastors and teachers, to prepare God's people for works of service, so that the body of Christ may be built up until we all reach unity in the faith and in the knowledge of the Son of God and become mature, attaining to the whole measure of the fullness of Christ.

13. Personal Calling: The Pentagon

Ephesians 4:7, 11–13

"But to each one of us…" It has been a traditional teaching that the fivefold ministries in this passage are five roles for leaders in the church. But that is not what the verse says. "To each one" refers to every member of the church, not just leaders. What the Bible says is that each one of us has received a portion of grace in one of five roles. That grace has come to us in the form of a call to be one of five types of people. There is no mention of leadership in this passage, so we can see that this is not just for those who have been ordained or have been through seminary. The fivefold ministries in Ephesians 4 are for "each one of us."

"…Grace has been given as Christ apportioned it." The fivefold roles apply to all members of the body of Christ in varying degrees. What Paul is saying is that Jesus, by the gift of his grace, has empowered and equipped each of us for service. We have all been given different-sized portions of grace and anointing. We each receive part of the whole. Christ's ministry fully demonstrates all five roles of apostle, prophet, evangelist, pastor and teacher. We, as members in his body, receive one of these five appointments, relying on one another for those areas we are not gifted in.

"It was he who gave some to be apostles, some to be prophets, some to be evangelists, and some to be pastors and teachers, to prepare God's people for works of service, so that the body of Christ may be built up." These five gifts of grace seem to be the elements needed for preparing people for service and building up the church. Each person receives a portion of grace to fulfill a ministry role as an apostle, prophet, evangelist, pastor or teacher.

"Until we all reach unity in the faith and in the knowledge of the Son of God and become mature, attaining to the measure of the fullness of Christ." When each person is working, by grace, in the role given by the Holy Spirit, the result is unity in faith, a continual growing in the personal knowledge of Jesus and maturity or wholeness, which all lead to the fullness of Christ. When we look at each part of the passage in context, it becomes clear that the gifts mentioned in Ephesians 4 are roles or functions given to each believer, and that the gifts mentioned in 1 Corinthians and Romans are tools to enable every believer to function more effectively in his or her role.

Let us look in more detail at each of the five roles as we see them in Ephesians 4. Then we will help you to identify your base and phase ministries and look at how best to utilize them.

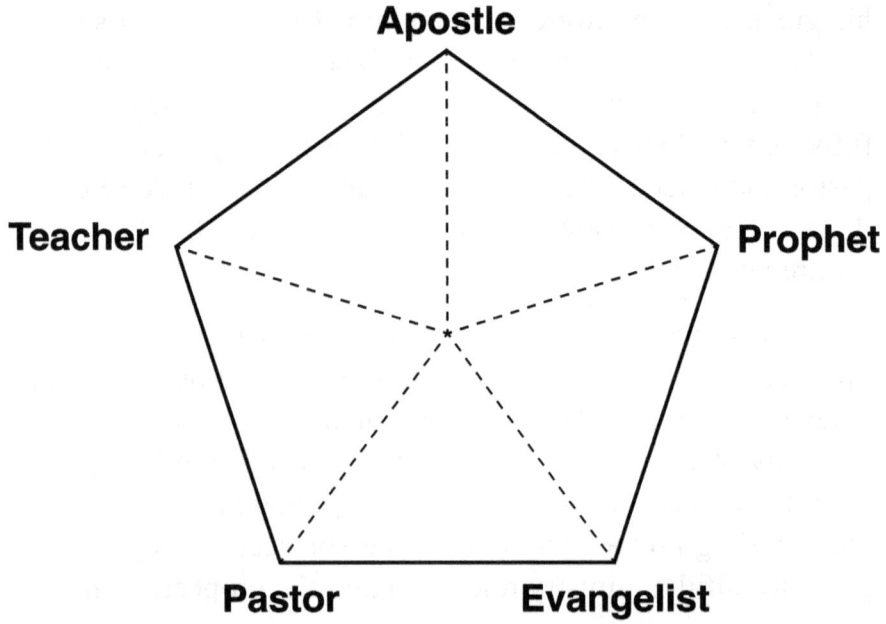

13. Personal Calling: The Pentagon

Apostle

From the Greek *apostolos* meaning "one who is sent out." Apostles are visionary and pioneering, always pushing into new territory. They like to establish new churches, ministries, non-profits, Kingdom-minded businesses or initiatives. They come up with innovative means to do kingdom work.

- Biblical examples—the Twelve, Paul, Priscilla and Aquilla.

- Jesus' example—Jesus was the one sent by God (John 3:16).

- Apostles enjoy dreaming, doing new and challenging tasks, change.

- Secular examples—entrepreneurs, explorers.

- Core question Apostles ask: Are we leading the people of God to their destiny?

- Characteristics of immature Apostles: They are unable to distinguish between the constant flood of good and innovative ideas they have and the God-ideas that are being given to them. It's about an inability to discern. They try out something new every week, never really develop any of their ideas and jump from one project to another. After a while, people stop following Apostles because they have a hard time staying focused on the task at hand, and people refuse to give their time and energy to something they know could change due to any whim of an immature Apostle.

Prophet

One who hears and listens to God (*prophetes*); the Prophet foretells and tells forth revelation from God. Often Prophets are able to stand back from circumstances to get a clear picture of what is happening and therefore see creative solutions and develop a vision for situations others don't see. Prophets understand the times and what people should do.

- Biblical examples—Anna and Simeon in Luke 2 as they prophesy over the infant Jesus. Agabus in Acts 11:28 and 21:10 when he predicts a famine and prophesies about Paul. Philip's daughters in Acts 21:9 were all known as prophetesses.

- Jesus' example—Every word spoken from the mouth of Jesus was revelation from God. Jesus often foretold events such as Peter's denial and the details of his own death. He himself is the fulfillment of Old Testament prophecy concerning the Messiah such as found in Isaiah 53.

- Prophets enjoy being alone with God, waiting and listening.

- Secular examples—people who speak out their perceptions. They're often creative types, musicians, and artists.

- Core question Prophets ask: Are the people of God hearing his voice and responding appropriately?

- Characteristics of immature Prophets: While they have a natural gift to "see beyond" what most people can see, immature prophets make two fundamental errors. First,

13. Personal Calling: The Pentagon

if they sense God is saying something, they provide the interpretation themselves and don't release the prophecy to a community of people outside of them. Just as Paul said, the prophet will give his or her sense, but it's up to the community to weigh and give an interpretation. The Prophets' job is to share, release what they've received, back away, and then see what other people make of it. The proper path goes like this: Revelation to Interpretation to Application. An immature Prophet, having received some sort of revelation, wants to go straight to Application. This is incredibly harmful and not the pattern that Scripture gives us. Second, Prophets assume they are always right. The problem is that often times they are right, and this builds a false sense of confidence that they get it 100 percent of the time. Because of this, they can become arrogant, haughty, and overly critical. In contrast, a mature Prophets are actually quite humble because they know that any revelation they receive isn't their own and they entrust it to the community.

Evangelist

One who brings good news and shares the message readily (*euanggelistes*). Evangelists love spending time with non-Christians and often remind other Christians that there are non-Christians still out there in the world. Evangelists are not necessarily all like Billy Graham; they may be "people gatherers." Evangelists know the Word and can make it relevant to non-Christians.

- Biblical examples—Philip in Acts 8:12. The people

believed Philip when he preached.

- Jesus' example—Jesus embodied the Good News. He was the Good News. We can see Jesus as Evangelist in John 3 with the Samaritan woman at the well.

- Evangelists enjoy discussion and sharing their point of view. Wherever they go, they seem to draw others into discussion about Jesus. Evangelists are passionate about sharing the Gospel. They are not timid about their faith and seem to easily share with others regularly.

- Secular examples—salesmen, politicians, public relations reps.

- Core question Evangelists ask: Are new people entering into the Kingdom of God?

- Characteristics of immature Evangelists: Like immature prophets, there are two things Evangelists typically do that can be truly harmful. First, they present a reductionist Gospel that's all about getting people out of hell, which, while important, doesn't always include Jesus' invitation to grace-filled discipleship and the availability of the Kingdom that was his central message. When they do this, they make faith and Christianity all about the afterlife and less about what happens here on earth. This is terribly destructive. Second, many immature Evangelists can have sort of a "Love you and leave you" strategy. Once you've "crossed the line" into becoming a Christian, they make the world's fastest baton pass-off to the local church or a small group and are never heard from again. They move on to the next person. Now this isn't to say that Evangelists need to

13. Personal Calling: The Pentagon

be there forever, but someone who is just starting the discipling process shouldn't have a jarring experience. Being a disciple is about relationships and immature Evangelists can make a bad first impression when it comes to how Christians exist in relationships.

Pastor

One who shepherds God's people (*poimen*), who cares for others with a tender heart, and one who sees needs, provides comfort and encourages others. Pastors spend most of their time with other Christians. Pastors can easily empathize with others and exhibit lots of patience with those in need.

- Biblical example—Barnabas in Acts 15:36–41. Barnabas clearly demonstrates a pastoral heart in his defense of Mark.

- Jesus' example—In John 10, Jesus refers to himself as the Good Shepherd who has come to lead his people.

- Pastors enjoy one-on-one chats and showing hospitality. They get burdened by others' problems and have a knack for speaking the truth in love. Pastors are good listeners and are easy to talk to and share inner feelings with.

- Secular examples—counselors, social workers, nurses and anyone in the care-giving professions.

- Core question Pastors ask: Are the people of God caring for and showing compassion for people?

- Characteristics of an immature Pastor: Pastors love nothing more than being with people in the midst of their brokenness, pain and suffering. However, Pastors can have a really difficult time in moving people from that stage to one where they are seeking healing, transformation, and redemption. Immature pastors sometimes don't have the confidence to push or challenge people to move forward, to take a step forward into the Kingdom, for fear that the person will be angry with them. The mature Pastor can live in this tension while the immature counterpart stays a mile away from it and lets people sit in their brokenness far longer than should happen.

Teacher

One who holds forth the truth and is excited by it (*didaskalos*). The Teacher looks for ways to explain, enlighten and apply truth.

- Biblical example—Apollos in Acts 18.

- Jesus' example—he was often referred to as Teacher or Rabbi. His "students" often remarked that his teaching was different because he taught with authority.

- Teachers enjoy reading and studying the Bible and helping others to understand it.

- Secular examples—lecturers, trainers, schoolteachers.

- Core question Teachers ask: Are the people of God immersing themselves in Scripture and incarnating it?

- Characteristics of an immature Teacher: The good thing about Teachers is their profound love of Scripture. The

13. Personal Calling: The Pentagon

bad news is that Scripture can be the end rather than God. Immature Teachers tend to forget that Scripture is a thing that brings us to God. Scripture isn't the point. God is the point. They can suffer from Bibliolotry in which they idolize Scripture and put it over their relationship with the living and breathing God that we come to know by means of reading and incarnating Scripture. There are few things more beautiful than watching a Teacher learn from a Prophet because the Teacher's ability to teach goes to a new level as all of his or her teachings drive people to the arms of the Father. In addition, immature Teachers can rely on their own intellect to "wow" people rather than on the authority that is given from Scripture and from the Holy Spirit. People commented about Jesus that his teaching possessed an authority that they didn't see in the Teachers of the Law and the Pharisees. Likewise, the writer of Hebrews says, "Remember your leaders, who spoke the word of God to you. Consider the outcome of their way of life and imitate their faith." A Teacher's authority doesn't come from how smart he or she is but from the Word of God and the power of a transformed life. An immature Teacher often forgets this.

Base and Phase

Each of us has a base ministry that represents one of the fivefold ministries in Ephesians. We believe that God gives each of us this ministry and it is ours for life. Hence, we call this our "base ministry." However, there are also particular periods when God leads us to discover and understand the other ministries for a brief time. This is what we call our "phase ministries." We all have our base and at least one phase ministry at any given time.

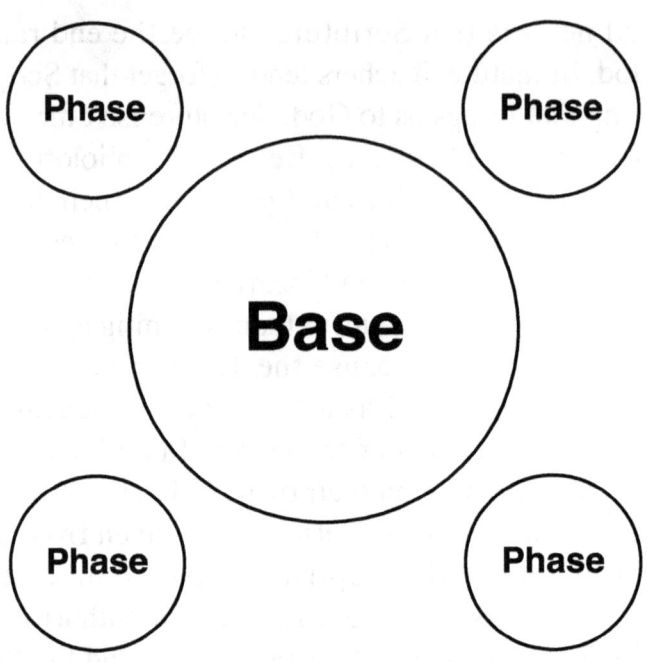

For example, the Lord may call you to teach a class on reading the Bible that you may not necessarily feel most comfortable with. Perhaps your base ministry is a Pastor, but you sense God calling you into a phase of being a Teacher. Your base ministry will be the one that refreshes you, the one you are most passionate about. The Lord, however, will mature you by taking you through the other ministries in phases. Many have experienced the Lord making their base ministry more rounded as they experience phases in the other areas. What God seems to be doing by allowing you time in the phase ministries is to strengthen your base ministry. By taking you out of what you're most comfortable with, he is also shaping your character, which expands your capacity to serve the body of Christ and the world he so loved.

So one way of understanding base and phase is learning

13. Personal Calling: The Pentagon

that our base is something that we do naturally, but God still gives us seasons when we have a phase of another ministry to learn the basics of it. One of the things that I noticed when I was a young man in my 20s was that I had different seasons of trying new things. I'd have a year or two when I went through a season of immersion into Evangelism, but eventually, the grace ran out and I just started something new. Then I'd have a season where I apprenticed myself to someone who was very Prophetic and learned a lot about what it is to act out of that Prophetic ministry, but the grace ran out and I started something new. This happened over and over: God would lead me into a season of learning a different ministry, in which I spent a good amount of time in that phase, but I kept returning to starting new things, which was my base ministry. I just couldn't help myself. Well, as it turns out, there was a reason for that. I'm an Apostle. I start new things. But I'm a far better and more well rounded Apostle because I had phases in the other four base ministries.

My general observation is that we enter into phases for one of two reasons. First, we have a clear sense that God is asking us to learn a ministry we don't yet have access to or aren't competent in yet. So while we both are Apostolic in nature, it is crucial that we also know how to be an Evangelist when the situation arises. Being an Apostle isn't an excuse for not fulfilling an important part of the Great Commission. I may not be as good as a natural Evangelist, but I spend time in a phase so I have at least a foundational level of competence in that ministry. So of course we are all called to be witnesses to the Good News, regardless of whether we are natural evangelists. Second, we enter into a new phase when circumstances arise that immerse us in a phase ministry we are unfamiliar with, but need to have access to in order to accomplish the work God has called us to. An example of this might be someone with a Pastor base who has been serving as a Discipleship Pastor at a local church stepping into a Teaching role because the Senior Pastor stepped down. Someone needs to teach, you've been put in the role, and now you have a quick learning curve!

What some people have wrongly assumed is that they should only operate out of a place of absolute strength when it comes to base ministry. "I'm an Apostle. I'm only going to do things that reflect that ministry." However, Paul clearly does not see it this way. When he says, "and become mature" in Ephesians 4:13, he is referencing the individual arriving at a threshold of maturity but also referencing the various ministries. Maturity, at least as Paul is defining it in this passage, seems to be an individual having a measure of competency in each ministry, "so that we will no longer be infants."

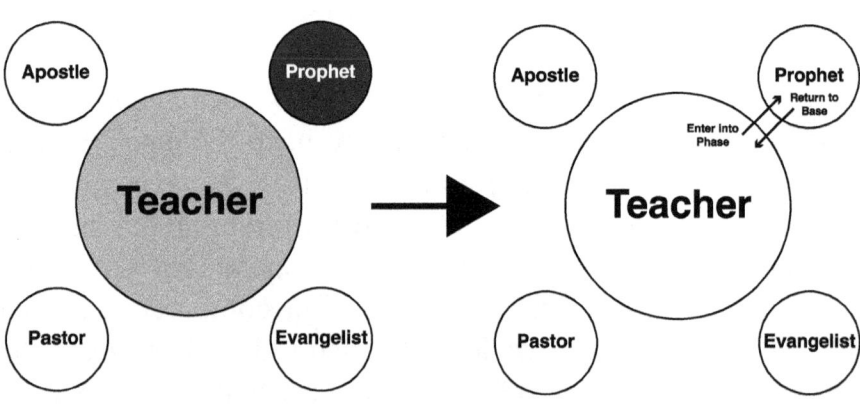

13. Personal Calling: The Pentagon

What we end up with is a spiritual formation process that leads us from infancy to maturity, but only when we have spent a phase within each ministry that is not our base. Spending time there, in a place that isn't our natural place of strength, gives us access to these phases at other times when we will need them. What we soon see when we reach maturity is that we are constantly faced with situations in which God is asking us to do his work in the world and our base ministry is insufficient. While we will certainly be far off from the person of Jesus, God is able to use the seasons of life where we have spent extended phases learning a different ministry to use us in that specific situation.

A warning: It is easy to fall into the trap of feeling as though you need to excel in all five ministries all the time. But this only leads to burnout and a failure to focus properly on your base ministry. Worse still, you will not be making room for others around you to explore their base ministries. What happens when grace for your phase ministry has been used up and it's time to return to your base? Generally, you will know you have run out of grace. Energy and enthusiasm dry up. You see less blessing and less fruit from your efforts, even though you are working at the same intensity level. Eventually you will experience less peace about what you are doing. You will have less joy in the task. Your thoughts turn to doing what you really love and what comes naturally for you.

Going back to your base ministry is the only thing that gives you a sense of peace.

Again, we need to learn a basic level of competency in each ministry, even as we will spend more of our life in our base ministry. So we are not all called to be Pastors, but we are all called to care. We are not all called to be Teachers, but we are all called to hold out the truth. We are all responsible for learning how to listen for God's voice, something that comes more naturally for the Prophet. We are all called to share the Good News with others, but this takes all those who are not called to be Evangelists out of their comfort zones. And we are not all Apostles, but must all learn to walk out into what God calls us to do. We are the body of Christ, which means that together, we represent the ministry of Jesus who was the embodiment of all five ministries in Ephesians 4. He is the perfect presentation of the ministry of the Spirit. By experiencing all five areas of ministry, whether as a base or a phase, we grow more into the likeness and character of our Master.

Once you have explained that every member of the body is equipped with one of the fivefold ministries as a base, the first question that will arise will be, "How do I know what my base gift is?" I have included a tool in the Appendix— the Fivefold Ministries Questionnaire—to help determine your gift. You can also take the survey online at www.fivefoldsurvey.com. Feel free to use this as you like; it is but one way to determine one's ministry role.

How To Find Your Base

Take a look at your own personality—a true, honest look. Are you an introvert or an extrovert? This has nothing to do with how confident you feel or how sociable you may appear. Being an introvert does not equal lacking confidence. And not all extroverts feel confident all the time, even though they may appear so on the outside. Being an introvert or extrovert has

13. Personal Calling: The Pentagon

to do with the world you find most appealing and where you recharge. It can also indicate your base ministry gift.

Extroverts think by talking things through with others. Being in the company of others and participating in group activities refresh an extrovert. The extrovert tends to work well with things that are immediate and can be seen quickly. Extroverts think out loud and are often more comfortable ad-libbing and speaking off the cuff. While not universally true, it would be fair to say that for the most part, Apostles and Evangelists tend to be more extroverted.

Introverts think by internally processing things. Introverts are refreshed and recharged by spending time either alone or with a small number of people they know very well. Introverts are committed to depth, and most of the great writers, painters and composers have been introverts. Introverted preachers are often comfortable offering their thoughts to a wider audience only when they have had time to prepare and feel that what they are sharing is as good as they can get it. The vast majority of Prophets are introverts, and more Pastors and Teachers have a natural preference for introversion. This is not, of course, a clear-cut way to define one's ministry. Consider yet another lens from which to look, the continuum of pioneers and developers.

Are You A Pioneer or a Developer/Settler?

Your reaction to or excitement over a new project or task can shed light on your base gifting. We call the two end points on this scale "pioneer" and "developers." Pioneers, for example, enjoy change and find the stress of doing new things exciting rather than threatening. Pioneers are committed to flexibility; instability does not frighten them. They reach out beyond their current experiences and relationships to discover new frontiers and challenges. Pioneers often find themselves bored and frustrated by the discipline necessary to sustain what has been established. They love to make breakthroughs and are always looking for the next frontier to explore and tame.

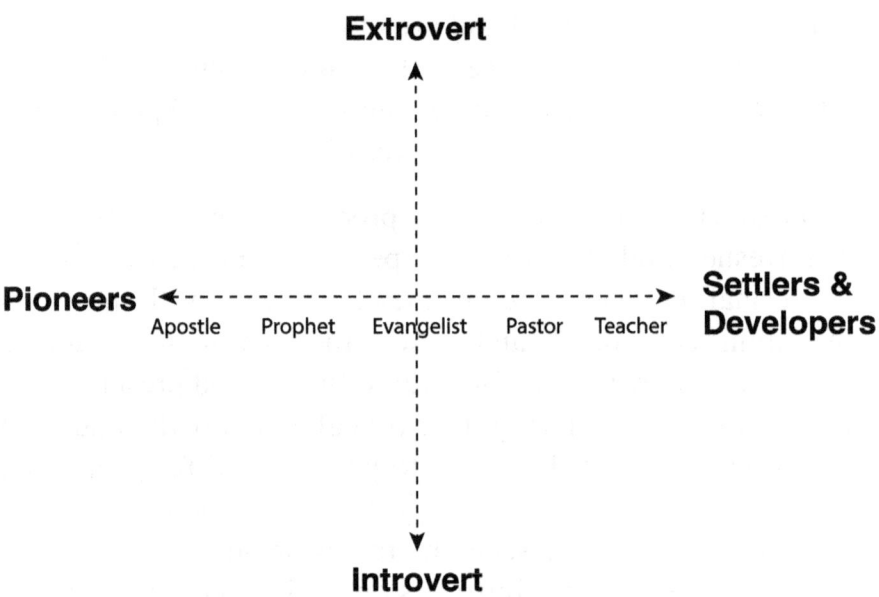

Developers are what we used to call "Settlers" but some people felt it sounded too negative - personally I like the word "Settler" because it has such a central place in the story of humanity. People have so often had to move and settle in new places. What you notice about Developers/settlers is that they invariably need to be committed to different things than the Pioneers, things like continuity, stability, and conservation. They prefer to grow and develop plans rather than scrap what they have and start over with something brand new. They are

13. Personal Calling: The Pentagon

great at implementation and processing; they like to see things through to the end. Developers are the steady, solid backbone of most communities. They like to know what to expect, and they feel most comfortable when things are moving smoothly according to plan. Instability can cause great discomfort for developers.

All through history there has been interplay between pioneers and developers. A look at American history reveals a continuing balance between those who go forth to explore new territory and those who follow to build houses, stores, schools and churches in these newfound places. Unfortunately, the two do not always exist well together. The pioneer gets bored and restless if asked to stick around to help paint and decorate the buildings once they are up, and the developer may not relish the thought of going to live in the wilderness in the same way the pioneer does.

Both pioneers and developers, however, are vital and mission critical. Without the pioneers, we will never find the next frontier. We will not reach beyond what we have already achieved. Pioneers are always looking beyond what we have already received to what lies ahead. Without the developers, we would never keep the frontier that was won by the pioneers. The pioneers will have pushed on to new territory, leaving the recently discovered land barren. Developers must come to build and occupy, to maintain and to increase through steady, deliberate efforts.

Pioneers look ahead to the frontier and seek to break new ground by putting visionary ideas into practice. Developers consolidate the frontier that has been won by the pioneer and play an equally important role in the continued health of the land. In church terms (generally speaking), the pioneers would be the Apostles, Prophets, and Evangelists. Pastors and Teachers tend to be of the developer nature.

Any healthy church needs pioneers and developers, yet the tension between the two must be understood and managed to keep from being swallowed by division. Pioneers naturally want to move into new ways and ideas to advance the kingdom. Pioneers are willing to take risks to join the Lord in new endeavors, often long before the developer even knows the Lord is moving in that direction. Off goes the pioneer, with excitement that cannot be contained, but that disturbs the developer who is still working to maintain and see greater life in the places we already have.

On the other hand, "There's still so much that needs to be done here" is the developer's life motto. Developers look to put down roots while pioneers are hacking through dense jungle growth in the search for new territory. Many churches split, not because of theology, but because they don't understand the interplay between pioneers and developers. In some churches, the pioneers are driven away by developers who do not want to explore anything new and gain new territory for the Kingdom. In others, pain is caused by pioneers who are not patient enough to wait for developers to catch up with them. There needs to be mutual respect, admiration, and acceptance of the role each of these play in the church.

Without pioneers, we will never gain new territory for the Kingdom Without developers, we will never keep the territory that was won.

We need both.

13. Personal Calling: The Pentagon

The Continuum: Get Flexible!

Using the lenses of pioneers and developers, or introverts and extroverts, is not an exact science, and we must be careful not to box anyone into an identity they are not comfortable with.

Testing comes into our lives to make us more flexible, to stretch us out of our comfort zone. God stretches us by taking us into territory where we do not naturally feel comfortable. Moving in a direction that is not to our natural liking (a pioneer acting as a developer, for instance) brings about maturity. We do not grow by staying in our comfort zone. Character and maturity are developed by moving away from our natural preferences. Once this period of testing is over, we then find relief by falling back on that for which we are gifted, our base ministry. If we never move into a phase ministry, however, we will not grow.

I realize, of course, that the application of the five fold ministry is enormously challenging given the long history of neglect that this particular New Testament teaching has received. However, my experience down through the years has been that on every occasion where congregations have come to understand, and embrace the idea that everyone in the congregation is "one of the five" then genuine, congregational transformation, begins to take place. From the poorest communities in inner city London to the richest retirement communities in America this teaching has had enormous benefit.

This benefit, of course, can be seen at the corporate level as congregations become much more dynamically involved in the ministry of Jesus, but I think it's at the personal level that the change is often most significant.

At an individual level it's always a wonderful thing to understand our identity and what it is that we've been made and shaped for by God (Eph 2:10). Watching people come alive to the idea that they are more than listeners and followers of others and discovering they are partners in the mission and ministry of Jesus has been beautiful to behold. I've seen young and old gain entirely new levels of confidence as they realize they were designed for "more". But recognizing that we need everyone else is also important. Watching whole congregations begin to understand that whatever our individual base ministry might be, we need to receive from all of the other ministries so that we grow to maturity – to the fullness of the stature of Jesus - is an incredible gift.

Listen Jason Z.'s story of his own awakening with the concept of Base and Phase within the Fivefold Ministry:

For years, I knew about the fivefold ministry in Ephesians 4:11-13. I could teach about apostles, prophets, evangelists, pastors, and teachers, and I understood, at least in theory, that these weren't just titles but gifts given to build up the body of Christ. But if I'm honest, I never really knew where I fit.

As a church leader, I wore a lot of hats. Some weeks, I was the shepherd, caring for people in crisis. Other weeks, I was deep in study, teaching and preaching. At times, I felt like an evangelist, constantly inviting people in. Other times, I was casting vision, pushing our church forward. I was doing everything—because that's what church leadership seemed to require. But I never knew what my lane was. I was a jack of all trades, always shifting gears, but never feeling like I was fully thriving.

Then I came across LifeShapes and the Pentagon. It wasn't

13. Personal Calling: The Pentagon

a new concept for me, but it helped solidify something I had been struggling with for years—base and phase. I finally had language for why I felt so scattered. I had been living in all five roles at different times, but only one of them was truly home for me.

I realized my base was as an apostle. That's where I come alive—starting new things, pushing into uncharted territory, dreaming about what's next. But in full-time ministry, I was constantly forced to phase into other roles, and while I could do them, they weren't my natural sweet spot. No wonder I felt stretched thin.

Now that I'm no longer in full-time vocational ministry, things are different. Being part of a house church has given me the freedom to live more fully into who God made me to be. I'm not pulled in a dozen directions—I get to focus on what I do best. Instead of feeling the pressure to be everything to everyone, I can step into my apostolic gifting without guilt.

I'm learning that when I operate from my base, I don't just feel more at peace—I'm also more effective. I can still phase into other roles when needed, but I no longer feel like I'm constantly swimming against the current. And perhaps more importantly, I'm surrounded by a community where others are stepping into their own gifts. The weight isn't all on one person; we build each other up.

The Pentagon has helped me see that the church was never meant to be led by just one type of person. It flourishes when all the gifts are activated. And now, instead of trying to be something I'm not, I get to fully live into the role God designed for me. For the first time in a long time, I feel free.

14. Definitive Prayer: The Hexagon

> *One day Jesus was praying in a certain place. When he finished, one of his disciples said to him, "Lord, teach us to pray, just as John taught his disciples." He said to them, "When you pray, say: 'Father, hallowed be your name, your kingdom come. Give us each day our daily bread. Forgive us our sins, for we also forgive everyone who sins against us. And lead us not into temptation.'"*
>
> *Luke 11:1–4*

The disciples—those whom Jesus called to be his full-time students—learned practical faith by watching Jesus in action. And, as we see throughout Scripture, Jesus spent much time in prayer. They recognized that Jesus' Up relationship with his Father through prayer was key to his fruitfulness in his ministry and relationships. Thus, when the disciples came to Jesus and said, "Lord, teach us to pray," we can assume they had been watching and listening to Jesus pray. There was something about the way their teacher went about prayer that was different and caused them to want to pray in the same way.

In the classic book With Christ in the School of Prayer, author Andrew Murray notes, "Jesus never taught His disciples how to preach, only how to pray." Perhaps, having done life with Jesus, they understood better than we that prayer is what believers need most to be effective disciples of Christ. In fact, Andrew Murray issues this challenge to us: "What think you, my beloved fellow-disciples! Would it not be just what we need, to ask the Master for a month to give us a course of special lessons on the art of prayer?"[91]

Asking for a model of prayer was the next step in the disciples' spiritual growth. Jesus told them, "When you pray, pray like this." He did not give them several methods to choose from—he gave them one model to follow. It has only six parts to it, but it covers everything Jesus taught us about kingdom life:

> *Our Father in heaven,*
> *hallowed be your name,*
> *your kingdom come,*
> *your will be done*
> *on earth as it is in heaven.*
> *Give us today our daily bread.*
> *Forgive us our debts,*
> *as we also have forgiven our debtors.*
> *And lead us not into temptation,*
> *but deliver us from the evil one.*
>
> —Matthew 6:9–13

---

91 Andrew Murray, *With Christ in the School of Prayer* (Old Tappan, NJ: Fleming H. Revell Company, 1984) 16.

14. Definitive Prayer: The Hexagon

As discipling leaders, we also have people watching us closely. Those we are discipling will learn from us and imitate our example. What will they learn about prayer by watching us? Much, if we model the prayer Jesus taught. When we pray the six phrases of the Lord's Prayer, we are planting the seed of Kingdom life in our hearts. This seed will sprout and grow, and the fruit will be meditative prayer, intercessory prayer, contemplative prayer, and so forth.

Notice I said model the prayer. Jesus only taught one method of prayer. If I or any other person were telling you, "This is how you should pray..." you could easily reply, "Well, I'll consider your thoughts, but I'm sure there are many other ways to do it." But when Jesus, the Lord of all says, "Pray like this," we need to pay attention and do just as he says. The Hexagon invites us to go back to Jesus to learn the art of true prayer.

God is most interested in a relationship—an open, ongoing relationship that Scripture often describes as "walking with God." Life is a process of learning to walk with God, learning to relate and communicate with God. How we interact with God is vital for our lives. Thus, when Jesus is teaching his followers to pray, he is showing them how to walk with God. If walking with God truly is what our lives are all about, praying the way Jesus shows us is a major part of our life.

The Lord's Prayer as taught by Jesus contains six elements. When we learn to pray these segments in the right way, we also will be learning to align our lives with God's will for us.

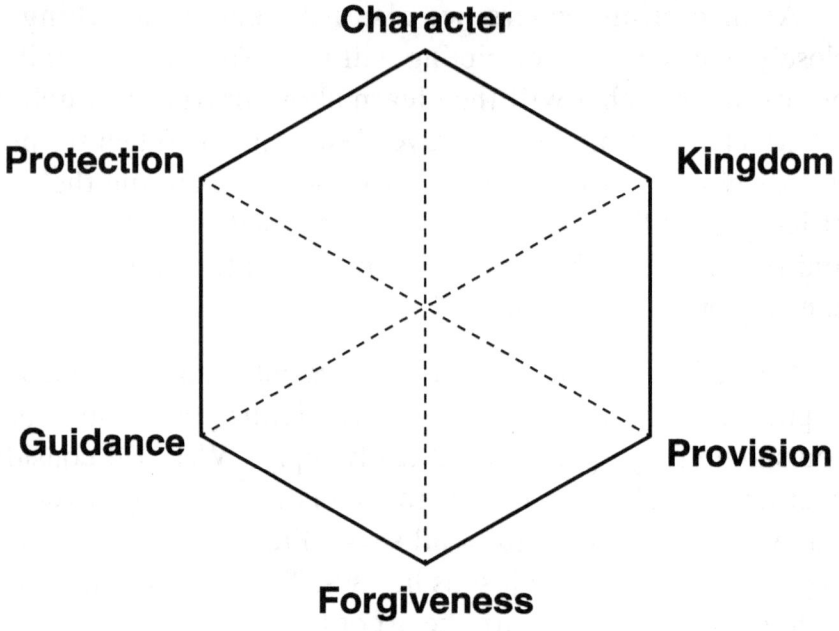

The Hexagon in the Lord's Prayer

Our Father in heaven. Hallowed by your name Jesus begins his prayer with a simple word that embodies an important relational concept: Father. Jesus uses the Aramaic word Abba, an informal name we often translate as Daddy. It's an intimate name for our intimate God. None of us will dispute that Jesus could legitimately start a conversation with the Almighty with such a familiar term. Yet how often do we fail to remember that in this prayer Jesus is teaching that all believers have the same right of relationship he enjoys? This relationship also transcends physical presence. God was just as much Jesus' Father during their physical separation—God in heaven and Jesus on earth—and he is just as much our Father now as he will be when we join him in heaven. And saying God is hallowed reflects how God is very close and yet very different. We offer respect to our

14. Definitive Prayer: The Hexagon

Father and our God for he is holy, with no darkness or sin. We pause to acknowledge that he is what we long to be. Our spirits yearn for this God-likeness to be a reality in us so that God's glory is revealed to others here on earth.

Your kingdom come, your will be done on earth as it is in heaven. Here Jesus says, "Yes, you've been fully adopted into God's family. You have every right to be talking to him but do you realize who your Daddy is? He's the King!" Not a king, the King. So we say, "I want what you want, Daddy. Your Kingdom is an awesome kingdom of light and love, and I want your Kingdom to advance in this world of darkness and hate. My desire is the same as your desire: to see everyone come out of this world of sin and into your Kingdom of forgiveness. I want your rule to advance and be known in this world."

Give us today our daily bread. As humans, we are needy beings. In prayer we can admit those needs. We have physical needs—food, shelter, clothing—that must be met daily. We need health in our bodies. We have spiritual and emotional needs—hope, someone to love, faith—that also must be cared for daily. We need strength in our spirits. All of this is included in "daily bread."

This is where we pull a chair up to our Father's table. We acknowledge that he has the means to feed us—whatever our hunger is. We go to him with our most basic needs anticipating he will feed us from his bounty. We ask because it demonstrates not only our need, but our trust in his provision for us.

Forgive us our debts, as we also have forgiven our debtors. God has given us territory that is ours, and his provision within that territory is full and without want. Yet for some reason we often stray from our land and try to take what is not ours. We trespass into our neighbor's land and incur a debt we cannot pay. When we transgress against another, we are saying, "God, what you have given to me is not enough." And for this we must ask forgiveness. We need to be aware that God has set a path for us; he has called us and given us a destiny. In this prayer we are asking God to help us not to stray from his place within his kingdom. And when other people stray from their path onto ours, hurting us and abusing us and causing us pain, then we need to forgive them as God has forgiven us. "Keep us, Lord, from being indebted to you in withholding forgiveness from others."

Lead us not into temptation. Up until now, the prayer has been dealing with our relationship with the Father and with those around us. Here the prayer changes, now dealing with us going out into the world with the message of God's love and forgiveness. "When you take us out into the world, Father, to do your bidding, to advance your kingdom, give us the strength to be in the world but not of the world."

And deliver us from the evil one. Our souls have an enemy, and his devices of evil include temptation to participate in that evil. If we are led astray by his temptations, eventually we will end up in his hands. The evil one comes only to steal and to kill, says Jesus. He wants to steal our health, steal our joy and our love. If he is successful in his endeavors, we will enter into an eternal death in which we will forever be separated from the love of Christ. We are praying that God would keep us safe as we venture through life in the Lord's service.

As you study each section of the prayer, you will see that it is a framework in which to pour all of the thoughts and concerns of your life. The following section will help guide you with

14. Definitive Prayer: The Hexagon

some practical steps on how to use this prayer for your own life and teach it to those you are leading. You'll also see how this model for prayer can add a new dimension to the prayer life of your community. You can take the thing most burning in your heart at the moment and pray through it using this prayer. Jesus teaches us as the model. In doing this, you are communicating with God as he has taught us to. It really is that simple.

By saying that there is only one prayer model given to us by Jesus, I do not mean to say that we pray these exact words and no more. When I say this model is simple, I do not mean that it is shallow. We must have a growing understanding of the six aspects of this prayer. We cannot remain static in our grasp of how Jesus taught us to pray—where there is no movement, there is no life. Too many churches have lifeless times of prayer, led by those who have remained in the shallow end of the pool. The model for prayer taught to us by Jesus is shallow enough for a baby to bathe in and deep enough for elephants to swim through. What a marvelous paradox!

Praying the Hexagon

As you pray through this prayer, watch and wait—anticipate that God wants to speak to you through one of these areas. Picture the prayer as filling a bottle. You can apply it to your life in two ways. The first is to take your requests and drop them into the bottle. Pray through this model prayer with your request in mind, and see where it sticks. For instance, you can pray for your day:

"Father, I know you are my caring, loving heavenly Father. You rule over all and will watch over me today from your throne in heaven. Let your glory be seen in all I do today. I want your rule and will to be done in all of my thoughts and actions today. Please provide for all of my needs today—spiritual, physical, financial."

Here is where it sticks: you begin to think about the drawer full of bills you need to pay, but you are not sure where the money is going to come from. You spend your time in prayer seeking God for the "daily bread" to pay your debts. This is the point in praying through the Lord's Prayer that you stop; you realize that it is the area of your life that you and God need to walk through together today. Tomorrow the stopping point might be for forgiveness or for help in times of temptation. Each day will have at least one place that sticks out and grabs you as you pour your prayer from the bottle.

The second way to use this model prayer is to pour it out over each request. If someone you know is sick and asks you to pray for them, you can pray like this:

"Father, your reign in heaven extends down to our residence here on earth. Let your glory be seen in the life of my friend. In your Kingdom there is no sickness, no pain. Let your kingdom come in my friend's life and body today. Providing our daily bread and our daily provisions includes having a healthy body so we can do all of your will, so please give my friend a healthy body today. Forgive my friend, as he forgives others, knowing that unforgiveness in our spirits can cause our bodies to react as well. Let him not be tempted to turn from you, his Healer, in this time of need. And protect him from the principalities and powers that want to cause him harm."

As you continue practicing the prayer, it becomes much easier to invite the Holy Spirit to prompt you to "stick" on one area at a time, whether you are praying for yourself or someone

14. Definitive Prayer: The Hexagon

else. For instance, as you pray through the Lord's Prayer, perhaps you will think, "I am really having a problem with so-and-so in my small group. He has stomped in my garden over and over again. He is out of his territory and into mine. Nevertheless, I forgive him, Lord, just as you forgive me when I stomp in someone else's garden." Perhaps you will stop on "your Kingdom come, your will be done" as you consider what is going on in our world. You may be thinking of an atrocity done to people in another country. You say, "Lord, this does not look like your Kingdom. Hate, not love, is reigning there, and that is not right. Let your Kingdom rule be seen right now in that situation, and let love—which I know is your will—be felt by those people."

There are several more ways I personally find it helpful to use the Lord's Prayer to deepen my communication with the Father. As you reflect on these methods, no doubt you and you and your community will come up with more.

How Deep Does The Hexagon Go?

Take one phrase per day from the Lord's Prayer and focus on it for your prayer time. Spend one day just thinking about what calling the God of the universe Father really means. If he truly is your Father, what responsibilities does he have toward you? What do you have in your relationship with him? What does it mean that he is in heaven? Reflect on Dallas Willard's words: "Heaven is God breaking into our reality."

Each day, pray through one of the phrases. Use that phrase to pray for the needs in your life and in the lives of those around you. If you feel you have reached the bottom of that phrase, that there is no more for you to get out of it, dig some more. Each of the six segments of this prayer is bottomless.

Another way to better understand the Lord's Prayer is to see it as a circular prayer; each phrase is fully developed by all of the others. Take one phrase, place a colon after it, and then continue with the other phrases. Ask, how is this part of the prayer fully articulated in the rest of the prayer. For instance, take "your kingdom come, your will be done":

"Give us today our daily bread." It is God's loving desire to meet all of our needs. In his kingdom, there is no want.

"Forgive us our debts." In God's kingdom, our sins are washed away, never to be revisited.

"As we also have forgiven our debtors." As we walk in the grace of God's forgiveness, we will forgive others. Freely we have received, freely we give. This is a law of kingdom life.

"Lead us not into temptation." It is God's will that we walk the path he has laid out for us. In his kingdom, we will be fulfilled by all he has for us, and will not turn aside for a lesser, temporary fix.

"Deliver us from the evil one." The kingdom of God is all light; in it, darkness disappears. Principalities and powers that haunt us have no power in God's kingdom.

"Our Father in heaven." The Kingdom is ruled by a King—and the King is our Dad! We can feel right at home in the Kingdom. We are not strangers, but sons and daughters. We belong in God's Kingdom.

You can do this with any of the phrases in the Lord's Prayer. Put a colon on the end, and keep reading the rest of the phrases. Consider how that segment is played out in your life in the light

14. Definitive Prayer: The Hexagon

of the rest of the prayer.

Let us suggest one final way to dig deeper into Jesus' model for prayer. I've mentioned praying until the Holy Spirit stops you. Using this method, focus on where you are stopped, and use your "sticking point" as a starting point. Ask yourself, "To what extent have I chosen to act like God in this area?" If you focus on daily bread, think about how you are taking God's place and are striving to meet your own needs. Then look left and right, as it were, at the other phrases. How are you supplanting God in these areas? This can lead to a time of repentance, cleansing us from the toxins that build up in us when we assume God's role.

These are just a few ways to explore these six short phrases Jesus gave us as a model for our prayers. As you can see, there is no end to how we can walk and talk with God using this model. As you begin using the principles of the Hexagon in your personal prayer life, you will no doubt uncover many other ways to apply this model. I encourage you also to begin teaching these principles with those you are discipling and allow them to cascade from there to the wider community. I believe you will see exciting changes in your own prayer life and that of those you lead. All that I've learned about prayer and the use of the lords, prayer as the model is based on a deep desire that God has prompted in me to know him better. For decades, I have met with a group of people each weekday morning to pray. That has been the foundation of my life and ministry for the better part of 40 years. For me, learning about prayer and inviting God to take me deeper has been one of the great adventures of my life, and I've often needed the help of others to take the next step.

When I first moved to Sheffield, to lead the church there,

I felt I should ask one of the nuns from the Order of the Holy Paraclete at Whitby North Yorkshire to pray for me - that I might grow in prayer. It was a humbling yet lovely experience to kneel in the presence of that holy woman and ask her to lay hands on me, but the effect was amazing and immediate; my hunger for prayer increased and the life of prayer in the church multiplied rapidly.

Do you need to ask God to increase your hunger for prayer and your desire to know him better?

Take a moment and read a note from my friend Mike R. about his experience with the Hexagon:

I suspect that what the disciples were getting at when they asked Jesus to teach them to pray, was their recognition that Jesus had a singular relationship with his Father. He had an intimacy with God that was unlike any they had ever seen. Who wouldn't want a piece of that once you have seen it, right?

I imagine his explanation of how to pray as a way to develop such a relationship. You might ask, what do I mean by that?

He begins by telling us to understand that He is a Father. Our Father, in fact. Parenting is what Fathers do. They reproduce and express their DNA in their children. They love their kids. They spend time with them. They try to impart to them all they hold important. Jesus then explains to us 6 facets of his Father's heart. These are the things He desires to impart to his children.

Since Jesus said we need to apply his words and not just hear them, I try to use the exercise of praying through these six components as a way to experience each of them. Rather than

14. Definitive Prayer: The Hexagon

being content to ask him for an expression of his authority, or for him to provide bread, forgiveness, or protection I try to enjoy the presence of my Father who's authority is absolute, who desires to give me what I need, whose character is holy, who wants me to imitate his willingness to forgive, who is willing to provide me with guidance. In John 15 Jesus says, "Remain in my love, let my words remain in you".

What I'm trying to say is that I think prayer is supposed to be focusing on the One who is all these things. That's why Jesus' explanation of prayer is all about the Father. It's all about who He is. Talking with him could be about experiencing the incredible gift of being with him, and knowing him. It's sad that we are often content with simply asking what He can do for us.

Part III

Huddles Sustain a Discipling Culture

Part III

Buddies Sustain a Discipling Culture

15. Using Huddles to Disciple People

As we move from Part 2 to Part 3, I want to be clear that Part 3 is immensely practical in terms of how to start a Huddle. If you're not ready to start a Huddle or some other method of discipling people, you can feel free to skim or skip it. However, I invite you to review the appendices for more information that you may find helpful.

One other caveat I'd like to make: My advice is to resist the urge to start a Huddle because you've read this material on how to lead one. The only way to lead a Huddle successfully is to first be in one. My experience is that people often assume that if they can read a book on the matter or have a short conversation with someone, they can now perform what they've just read or heard about. There are times when this is true and times when this isn't true. Leading a Huddle is a time when you will need more than a book to help you develop the necessary skill set. In the same way that you would not want a person performing open heart surgery on you because they once read a book on it, our position is that you wouldn't want someone discipling you and shaping you to be like Jesus because they read a book on it. You want someone who has been discipled in how to disciple!

If you are in a church community that has Huddles and you aren't in one, ask one of the leaders if you can be discipled in a Huddle. If you are in a church that doesn't have Huddles yet and you'd like to pioneer that in your context, our movement offers coaching opportunities that you can be a part of.

What is a Huddle?

- A place to directly disciple your current or future leaders in mission and discipleship

- Helps people answer two questions each time they meet:
    - *What is God saying to me?*
    - *What am I going to do about it?*

- A place to give and receive encouragement and accountability

- For a group of 4 to 10 people (I recommend starting with four to six people)

- Regular and consistent in their rhythm of meeting (at least every other week)

- Led by the Huddle leader

- Something you are invited into by the leader—this is not something people bring a friend to. If you lead a Huddle, then it is your Huddle, and you set the terms, including who you have chosen to disciple and invite.

- Relaxed and fun—laughter should happen regularly!

- Dependent upon openness and honesty within the life of

15. Using Huddles to Disciple People

the Huddle

- For a season only, not forever—I tend to ask people to commit for a year at a time. Obviously, your current leaders remain in Huddles for as long as they are leading people, but you will want to shake things up from time to time.

- Measured by growth in maturity and fruitfulness of members

- Something that multiplies over time, as members start their own Huddles

How is it Different From A Small Group?

Huddles do have a few similarities to small groups; most notably, they are similar in size (four to ten people), meet regularly and at the same location. However, there are some key differences as well.

Differences

- Huddles are not open to the public. They are a group of people who are committed to attending each Huddle and are invited to be a part of the group by the leader. Huddles don't grow by adding more people to an existing Huddle. Huddles grow when current members start a Huddle of their own.

- Huddle leaders act as the primary disciplers of the members of the group, not as facilitators. They are giving their lives as something worth imitating, giving their members access to all parts of their lives. Huddle leaders are inviting the members of the Huddle to imitate the parts of their lives that look like the life and ministry of Jesus.

- In small groups, creating a warm, friendly environment with few-to-no challenges is the most important thing as new people might be attending. In contrast, the job of the Huddle leader ultimately isn't to create the warmest, most comfortable environment. The leader's job is to create an environment that is a safe place to be honest, but one of accountability, learning, encouragement and challenge. It is not uncommon for a Huddle leader to say something that might be difficult for someone to hear, but it is said in love for the sake of transformation.

- People miss small groups if things come up or perhaps people may not feel like attending that night. In Huddles, the expectation is that you never miss a Huddle unless it is absolutely unavoidable. Huddle leaders hold their members accountable to this expectation.

- Small groups often revolve around particular curricula, courses or a very specific Bible study theme/topic often decided by the group as a whole. The direction and trajectory of Huddles are guided by where the Huddle leader feels the Holy Spirit is leading the group and by the particular *kairos* moments the people within the group are experiencing.

15. Using Huddles to Disciple People

Why Do Huddles Work?

Learning

As I have previously discussed in this book, through the relationship of a Huddle leader and the members of their Huddle, people are able to learn through classroom teaching, apprenticeship, and immersion. Go to chapters 4-6 for more on these ideas.

Language

Huddles work because people are slowly learning an agreed-upon discipling language that not only will they be able to teach others but also is shaping and transforming who they are. The language isn't just head knowledge; the language is becoming incarnated into who they are. Within the group, it is creating a culture of continual maturation as people become more and more like Jesus. They are orienting themselves to becoming lifelong learners of Jesus. Go to chapter 7 for more on these ideas.

Multiplication

From the beginning, Huddle members know that one day they will start a Huddle of their own. One of the non-negotiable that Jesus makes clear in his last words is that disciples make disciples. So Huddle leaders tell members from the beginning that the expectation is that in 6-12 months they will start one of their own. Now we won't tell people they have to start a Huddle or when they have to start it; God will make it clear when. But they know the expectation heading in.

As you might expect, this puts a bit of pressure on Huddle members.

I have found this to be good pressure. What it says is that my spiritual health and maturity affect not only me but also the people I will soon be discipling. People often become stunted in their spiritual development if they assume it only affects them (though this is never really the case), but knowing that other people are depending on them changes the game in their minds and makes them take their own spiritual development more seriously.

High Commitment

As you are probably gathering, a Huddle is high commitment. This is one of the reasons a Huddle is so successful in discipling people. When the bar is raised, people either bow out or step up. Most of the time people step up. It is our experience that people want to grow but are unable to will themselves to transformation. They need relationships and structures that keep them accountable and moving toward Jesus. They also know the only way this can happen is with high commitment.

Group Learning

Huddles work because they expose people to the learning of a group rather than only one-on-one mentoring. What a member gets to see is not only how the leader is discipling them, but also how the leader is discipling other people as well. Because each person is different, different skills and practices are needed to disciple various personality types. Discipleship in a committed group of people allows people to learn how they will disciple other people in the future who aren't like them. Such committed discipleship also allows what is being spoken into the life of another person to possibly be true of you as well.

15. Using Huddles to Disciple People

Furthermore, it adds a layer of accountability that is unique to group settings. If each time the Huddle meets you are the only person who doesn't follow through with what you say you are going to do, you begin to feel the pressure of your actions. The advantage of the group setting is that it is easier not to follow through when there are only two people in the discipleship relationship. When you inject another 5-8 people into it, the group dynamic helps people take accountability more seriously.

Time

The fact of the matter is that we only have so much time in each day and each week, and we need to use that time wisely. We have found that regular, one-on-one mentoring can work sometimes, but it can be very time-consuming to do this with more than just a person or two. Huddles allow us to disciple a good number of people while still being wise with one of our most precious resources: our time. Rather than having eight one-on-ones each week for an hour each (for a total of eight hours per week), a Huddle allows you to disciple, say, eight people every other week in one two-hour meeting. Huddles work because they allow the maximum amount of investment in a group of people without taking too large of an investment of regularly scheduled time.

Balance of Invitation and Challenge

Jesus was skilled at discipling people because he understood invitation and challenge.

He invited people into a covenant relationship with him, and they had access to everything.

Jesus also had a clear vision of who God had created the

disciples to be. Jesus knew they were adopted sons of his Father and that meant their identity was royal. That meant their role, their purpose in life, was to represent their Father (the King) in this world, exercising his authority and power. The challenge is to live into this identity and into this calling; to live into the reality of the Kingdom of their Father.

Huddles work in this way because, once people experience invitation and challenge, it's addictive. Why would you want to leave that kind of relationship? Someone who cares enough about you to give you all of their life, but loves you enough to take you to the place where you live out of your true identity... even when getting you there may be hard sometimes. This allows the person to live out of a place of security rather than insecurity. They aren't questioning your motives for bringing the hard truth. That person knows you are committed to them for the long haul.

Our experience is that many people (though not all) experience more spiritual growth and breakthrough in their first 6-9 months of Huddle than in their previous five years. When people have this kind of growth, they are ruined for life. They can't go back to a place where they aren't experiencing both invitation and challenge. They want that kind of discipling environment and relationship. Go to chapter three for more on this idea.

Continued Investment

Once you begin a Huddle of your own you continue to be in a Huddle. As you invest, you can continue to be invested in. Typically speaking, most people experience the most spiritual transformation not when they are first being discipled, but when they start discipling people themselves. I believe that any

15. Using Huddles to Disciple People

time you intentionally release a leader to influence, lead and disciple others, it must happen in a system of accountability. Huddles work because every person who Huddles others is also being Huddled.

Spiritual Formation Process

Phase One: Language

As I have already discussed, language creates culture, and I believe LifeShapes is a powerful discipling language. It's important to understand here that this language lays the foundation for everything else. It helps establish the biblical worldview of Jesus and gives people a lens to see the world in the way that Jesus did. What Huddle does is slowly teach people this language. The first few months of Huddle are similar to learning Spanish 101 and 102. You have to know some of the nouns and pronouns and how to conjugate verbs before you can really start to immerse yourself in the language and become fluent in it. It's all about the basics.

Learning the basics of the language is key, particularly as people are learning to engage the two central questions:

- *What is God saying to me?*

- *What am I going to do about it?*

This is foreign for so many people. Most people don't even know how to hear and discern the voice of God, much less respond to it.

We clearly see Jesus establishing this foundation of language. On the first day of his ministry, he introduces the idea of the Kingdom, and very soon after that he delivers the Sermon on the Mount, exploring more fully the reality of the Kingdom of God. Everything that Jesus teaches, every story he gives and every action he makes is wrapped up in the language of the Kingdom of God.

Phase Two: Rhythms

This phase is about learning the rhythms of life that Jesus talks about in John 15, how there is an ever-swinging pendulum between rest and work that was written into our bodies from the creation of the world. Jesus is trying to draw out this principle: We are designed to work from a place of rest, not rest from work.

He makes it quite clear that real rest is found in him being connected to his Father. It is in times of rest that we not only receive the Father's life and energy, but we also hear his voice.

Because so few people have ever been able to sustain daily or weekly rhythms, it usually takes months for this to happen in the lives of the people in your Huddle. Most people, in order to do this, need to start getting up early every day and spending time in Scripture and prayer (though this isn't how everyone will function, and that should be OK). It isn't law and certainly some people don't start their day this way, but for us it's been a general observation. This tends to be a hard adjustment for most. You will likely find that most people don't get up at the same time and rarely go to bed with any consistency.

This isn't an easy process. It will be something the people in your Huddle struggle with. Undoubtedly, they will want to give up. And as the person discipling them, remember, you lay down your life to get them through this. If they can't get these

15. Using Huddles to Disciple People

rhythms down, our enemy will render them virtually ineffective because he has cut off their source of life and energy: the Father.

They will want to give up during this phase, but give them a tremendous amount of grace and keep reminding them why they are doing this. One helpful tidbit: I've found it helpful in our Huddles to text them each day, for six weeks straight, the passage of Scripture you're reading as a way of holding them accountable. I've found that if we can win this first, all-important battle of the day, the other battles of the day go our way a lot easier.

The same goes for taking a day off (Sabbath), an important weekly rhythm. You have to give a massive challenge and a massive invitation for them to make this happen in their lives. They might fail more at this than they do in their daily rhythms. Many people are addicted to work, to emails, and to doing, doing, doing. It's so very difficult in our culture to take a whole day off. But you have to help them fight for it, and the best way to do that is to model it in your own life. Invite them and their family to spend their day off with you and your family. Show them what it's like and why it's such a beautiful thing.

Phase Three: Boldness in Mission

Very clearly, we are to be about our Father's business. We are the agents of the Kingdom. We definitely have an interior world, but as we become deeply connected to the God of mission, we respond in kind since we have been made in the same image. We carry his authority and have been told to exercise his power. So every day, there is a mission.

What a Huddle allows you to do is disciple your members in such a way that they integrate the mission into their way of seeing the world and balancing their relationships. It isn't that you necessarily take your Huddle out on a mission together (though you can certainly do this); it's that you hold them accountable to living out the out component of Jesus' life through concrete, actionable plans.

Every disciple is missional. It's part of the deal! Most of us simply don't live that way.

Now, when we first start interacting with this, there will be some timidity to it. More than likely, we will stick to the "People of Peace" that we know well, and in front of whom we won't risk embarrassing ourselves. But what happens when we sense we are supposed to pray for someone we don't know? Or ask someone we have only met once a personal question? Or ask for healing for someone we just passed on the street? Maybe spend time in Section 8 government housing where people have to choose between buying food or paying rent? Or make a spiritual insight into someone's life that you know very well and are scared of what they may think of you afterward?

If you are anything like me when I was first starting out, the thought of this petrifies you! But we can't read Scripture and not think that God isn't preparing people for us to be present with others and for a specific purpose. This third phase is an exercise in learning boldness and walking in the economy of a different kind of kingdom.

Does that mean you don't engage in a mission in the previous two phases? Of course not. It simply means that as people learn the language, as they have rhythms of listening to the Father regularly governing their lives, out of the overflow will be an increased intentionality, authority and boldness that weren't present before. It starts from the inside of you and works

15. Using Huddles to Disciple People

its way out.

Now something very beautiful starts to emerge in this phase, something Alan Hirsch calls *communitas*. In *The Shaping of Things to Come*, Hirsch describes communities that are deeply formed through a uniform and profound experience.[92]

A few examples of *communitas*: Hostages are with people they have never met, share five days together, but an unmistakable bond and kinship are formed through that harrowing experience. The former hostages stay close for years after the crisis. A college basketball team plays, trains, practices and strategizes together for months, hoping to make it to the Final Four of March Madness. The shared experience forms something deep between the players.

It is one thing to form a community. It is something entirely different to form *communitas*.

Bill Easum comments, "Christianity is concerned with the unfolding of the Kingdom of God in the world, not the longevity of organizations."[93]

Study after study has confirmed that groups that try to start with a goal of a community, and hope somehow to move toward a mission, almost never get there. A mission must be the organizing principle of the group. When we start with a mission, we always get a community, because we band together for a common goal, because we'll need to care for one another in the midst of the battle of the mission.

---

92 See *The Shaping of Things to Come: Innovation and Mission for the 21st Century Church* by Michael Frost and Alan Hirsch.
93 Bill Easum, *Unfreezing Moves: Following Jesus into the Mission Field* (Nashville, TN: Abingdon Press, 2002) 17.

In fact, studies have shown that groups with a mission focus cared for one another better than those with a community focus.

Why?

Because these groups have developed *communitas*. In this Third Phase, Boldness in Mission, *communitas* starts to develop.

Phase Four: Leadership

One of the stated expectations of a Huddle at the very beginning of Phase One is that if you're in a Huddle, you will start one of your own someday. This is how we keep the gospel imperative of the Great Commission: Make disciples who then make disciples who then make disciples. A Huddle isn't just for our sake (though we receive great spiritual benefit from participating).

If we receive anything, it's so we can give it away. Once people know the agreed-on discipleship language, their lives are evidence of this, and when they have sustainable rhythms in their lives and are learning to boldly enter into mission, then the expectation is that they will begin a Huddle (or another missional/discipling endeavor) of their own. Every disciple leads someone, even if it's just four people.

Spiritual Formation Process:
While there isn't a formula, there is a form

What is the general path that allows people to learn and incarnate these principles over the course of a year in a Huddle?

1. Use the first 5-6 Huddles on the Learning Circle. This is the foundational shape and the one that is returned to in every Huddle to come as we learn to hear God's voice

15. Using Huddles to Disciple People

and respond to it.

2. Observe and discern through the Spirit where God is shaping this group of people:

- If they are struggling with Identity, spend several Huddles on the Twin Triangles of Covenant and Kingdom.[94] Although the twin Triangles of Covenant and Kingdom are not LifeShapes, you will find them hugely important in discipling people.

- If they are struggling with being over-scheduled, exhausted, stressed or tired, spend several Huddles using the Semi-Circle.

- If they are struggling with prayer and connecting with their Father, use the Hexagon for several Huddles.

- If they are struggling with surface relationships or living isolated lives, use the Triangle for several Huddles.

3. After the Circle, the best introductory shapes for spiritual formation are the twin Triangles, Semi-Circle, Triangle, and Hexagon. Continue to observe and discern how the Spirit is shaping the group and use these shapes in the order that seems appropriate to how God is shaping the group. The object isn't to get through these four shapes as quickly as possible, but to learn them in such a way that they become incarnated into the lives of the Huddle members.

4. Once the Huddle members really seem to be living into the Circle, twin Triangles, Triangle, Hexagon, and Semi-

---

94 See Mike Breen's *Covenant and Kingdom: The DNA of the Bible.*

Circle, they will start to see a good amount of spiritual transformation. They will also be living out a sustainable spiritual life without the extremes of "off" and "on." You will notice that the members of the Huddle are becoming much more alive and healthier people.

5. Once you are confident in this, teach the Pentagon for several Huddles, helping people identify which of the fivefold ministries God has created them to be (their base gifting), how they are already naturally living it out and what phase God is currently leading them into.

6. Teach the Heptagon and teach them how this is playing out in the spiritual family they are a part of. Help them assess how they can contribute more fully to the life of their Missional Community.

7. Teach the principle of Person of Peace for several Huddles, helping them identify the People of Peace in their life who are spiritually open and how they can more fully invest in those relationships so God's Kingdom can break through into their lives.

8. In this process, it's important to leave space for the Spirit to deal with things as they come up and not try to plow through in teaching a new shape when there's more immediate work that God is trying to accomplish.

9. It is often helpful to return and review shapes between learning new ones, as well as simply returning to the Circle for a Huddle, and leaving it open for people to answer what God is saying to them and what they are going to do about it.

10. At the conclusion of every Huddle, regardless of the

15. Using Huddles to Disciple People

shape, each Huddle member should be able to clearly articulate, 1) What is God saying to me, 2) What am I going to do about it in the next 2 weeks?

16. Huddle Launch Guide

Before Your Huddle Begins

- If at all possible, make sure you've had a chance to participate in a Huddle before you begin leading your own. Don't assume that because you have led a small group in the past that you can easily lead a Huddle. They are vastly different. The best way to learn to lead a Huddle is to be in one.

- If you're a pastor, don't teach a LifeShapes sermon series. It will be in one ear and out the other of the people who hear it. The power of LifeShapes is when they are actively applied in someone's life in a small, committed community.

- Obviously this book, *Building a Discipling Culture*, is the foundational text for the language of LifeShapes. There are more helpful resources and content at 3dmPublishing.com

- Really ask God who should be in your Huddle. Spend at

least 3-4 weeks praying about this. The inclination will be to think strategically. That's fine. Think strategically. But don't let strategy interfere with who God wants to be in your Huddle. God will often surprise you with who he brings into the Huddle and who doesn't end up being part of it. Look for the People of Peace whom God has prepared for your Huddle. That's who you want. Maybe write down the people who would be obvious choices first. Then, come back a week later and ask God to give you a few people who wouldn't be obvious choices.

- More than likely, you will run into a few skeptical people when discussing Huddles. If they are massively cynical about Huddles and you find yourself trying to prove that a Huddle is of value, just pass on them for the time being. It's difficult to actively disciple someone who is cynical. There's a good chance that person will come around, but it will be the transformed lives of the other people in your Huddle that convince them. There are plenty of people who are looking for people to invest in: Find those people.

- Make sure the people in your future Huddle know the enormous commitment level: specifically about keeping the Huddle time sacred on the calendar. You put a Huddle on the calendar, and then schedule the rest of your month. Obviously, you don't want to say it quite so forcefully because they won't understand the importance of it from experience yet. Let them know it's OK to miss a Huddle for unavoidable things, but being tired, busy, or stressed isn't a good reason to miss. They will always be at least one of those three things (if not a combination of them).

16. Huddle Launch Guide

- A Huddle is all about investment. You are investing your life into theirs. This is, essentially, what you are saying to them: "I want to invest my life into yours and the places that look like Jesus, copy those things. The rest, well, that you can scrap!" This is a profound thing because most people either 1) have never thought they were worth investing in or 2) all investment was tied to what they could produce or give back to the organization. In other words, often they felt like they were being used. You are offering them something beautiful: an invitation to your life.

- Don't oversell yourself as the Huddle leader, especially if this is your first time leading a Huddle. Just as there is a learning curve for the people in your Huddle, there will be a learning curve for you. Make sure they know this will be a journey, a learning process, for you and for them. They are learning how to be discipled, and you are learning to disciple. Remember the quote from G.K. Chesterton: "If it's worth doing, it's worth doing badly." Leading a Huddle is a skill you have to learn and develop like anything else in life. No one was born a great Huddle leader. You will be naturally more skilled at either invitation or challenge and will have to concentrate on improving the other. You have to put in time and effort and have patience. There will be times when you don't feel like you're doing well at leading your Huddle. That's normal! Pray more, stick with it, get coaching from a strong Huddle leader, and over time you will develop the skill set.

Your First 10-12 Huddles

- Your sweet spot for a Huddle meeting is going to be right at 1½ hours, or maybe 2 hours at the longest. The purpose of a Huddle isn't to get out every feeling that someone has. It isn't group therapy (I'm not knocking therapy; it's just that a Huddle isn't that place). The purpose is to process what God is saying to you and how you should respond. If someone is dealing with a strong emotional reaction to an event, that emotion was produced by either a *kairos* or string of *kairos* moments. We are looking to process these moments and the invitation to walk more fully in the Kingdom, not to simply get out what we feel. A Huddle has the ability to help you process what God is saying to you and, over time, do so with a quicker and more discerning eye.

- Take 10-20 minutes in the beginning as people are arriving to hang out and catch up. I've always found it quite helpful to have food and drinks available. It helps to create a safe, warm environment. Help people understand this isn't time they want to skip, but part of the Huddle experience.

- Even when teaching a new shape, try to never teach longer than 12-15 minutes. You want to give them enough so they have a significant *kairos*, but not so much that they zone out or become overwhelmed. Many times, you won't have to teach more than five minutes to get people to the place God has for them.

- Just because you have a Huddle doesn't mean there needs to be teaching. There will be many times when processing people's *kairos* moments is more

16. Huddle Launch Guide

than enough.

- This will probably be your biggest learning curve: You have to keep one eye on what a person is saying and another on what God's Spirit is saying. In this way, a Huddle is very much prophetic in nature. Again, this is something that you can learn to do, but it will take some time. To help with this learning curve, write notes as people talk. What phrases pop up? What verses from Scripture? A story? An image? A metaphor? What's the central theme of what they are saying? This is an easy way to learn to keep both eyes open. You may also want to carve out 15 minutes before people arrive when you can be silent and listen to God, pray for the people in your Huddle and ask God's Spirit to be present with you.

- I have found it helpful to teach the Circle first, the Semi-Circle second, the Triangle third and, after that, whenever a new shape is appropriate (the Sample Huddle Outlines will go into more detail about how you might teach these and how long I usually spend on each so that the language is learned). But again, your Huddle might be different, and a different order might be appropriate. There is no magic formula to this.

- I strongly recommend you take your first five to six Huddle times to focus only on the Circle. I also suggest dedicating one of these Huddles to teaching the Covenant and Kingdom Triangles[95] after Huddle members are familiar with the Circle in order to see what the *kairos* moment produces and then take it around the Circle.

---

95 For the Covenant and Kingdom Triangles, read my book *Covenant and Kingdom: The DNA of the Bible.*

Building a Discipling Culture

While not in the LifeShapes catalog, it is immeasurably helpful as it really helps paint the reality of scripture and the world we live in. Furthermore, all the LifeShapes are built on the principles of Covenant and Kingdom and flow out of them.

- Do not rush through the LifeShapes. There is no prize for getting done with the shapes. You'll want to resist the urge to view the shapes as curriculum. Your job as the Huddle leader is to see the shapes incarnate themselves into the people you are discipling. This takes time and does not happen overnight. Slower is better.

- If you sense that someone should be prayed with after sharing and making their plan, pray for them right then. Don't just say you'll pray for them. Do it then!

- Do not assume that because you have taught it once, you have taught it for the last time. Remember, language creates culture. This culture is established when 1) they can teach you the shapes and the language becomes "everyday language" and 2) their lives look like the shapes have been incarnated. So take your time. For example, after the third or fourth Huddle, have one of them teach the Circle to the group as if they were the Huddle leader. In doing this, you are once again planting the seed that one day, they, too, will be Huddle leaders.

- Bring challenge early in the Huddle experience. The longer you put it off, the harder it will be. By bringing challenge early, you set the tone for what kind of group it is and how it is vastly different from other groups people have joined. Obviously when you give challenge, it needs to be with a strong measure of humility and

16. Huddle Launch Guide

said in a way that is meant to build the person through the challenge rather than embarrass or break them. Sometimes, challenge happens best outside of the Huddle. You'll want to discern the best place to give it.

- Not everyone gets equal time. Some people are having more significant *kairos* moments than others, and so more time is needed to dig into that. That's fine. That doesn't mean there isn't equal learning. From the beginning, make sure people know this. They should be thinking about how what is being said provides insight into their lives and what they might be saying if they were the Huddle leader. The learning doesn't stop just because they aren't the one talking.

- When your Huddle is just beginning, very rarely let other people interject with their own thoughts or opinions. I know. This comes off as harsh, doesn't it! Here's the thing: They will be invited and welcomed to interject when they know the language and their lives show it. Explain this to your Huddle. Go back to the Square as you think about this one. (Turn to the chapter on the Square as a reference for the rest of these comments.) In D1, an L1 leader needs to be very directive. No one knows what they are doing! They have to be told what to do: they are excited, but have very low competency and an exaggerated sense of confidence. In D2, the L2 leader has to coach quite a bit and still be very directive. The Huddle members are hitting a wall, can't get through it, and only you can get them past it. For instance, if they are just starting to do missional engagement, they probably won't be terribly good at it in the beginning and will want to give up. D1 and D2 are where the first few months of your Huddle will be as most people will quickly learn the language, but it won't be bearing much fruit in their lives yet because they don't have the sustainable rhythms of the Semi-Circle. However, in D3, the L3 leader builds consensus, invites people in and asks for their opinions. This is a critical turn in Scripture when Jesus says in John 15, "I no longer call you servants but friends!"

- In the first few Huddles, help them in the process of what God may be saying to them and what a plan might be. You want to do this plainly and with lots of humility. Maybe you can say it like this, "Well, it sounds to me like God might be saying _____. How would you feel about doing _____ as your plan? How does that strike you? Does that hit you as true? Am I off on that one?" By helping them along the first few times, you're giving them a real-life example of what it should look like. But always give it with humility because you could have missed it. Be open to the fact that you could be wrong!

- At the conclusion of a Huddle, make sure each person can answer these two questions:

    - *What is God saying to me?*

    - *What am I going to do about it?*

- It is very important that they are able to articulate what God is saying to them on their own (not just what you said) and the plan. Have them write it down. Once everyone has done this, have each person quickly read it back. Doing this for the first four to five months will help in changing the way they think and respond.

After Your First 10-12 Huddles

- There will more than likely be a gap between when you teach the Circle, Semi-Circle, and Triangle and the other LifeShapes. However, there is also a good chance you will need to teach the Hexagon (the six phrases of the Lord's Prayer) in order to help people learn to pray as they are engaging in their daily rhythms. These four shapes usually give you the foundation you need to build on to move out of the first two phases of a Huddle.

- If the four phases of a Huddle are language, rhythms, boldness in a mission, and leadership, it's pretty easy to evaluate where people are by looking at the Square. Are they unconsciously competent in teaching the shapes? Are they hitting a wall with boldness in a mission? Have they even received a prompting to lead anything yet? You get the picture. Knowing where people are will help you discern as you pray where God wants you to take your Huddle.

- You can use the Learning Circle as a way to use Scripture in your daily rhythms (see the Sample Huddle Outlines for more notes on this).

- You can teach the Square to the whole group or individually as people need it. If you do it individually, people will need it at different times based on where they are tracking spiritually.

- Start actively training your Huddle members to be

Huddle leaders. As someone is sharing, ask someone else randomly, "If you were the Huddle leader, what would you say right now?" This wakes everyone else up, but it also gets the wheels turning in their brains about what they would say to each person. This is a big piece of a Huddle: You're also in a Huddle to learn how to lead a Huddle for other people! Maybe every once in a while have each person take notes as everyone shares as if they were the Huddle leader to practice "seeing with both sets of eyes."

- There's the potential to get addicted to being directive and having everyone like the insightful comments you provide that cut them to the core. The point isn't that people see you figure out what God is saying to them; the point is that you teach them to do this for themselves and others. Don't stay as the L1/L2 leader but for so long. As soon as you can, invite people into the conversation. I can't overemphasize the importance of this point.

- Once you feel like your Huddle is through the first two phases (Language and Rhythms), give everyone a copy of *Building a Discipling Culture* and have everyone read a chunk of it between each Huddle. Then, discuss it for a few minutes to start the Huddle. By doing this, you are:

- Giving them a chance to refresh their memory and go deeper with each shape.

- Reminding them that mission is the point of all of this as they will soon be leading a Huddle of their own.

- Teach the Pentagon, Heptagon, and Octagon as seems appropriate for your Huddle. Does it seem like some people in your Huddle aren't dealing well with something toxic in their life (anger, bitterness, etc.)? Well, the Heptagon is all about organic health. It's the tool you use to evaluate how healthy you or your community is. Are people really starting to delve into their identity as they are thinking about a mission? Teach the Pentagon. It's all about personal calling. Are people asking questions about how to do evangelism and a mission? The Octagon is the shape of choice. Feel out where your group is. Pray about where God needs your group to go. Teach the shape that will help you get there. But again, the goal is to let it sink in and become part of you.

- Remember, when leading a Huddle, you're teaching the Huddle members the very basics of following Jesus, and the big goal is getting them to a place where they can give their own lives as a living example by leading a Huddle of their own.

Teaching People To Do Mission In Huddle

The following are a few examples of how you can use Huddle as a missional training ground for the people you are discipling:

- Have everyone come to Huddle at the normal place, but have each person bring $5. (They don't know why.) Each person is then assigned to go spend that money at a restaurant/coffee shop somewhere, buy a drink, ask the Holy Spirit to reveal to them a person of peace, and have ONE substantive conversation in that one hour they are there. Doesn't have to be Jesus related... but something deep. Then, the whole Huddle gathers at a place after that to process and go around the Learning Circle as they enter into the *kairos* that has been created.

- Go out for a dinner one night with your Huddle where everyone brings his or her Persons of Peace. Process the night through the Learning Circle in the next Huddle.

- Have everyone in the Huddle bring their families (if applicable) and invite Persons of Peace with their families and go to the park for a cookout and family games.

- Have every person in the Huddle share your communities' language for the gospel with one person of peace they are close to. Have them explain to the POP that they are simply practicing and are neither asking for or expecting a response. Have the POP give feedback. Did it make sense? What questions would they have? Did they feel pressured? Process in Huddle.

- Have the Huddle regularly serve with the poor and regularly process in Huddle.

- Move into bolder expressions of mission with your Huddle. Set up a "Free Prayer Table" on the sidewalk of a crowded street or shopping center and offer free prayer to people as they pass. Process the *kairos* in Huddle.

- Have everyone in the Huddle commit to praying for one specific Person of Peace every time they are in Huddle and have them commit to pray frequently in their own prayer times until they see breakthrough. Process the *kairos* of frustration and breakthrough in Huddle.

- Have everyone in the Huddle meet during lunch on a workday and go to a place where people are and engage in random acts of kindness. Process the *kairos* in the following Huddle.

- Have the Huddle meeting in a public place like a restaurant or coffee shop and use the time to pray for people in the place, asking for the Holy Spirit to show someone who is a Person of Peace and engage appropriately.

- Use one of your Huddles as a time to practice sharing the gospel in a relational way. Allow time for feedback, encouragement, coaching and critique.

- Use your Huddle time to explore the differences between Persons of Peace who are passing relationships (you meet them randomly) and permanent relationships (a regular part of your life). How is mission done with the Octagon with these different types of POPs?

- Have everyone in your Huddle knock on five doors of people living around them bringing cookies and engage in conversation. Follow up with a dinner invitation if the relationship seems ready. Process the *kairos* in Huddle.

- Have everyone in the Huddle ask God: 1) what missional context they should be trying to reach into, and 2) what the gospel touch point is for that missional context. Share in Huddle and then have their plans respond appropriately.

After You've Got All The LifeShapes

Because a Huddle isn't based on a set curriculum, from the very beginning (and after you have taught LifeShapes), you'll need to rely completely on the Holy Spirit's guiding of where your Huddle is going (generally) and what each specific Huddle should be about (specifically).

Spend time before each Huddle praying and asking God what this specific Huddle time needs to be about. Is it about building faith? Character? Skills? How does God want you to go about doing that? Often Huddles will come out of what God is teaching you. You have walked through a door that God has led you through and experienced breakthrough, and then you pass it on to those in your Huddle.

There are three different kinds of Huddle experiences:

1. Faith Huddles—Each person brings a *kairos* and the Huddle helps them determine what God is saying to them and what they will do about it.

2. Character Huddles—Use the character questions that come with the Triangle (see the Appendix for this set of questions) to help lead a balanced life of integrity.

3. Skill Huddles—Allows you to teach and hone a particular skill in your Huddle members. This could be listening to the voice of God, prayer, casting vision, mission, Huddle leadership, honing invitation and challenge, etc. Any skill set that Jesus used, we want to be able to pass on to those in our Huddles.

The following are just a few ideas for what you can do once the shapes have been covered:

- How are you doing? How is what you're leading doing? Mine out the *kairos*.

- Give a mini-teaching for five to ten minutes of a *kairos* you've had and what God has been saying to you. Then ask them what *kairos* this has produced in them. This is a great practice to get into. What you will quickly discover is that, by sharing the breakthroughs God is giving you in your life with them and creating a *kairos* for them, God will often give the people in your Huddle the same breakthrough.

- Revisit any of the shapes and come at it from a fresh perspective. Mine out the *kairos* by digging into what *kairos* moment was produced by revisiting that shape, what God might be saying, and how they might respond.

- Have everyone bring a Scripture that has stuck with them for the past two weeks. Mine out the *kairos*.

- Start it this way: "God, who is your Father, is so close to you that you can almost touch him. He loves you. He wants good things for you. What do you want to ask your Father?" Mine out the *kairos*.

- Go on a mission together. Mine out the *kairos* afterward.

No doubt you've noticed how each of these ultimately leads back to mining out a *kairos*. Remember, disciple in Greek means learner. By constantly coming back to these two questions through the use of *kairos* moments, we are allowing God to shape us into life-long learners. God is always speaking. We are always responding.

17. Sample Huddle Outlines

These outlines are meant to be a guide, not a curriculum. They are one person's notes on how he led his first few Huddles. Hold these outlines in your hands loosely, and don't cling to them. These are meant only to give a little more flesh and blood so we can take the concept of leading Huddle from the theoretical to the practical. The outlines cover several Huddles for the Circle, Semi-Circle, and Triangle, but none of the other five LifeShapes.

This is deliberate.

By reading and using these outlines, you will see patterns in the flow of a Huddle and how teaching happens in Huddle as well as discussion and accountability. Once you get a sense of that, you won't need outlines from anyone else. If you know the LifeShapes well, are willing to grow in your abilities as a Huddle leader, are willing be held accountable for the Huddle you're leading and really listen for God's voice to lead your Huddle, you're good to go.

Example of a first Circle Huddle

Pre-Huddle: food and drinks.

Opening prayer.

Objective: If you make disciples, you get a church. If you make a church, you don't always get disciples. The only number that Jesus is counting and the only thing he talks about in his last instructions are disciples. The Greek word is *mathetes*, which means learner. However, this word doesn't refer just to someone who can remember information; someone who becomes a lifelong learner, *mathetes* is someone who is always changing, growing, stretching and becoming more like Jesus. Jesus is literally suggesting that you can do everything that he does; you just have to learn it.

To become disciples, we really need a common language, something we can all understand and reference. (Spanish 101, 102 and 201 for example: You go to Barcelona and have a lot more fun if you know the basics of the language, but you become fluent once you are in Barcelona.) We become fluent when we are on a mission.

Shapes as a language: This isn't a way to teach and apply thousands of biblical principles. Rather, these notes are designed to form you into a lifelong learner by linking Jesus' key discipleship principles to memorable, easily explained images... shapes! Disciples are those who have a new framework of truth, enabling them to build biblical principles into their lives and grow together in authentic community. This is the whole point of the shapes. We can make disciples who, because they

17. Sample Huddle Outlines

have an easily understood language that is making them more like Jesus, can in turn make disciples themselves, thus building a community (the church) in the process.

Introductions: Have everyone introduce themselves with their name and a brief answer to this question: *Where are you today in your journey with Jesus?*

Layering information: We're starting with the Circle today, and I'm going to give you the very basics of it. But as we meet more and more, I'll continually give you more information about various shapes, adding to your depth and understanding. I'm going to give you just enough information for you to understand and apply to your life.

Read: Mark 1:14–15.

Explain *kairos* **and** *chronos* **time:** Use the speed bump and brick wall example. *Kairos* moments are opportunities (and can be anything—lyrics, Scripture, a conversation, looking at the sunset, a car accident, self-realization about something, anything) to step more fully into the Kingdom of God—this place where God's reality and our reality are colliding. Much of what I'll be working with you on is teaching you to see these moments that are happening all around you.
So we have this moment, this opportunity to step more fully into the
Kingdom. How do we do that?
Exactly as Mark writes—repent and believe? That sounds nice, but how do we do that? What does that

practically look like?
Walk through Circle: Observe, reflect, discuss (this is repent and leads us to the answer to this question: What is God saying to you?). Plan, account, act (this is believe and leads us to the answer to our second question: What are you going to do about it?).
These two fundamental questions of Christian spirituality allow us to be changed from the inside out: What is God saying to me? What am I going to do about it?
So what does this look like in action? (Walk through a *kairos* moment of your own through the Circle for them. Allow some vulnerability and let them clearly see how this plays out in a real-life example.)

Helpful tips:

- At this point, look at the time. You need to evaluate how large your group is and how much time you've taken up. You do not want your first Huddle to last longer than two hours total. So evaluate how much time you have left and decide if you have enough time to allow everyone to talk. If you don't, let the group know that only a few will be sharing this time. Another way of doing this is grouping people with similar themes together and working with two to three people at a time, rather than one person at a time.

- Before starting, read Psalm 139:23–24 a few times as a prayer and ask the Holy Spirit to work and be present.

- Explain that part of stepping into *kairos* moments is cutting through the clutter and learning to do it quickly: "This is a specific moment in time, not your whole life

17. Sample Huddle Outlines

story, just one moment. Jesus has given it to you for a specific reason. So I've got a timer that I'll be watching that will go off at ten minutes. My goal is to teach us to walk through the whole Circle in ten minutes. Not because you aren't worth more time, but because this is how we can learn to think through the moments God is giving us. Now I am going to guide the conversation, and those of you who aren't talking yet, just listen because what I'm saying to this person will often have as much to do with you as it does for them. You can learn just as much by listening."

- Walk through the Circle with each person, obviously pointing out each step in the Circle. Make sure everyone knows exactly what God is saying to him or her and exactly what his or her plan is.

- Have each person write down his or her plan in a journal or Huddle Guide (if you've purchased from 3DM or created your own). You'll be asking them about their plan at the beginning of the next Huddle.

- Remind them you will meet every two weeks and give them the next date.

Closing prayer: Ephesians 3:14–21.

Example of second Circle Huddle:

Have people be ready with a *kairos* moment from the previous week when they come to the Huddle. Send them a text or email to have this ready. In addition, mention this in the previous Huddle.

Pre-Huddle:
- Food/drinks, time to informally talk.
- Go around the group. What were their plans? Did they do them? How did their plans go? Remind everyone again about what layering information is.

Give them an outline of the night:
1. Hear back on how the plans went,
2. Delve deeper into why we always report back on plans, and
3. Discuss the Circle.

So here is our underlying premise: We want to find out how Jesus did things. Assume he is better at it than we are. Do what he did. It's that simple. So how did Jesus make disciples? Well, he developed this pattern for his disciples:

1. Get a group together (the call of the twelve).
2. Determine a language that supports what will be happening in the future. He introduces the concept of the Kingdom of God and keeps coming back to it over and over again and then gives specifics (Sermon on the Mount). Pretty much everything that Jesus teaches from that point on just goes back to those original principles.
3. Allow his disciples to watch and get in on the daily workings of his life and rhythms.
4. Send them out to do the same! (Read Luke 9:1–6).

17. Sample Huddle Outlines

5. They come back and talk about what happened. "Wow! This stuff actually works. We can do it too! But this one spirit we couldn't drive out? What about that?" Jesus tells them that this particular spirit can be cast out only with prayer and fasting. So they go back, report, share their experiences, get coaching and advice.

6. He sends them out again.

7. They come back and talk again.

8. (This pattern continues.)

Our Huddle will do the same thing. We will be spending many of our first Huddles doing what Jesus had his disciples do: learn a new language. (Use the learning Spanish and Barcelona example again.) We want to find out how Jesus did things. Assume he is better at it than we are. Do what he did.

The Circle

Review: Read Mark 1:14–15. So there is chronological time, but there's also another kind of time called _____? (*kairos*)

Explain:

- What is a *kairos* moment? (Have them answer.) God's future has burst forth into the present, and the invitation is to live in God's future more and more now.

- Tell a story: Francis Schaeffer and the two snowflakes at Le Brie:

    Schaeffer would take his disciples to the peaks of the

Alps and show them two rivers: the Rhone and the Rhine. To the left was the Rhine, the dirtiest river in the world, and to the right was the Rhone, the cleanest river that goes by beautiful French countryside and ends up in the balmy Mediterranean. As the snow fell on the ridgeline, he would say that each snowflake would end up in one of these two rivers. If it went left of the ridgeline, the Rhine. If it went right, the Rhone. A *kairos* is a lot like this: there is a razor's edge, a decision to engage with how God is breaking into our life or not to. Up until now, up until Mark 1, we could only go left. But now we can choose to go right. *Kairos* moments are like these snowflakes. There are many of them, and we choose what we do with them. Do we ignore them (and thus the snowflake going left) or do we engage with them to discover what God is trying to say (and thus the snowflake going right)? We choose every day.

Now we can choose what to do with these moments. You have the opportunity to live in and engage with an entirely different reality or shrug it off like you always have.

So if you want God's future, what do you have to do? Repent. Believe.

But these words come with some baggage, don't they? They almost sound ugly because of what they come with now. They don't even mean what they originally meant anymore.

Repent means *metanoia*: to change your mind, to

17. Sample Huddle Outlines

completely and fundamentally shift the way you think about something. This is an inner change that leads to an outward reality. Generally, we understand repentance as something we change or correct outside. But real repentance is a change in our inner being.

A good male example of this: Correcting looking at porn doesn't change the fact that you still objectify women and are constantly dominated by your darker desires. (Jesus with cleaning the inner cup rather than just the outside. Luke 11:37–44.) If you get the inside right, the outside will follow.

A good female example of this: We often assume losing weight, being trim, and looking as good as possible will make us feel better about ourselves and more valuable. While being healthy is important, being diet/weight obsessed doesn't deal with our core issue: We are insecure about who we are and care quite a lot about how people perceive us.

Believe means *pisteuo*: certainty, foundational, solid.

This is an active transformation. This is a certainty that has developed within ourselves so strongly that it produces an outer action. (Believe can be used interchangeably with faith.) When we say *believe*, we don't mean *hope*. Hope is about aspirations, but it isn't always grounded in certainty. Belief is a response to an inner change. Belief is always action-oriented. We set our alarm in the morning because we *believe/have faith* that the sun will rise and a new day will dawn. Belief/

faith is about certainty stemming from our inner core thoughts.

But look what we have done. We've reversed the two! We've said *repentance* is about changing your outer behavior and belief is something that is private, inward, something you believe, like some random facts in the sky.

But repentance and belief are connected. Jesus says to transform the inside and then the outside falls in line because we are now fundamentally different on the inside.

So to live in God's future, to step more fully into a *kairos* moment, we are asking God to fundamentally change the inside of us so that it produces an action. That's why these two questions are so central: What is God saying to me? (This will help change the inner parts of me.) And what am I going to do about it? (The inner change has to produce an action!)

Quickly review the Circle:

- Walk each person through the Circle with a personal *kairos*.
- Have all members fill out the pages in their *Huddle Guides* saying exactly what God is saying to them and exactly what they are going to do about it (the plan).

Closing prayer: Ephesians 3:14–21.

17. Sample Huddle Outlines

Example of Third Circle Huddle

Communicate to everyone ahead of time to have a positive *kairos* moment ready to share.

Pre-Huddle:
- Informal social time with food and drinks.

Give them an outline of the night:
1. Shape review,
2. Reflection on plans,
3. Closing thoughts.

Review Circle: Have people in the group draw and explain; do your best not to help.

Reflection time: How did your plans go in the past two weeks? (Each person shares; ask and prod as necessary.)

Pray: Psalm 139:23–24.

Explain: Everyone shares a positive *kairos* moment and you can walk through the Circle with them. Start with a *kairos* moment of your own and walk through the Circle with it.

Everyone shares. Use each positive moment as a time to affirm who they are in Christ. We are God's kids, he's our daddy, he wants to give us the very best kind of gifts (from James 1:17, "every good and perfect gift is from above" and from Matthew 7:7-12, "if you, who are sinful know how to give good gifts to your kids, how much more will your Father in heaven know how to give the very best gifts to his?" verse 11).

In the Circle, we are trying to answer two questions with these positive *kairos* moments: What is God affirming in you? What should you do about it to live more fully in this affirmation? (the plan).

Closing thoughts on imitation: Read 1 Corinthians 4:14–17 (from The Message version):

I'm not writing all this as a neighborhood scold just to make you feel rotten. I'm writing as a father to you, my children. I love you and want you to grow up well, not spoiled. There are a lot of people around who can't wait to tell you what you've done wrong, but there aren't many fathers willing to take the time and effort to help you grow up. It was as Jesus helped me proclaim God's Message to you that I became your father. I'm not, you know, asking you to do anything I'm not already doing myself. This is why I sent Timothy to you earlier. He is also my dear son, and true to the Master. He will refresh your memory on the instructions I regularly give all the churches on the way of Christ (MSG).

Look, you've had plenty of people slap you down, plenty of people tell you only when you are wrong. You need someone to invest everything they have into you. Discipleship happens only when someone says this: "Imitate my life."

This is what Paul says in another place: "Do exactly as I

17. Sample Huddle Outlines

do just as I imitate my behavior from Jesus."

So like Paul, we need someone to imitate, someone to see the life of Jesus in real flesh and blood. We don't need a perfect example; we need a living example. We struggle with this for two reasons:

1. Culture: Language is what creates culture. You can quickly build a culture of violence and creativity or a corporate culture if you have the language to build it (by language, we mean verbal and nonverbal). Sadly, most churches simply don't have a language (and thus a culture) to create an environment for discipleship. We don't know how to talk about it. That's what we are doing in these early Huddles: giving you an easily understood, transferable language that we can all understand. We are creating a culture where discipleship can happen.

2. Confidence: At some point, we have to deal with the fact that we are all mixed bags. Some things are worth copying, and some things aren't. We have to get to a point where we can disciple people; we have to believe our lives are worth copying. Would it be a good thing to copy my life? We have to confidently give ourselves as the living example of the thing we're speaking about.

I'm saying this to you for two reasons:

1. I picked you for a reason. You're in this Huddle for a reason. I need you to understand this clearly: I am committing to you that I will invest my life, as much of me as I can, into you. You guys are my

number one priority. Nothing in my ministry life is more important than you. And here is what I'm asking of you: Whatever parts of me that clearly resemble Jesus, I want you to imitate. Do as I do just as I'm imitating someone else's life, too.

2. Begin to wrap your mind around and orient yourself to the idea that at some point, you will be giving your life to someone to imitate. You will be the living example. That may not be next week, that may not be six months from now, but being a disciple means you are discipling others.

Closing prayer: Ephesians 3:14–21.

Example of the first Semi-Circle Huddle

Pre-Huddle: informal social time with food and drinks

Give them the outline for the night:
1. Review plans,
2. Learn the Semi-Circle, and
3. Reflections on the Semi-Circle.

Have all members talk about how their plans went and make sure they followed through thoroughly. Introduce this time by saying this:
1. I want you to give an account for the plan we came up with last time.
2. Give us an example of one place where you've failed/slipped in the past two weeks.

Pray: Psalm 139:23–24.

17. Sample Huddle Outlines

Explain: Tonight, I'm going to teach the Semi-Circle: This will be a big learning day. I know we've talked about support and challenge as well. I feel like I should be up front with you and say that the *kairos* you're going to be experiencing today is going to be one of challenge. This will probably squeeze you.
1. Read John 15:1–8.
2. Give the context of these verses:
    a. Every Hebrew has a vine.
    b. The vine grows for three years. They keep pruning so no fruit comes, and then cut the vine back to within a millimeter; the vine grows over the branch, creating a stump; then the branch spends three years being nourished and growing in strength (this is called the abiding time).
    c. As soon as fruit comes (and it is gigantic and can last on the vine for six months), it is pruned again.
    d. Vines develop this rhythm: Abide for a year, then comes a fruitful season; abide for a year, then comes a fruitful season...
3. And this is the fundamental rhythm that Jesus says his disciples are to have, because if we don't have an abiding time, we can't produce the fruit as we're called to do.
4. This is the argument Jesus makes to us:
    a. We are called to bear tons and tons of fruit.
    b. We can't bear fruit unless we spend time abiding (not bearing fruit).
    c. Therefore, in order to bear tons of fruit we must abide in the vine, being nourished and

strengthened.

5. Ordering of Creation from Genesis 1:
   a. God makes man and woman in his image.
   b. They get their marching orders: Work! Be productive!
   c. God rests on the seventh day.
   d. If man is made in God's image, who else would rest? Adam and Eve!
   e. So mankind's very first waking day after getting their marching orders is rest!

6. The fundamental revelation Jesus is bringing to John 15: We are created to work. *But we are designed to work from rest; not rest from work.*

7. Draw the Semi-Circle and talk about the seasons with the pendulum. What happens when we push the pendulum and keep it toward work? Eventually, we crash. We don't rest; we recover. We don't vacation; we recuperate. It isn't an accident that our best ideas always come on vacation! We finally have enough space for our mind to breathe new ideas.

8. And here's the thing; it is only in rest that we receive revelation—every child of God's birthright—the ability to hear God's voice, to be able to answer the question, "What is God saying to me?"

9. We want to develop these rest and work rhythms yearly, weekly and daily.

What is rest? We are asking the question, "What is it that recreates me? What gives me energy? What things reconnect me with myself, to God, to the people I love?" Rest is about learning to play! Rest allows us to see the gifts God has given us (the best gifts being our relationships) and then the ability to enjoy them. And we should note that rest will look different for everyone. We are all re-created in different ways.

From this nourishing energy our work can flow, rather than pushing and pushing and pushing. By operating from rest, we work from the Lord's energy and not our own.

We do know that God takes this pretty seriously. In the Ten Commandments, not taking a day off puts you in the same lots as adulterers, murderers, porn addicts, etc. Because not resting is a type of suicide, it's a stripping of humanity, and it's destroying the image we were made in.

Have a moment of silence for people to hone in on one point that struck them.

Have each person share the point that hit him or her the hardest. As the members share, help them develop a prayer they can pray over and over and over each day to bring them to a big *kairos* moment that you'll discuss during the next Huddle.

Explain that in the next Huddle, you will begin to help them construct a sustainable daily and weekly rhythm for each one.

Closing Prayer: Ephesians 3:14–21.

Example of the second Semi-Circle Huddle

Pre-Huddle: informal social time with food and drinks

Review the Semi-Circle

Talk about the fundamental need to develop a rhythm of life based on resting first. Share how your life has changed by making this rhythm the dominant reality of your life. Give some real details and a picture of the life you are now living by doing this. If we want to be disciples, this is a nonnegotiable; Jesus really makes that crystal clear. Now that doesn't mean we have to nail it and swallow the whole elephant at once, but we do need to start the journey.

Have each person share again what stuck out to them the week before and the prayer they were praying in the past two weeks. Listen to what surfaced. Walk through the Circle with them and land on a very solid plan on how to start living in this rhythm of life.

1. Daily rest means we need to at least spend some amount of time reading Scripture and in intentional prayer, gathering the energy and life of that abiding time in the Father as we get our "marching orders for the day," using his breath, not ours.

2. Weekly rest means we have a whole day where we do not do work (of any kind). That whole day is a day of play, a day to be enjoyed. Don't check your email. Turn off your cell phone. If you had to design a perfect day, what would it look like? Then make it happen each week. This is a day of play.

3. Yearly rest means scheduling vacation on our calendar before we schedule anything else. It means vacationing in a way that allows us to get off the workhorse and rest, relax, settle, reflect, wind down

17. Sample Huddle Outlines

and enjoy the people we love.

Talk about how you will be contacting them frequently (maybe even every day) to check in and give encouragement and accountability to follow through with this. Do not worry about the prayer "working" or even feeling rested right now. Let's start with the rhythm, and we'll tweak it once it's set.

Give a strong, encouraging word about how you believe in them and all of the life this is about to open for them.

Closing Prayer: Ephesians 3:14–21.

Example of another Semi-Circle Huddle

We'd use this after a few Huddles during which members are grappling with their new rhythms, once they begin to set in. More than likely, your members will be running into some brick walls with their rhythms, so don't overload them too much. Use this as they begin to make the turn into finding workable, sustainable rhythms. If your Huddle is doing well, you probably won't need a Huddle like this right now.

Pre-Huddle: informal social time with food and drinks.

Accountability: How have your daily and weekly rhythms been going?
(Everyone shares honestly.)

Explain: Tonight, I want to teach you an incredibly practical way to read Scripture. In fact, if I were to teach someone how to read Scripture that had never picked up the Bible, I'd really do two things: a) teach them about

Kingdom and Covenant and b) teach them the Circle. "Why don't we take a minute and think about a passage of Scripture that was a *kairos* moment for you."

- **Observe:** Of the Scripture you read this morning, which verse(s) stuck out? What grabbed you? What rose to the surface of your spirit? This is the *kairos* moment. Read your verse.

- **Reflect:** Why? Why this verse? Why does it speak to you more than the others? (Honesty is very important here.)

- **Discuss:** What does this verse say about my life? My relationship with God? With my husband or wife? The way I live? What truth is it speaking into my life? What should I start? What should I stop? What does God need to affirm about me? Is this verse speaking to Covenant? To Kingdom? How would a Father use this verse to speak to me? Specifically, what is God saying to me?

- **Plan:** Just today, not tomorrow or the day after that, just today, how should I live because God has spoken this to me? What's my plan for the day going to be in the next fifteen waking hours?

- **Account:** Well, this conversation is happening with two people: you and God. You are asking God (prayer!) to hold you accountable to follow through on your plan for the day. You are asking that when you start to step outside the plan, his Spirit would check your spirit.

- **Act:** Go into the day and do as you've told God you

17. Sample Huddle Outlines

would do.

Have one to two other people give you a Scripture and walk around the Circle with them.

"Because you have started to build some sustainable rhythms in your life, here is what I want you to do to enhance them:

The Plan: Every single day (including weekends), as you are doing your daily rhythms in the morning, reading Scripture and praying, I want you to write down the following things and bring them to our next Huddle:
  1. Write down the specific *kairos* verse(s) that stood out.
  2. Write down specifically what God is saying to you (in one succinct, short sentence).
  3. Write down your plan for the day."

Have everyone verbally agree. Give examples of what this has done for you (because you need to be doing this before you give it to anyone else).

Closing Prayer: Ephesians 3:14-21.

Example of a First Triangle Huddle

Pre-Huddle: informal talking with food and drinks

Review:
- Have someone fill in the Circle on a whiteboard with the help of the group, and then the Semi-Circle.
- Remind them that they will want to know this well enough that they can easily explain it to someone else

and walk them through it.
- Give each person thirty seconds to talk through how their plans went from the previous Huddle.

Teach the Triangle:
So if we are to become like Jesus, it's important to understand the intricacies of his life. And as we study and learn from him, we clearly see three dimensions emerge that his life revolved around. You could say that he had three great loves and he was constantly attending to these loves, allowing him unbelievably deep relationships:

1. UP (toward God, his Daddy, his Father)
2. IN (toward his disciples, the body, the church)
3. OUT (toward the world); we see Jesus' heart breaking in two places for the world: for people who didn't know God, who weren't in relationship with him, and for people who were experiencing injustice and being stripped of human dignity, stepping against systems of injustice.

Tent analogy: You need all three rods to have a tent stand up well as they pull against each other. Pull one rod out, and the tent starts to fall in; pull two out, and it collapses. We are called to have the same three great loves as Jesus. That means we have to attend to all three dimensions: UP/IN/OUT.

Churches reflect this as well. Most are good only at one, very few are good at two, and you almost never see a church good at all three. Why is this? It's pretty simple.

17. Sample Huddle Outlines

Churches clearly mirror their leaders. One leader put it this way: I won't elevate a leader until I'm ready to see ten more of them running around.

Maxim: We replicate who we are.

Churches, over time, resemble their leader, just as worship teams, over time, resemble the worship leader, just as small groups, over time, resemble their small group leader. We have to embrace this idea of the three great loves, the UP/IN/OUT, if we want the people we lead to be healthy, vibrant disciples, as well as ourselves! So let's move into a time of reflecting on this.

Pray Psalm 139:23-24.
Let's spend a few moments in silence. Why don't we each identify which of the three dimensions of UP/IN/OUT we feel we are strongest in and weakest in.
Have everyone share for each of these.
Bearing in mind your weakest, turn to your Huddle Guide. After the Triangle there is a list of questions for each dimension. Go to the Character Questions of the one you are weakest in (UP, IN or OUT) and take a few minutes to read through the questions. (These questions are also located in the Appendix of this book.)

Pray Psalm 139:23–24 again.
- What I want you to do is identify which question you'd least like to answer.
- Have each person share his or her question. Then, one by one, have everyone explain why he or she least wanted to answer that particular question

and then the *kairos* moment of this question. Walk through the Circle with them, producing a plan and answering the two fundamental questions.

Closing Prayer: Ephesians 3:14–21.

Examples of Future Triangle Huddles

- Have all members pick the dimension in their life in which they are strongest. Have everyone look at the Skills Questions (see page 247 in the Appendix for these questions) that people regularly go over for that specific dimension. Which question, if they were leading a group, would they feel most comfortable answering? Why? Mine out the *kairos*. Use this as an opportunity to start thinking and talking about the future. Create a plan where they use the *kairos* as a means to start dreaming what leadership for them could look like.
- Have all members bring a calendar of their next two weeks and look how they have scheduled their weeks. Do they show a balance of UP/IN/OUT? What do they need to subtract? What do they need to add? How could they continually keep their lives balanced this way?
- Have each person decide which dimension of UP/IN/OUT he or she is strongest in. Look at the Character Questions for that dimension and have each person find the question that gives him or her the most joy because he/she is doing it well. Have each person talk about that. Mine out a *kairos* moment from this and use it to affirm them and produce a plan that continues this affirmation.
- Spend some time before the Huddle praying and discerning one Character Question God wants you to bring to the

17. Sample Huddle Outlines

group to discuss (see Appendix 1). What does this say about the group? About the individuals? About what needs to be affirmed or challenged? Mine out a communal *kairos* moment, discern what God is saying to the group, and have a plan that everyone in the group is held accountable to.

Appendix

APPENDIX

Appendix 1.
Triangle Questions
for Up/In/Out

Discipleship is about becoming more like Jesus in every area of life. In *Building a Discipling Culture*, I have outlined a framework for growth through Up, In, and Out, each with two key dimensions: Character (who we are) and Skills (how we lead and disciple others).

These questions will help you assess both your inner transformation and your effectiveness in discipling others. Use them as a tool in huddles or for reflection and growth as you follow Jesus more fully.

Up Questions

Character Questions for UP:

- Do I make enough space for prayer?

- What situation or what person is weighing on my heart?

- Am I noticing God's strength and power more and more

in my life?

- Do I still feel pleasure?
- Am I living in a state of peace?
- Am I afraid or nervous?
- Am I obedient to God's prompting?

Skills Questions for UP:

- Do I sense peoples' lives in my group pointing more toward God?
- Do I find it easy to receive guidance for the next step in the life of my group?
- Do I find it easy to talk to a whole group in front of everyone?
- Can I teach effectively using God's word?
- Does my group share the vision God has given me?

In Questions

Character Questions for IN:

- Do I love the people in my community?
- Am I resting enough?
- How are my relationships with my friends?
- Am I experiencing intimacy in relationships?
- Do I keep my promises?

Appendix 1. Triangle Questions for Up/In/Out

- How easy is it for me to trust people?
- Am I discipling others?
- Is my family happy?
- Am I sleeping/eating well?
- Am I making myself vulnerable to others?

Skills Questions for IN:

- Do members of my group feel cared for?
- Am I effective at resolving conflict?
- Do I take on the discipline of confrontation?
- Is my group living as a community?
- Have I defined my own boundaries well?
- Am I flexible?
- How are my weaknesses as a leader compensated for by others?
- How do I cope with overly dependent people?
- How do I cope with controlling group members?
- Are there difficulties in my relationships with co-leaders / assistant leaders?

Out Questions

Character Questions for OUT:

- Do I have a heart for people not living in the

story of Jesus?

- How often do I share my faith?
- Do I leave time for relationships with non-Christians?
- Do I have a vision?
- Am I dying to success?
- Am I proud of the gospel or ashamed?
- Am I a servant?
- Do I intentionally spend time with the poor?
- Do I find it easy to recognize People of Peace?
- Can I take risks?
- Am I generous with my finances to those who don't have enough?

Skills Questions for OUT:

- Is my group growing?
- Am I too controlling as a leader?
- How welcoming is my group to new people?
- Can all group members identify at least one Person of Peace?
- Am I using leaders in my group effectively?
- Do I find it easy to multiply groups?
- Are those I am discipling turning into effective leaders?

Appendix 1. Triangle Questions for Up/In/Out

- Is my group effective in regularly doing OUT activities?
- Does my group have a specific "people group" in mind?

Appendix 2.
The Temptations of Jesus and the Enneagram

A few years ago Sally and I took a sabbatical together to reassess our journey with Jesus. Sally's area of reflection was the faithfulness of God— mine was the temptations of Jesus. Before leaving, some friends recommended I look into the Enneagram. I found Richard Rohr's materials particularly helpful. In one of his DVD series, he suggested that the Enneagram derived from the work of the Desert Fathers.

The Desert Fathers and Mothers left the cities and settlements of the Roman Empire and entered the Egyptian desert. Here they retreated from the world and engaged the devil on his own territory. The place of temptation and battle would become a place of victory. First Athanasius and then John Cassian brought the testimony of their remarkable lives and also their teaching to the world. Though I've not been able to confirm Richard Rohr's contention, it seems entirely plausible to me that people who gave themselves to the study of the vigil in the desert would come up with such a useful tool.

As a personality test, I find the Enneagram particularly helpful because it deals with our fundamental brokenness and thus does not seek to celebrate our strengths before addressing our weaknesses. Each of the nine personality types articulated in the Enneagram reflects something that was an original blessing in creation. Each personality type in some way looks back to the way in which we were first created and longs for how we will be in the new creation.

It's not possible for me to expound at length on the Enneagram here, but I encourage you to read further. Some great apps are available should you wish to explore more. But just to get us started, here's an introduction the nine personality types:

1. **The Reformer:** Very committed to truth, and often dutiful and practical in their application of it. They're always trying to be good.

2. **The Helper:** Always trying to find ways to serve others can become overwhelmed by this responsibility. They seek love by being loving.

3. **The Achiever**: Reaching the top is enormously important, but it's also important that getting there is done in such a way that others respect you for it. Seeking the attention of others is the Achilles' heel.

4. **The Individualist/Artist:** Seeing the world from a unique perspective is very important to this personality type. Creativity is greatly valued. They believe they are especially special.

5. **The Investigator/Scholar**: Expertise and careful analysis of information to arrive at illumination is

Appendix 2. The Temptations of Jesus and the Enneagram

tremendously important. Pressing through theory to arrive at reality is highly valued. Withdrawal from social engagement and personal interaction is a common trait.

6. The Loyalist: Deeply committed to long-term relationships. As people they are dutiful committed and loyal, but they have a tendency to fear.

7. The Enthusiast: Usually delight in life believing that more is better. They have deep commitment, joy, freedom, spontaneous, and positive lifestyles. The desire to escape difficult situations means that some things are left unfinished.

8. The Challenger/Leader: Often larger than life characters. Earthy, strong, and immediate in this style, these leaders often rely on instinct to guide them. Can be very confrontational.

9. The Peacemaker: Committed to wholeness, unity and peace. They promote acceptance and harmony and often offer great diplomatic skills. They tend to retreat into their own shell under stress.

I'm sure to Enneagram experts, these are woefully inadequate introductions to the nine personality types but they just intended to be a start.

Now, let's place these nine personality types on a triangle marked by the three A's —approval, ambition, and appetite. They look like this:

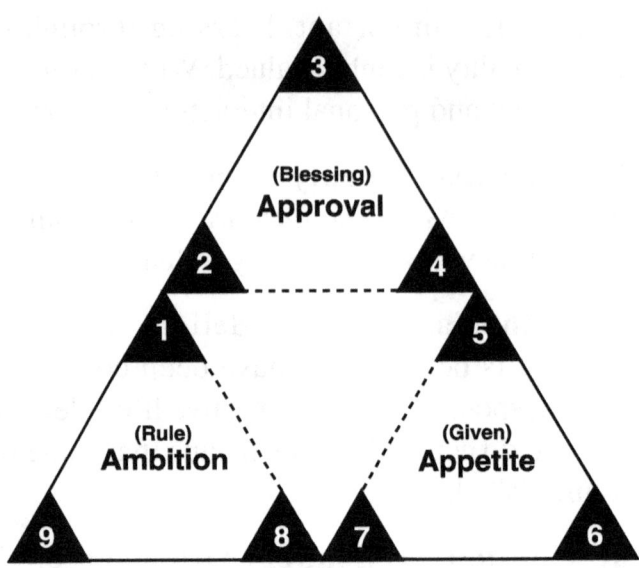

Those in the Approval triangle (types 2, 3, and 4) have an echo of God's first blessing in their hearts—"God blessed them" (Genesis 1:28)—and are defined by the longing for God's fathering presence.

Those in the Appetite triangle (types 5, 6, and 7) recognize the loss of Eden's abundance—"I give you every seed bearing plant on the face of the whole earth" (Genesis 1:29)—and are defined by a longing for its return.

Those in the Ambition triangle (types 1, 8, and 9) feel the loss of God's first commission—"rule over... every living creature" (Genesis 1:28)—and long for God's justice authority and power to be revealed.

Appendix 2. The Temptations of Jesus and the Enneagram

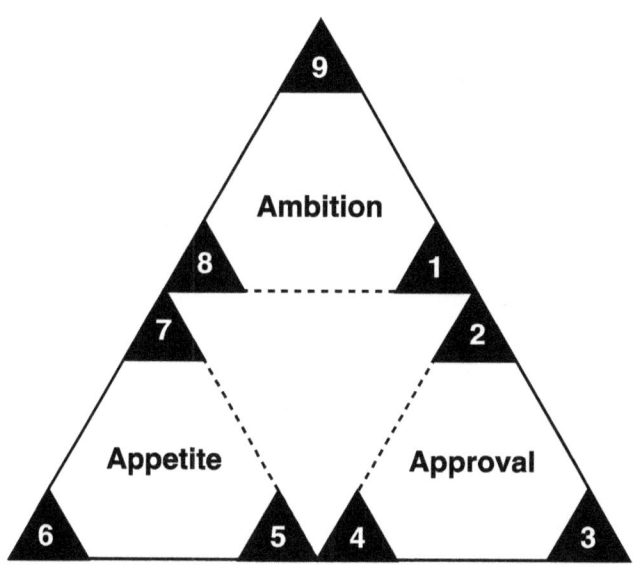

I hope you find this to be a useful tool to help you reflect on how you might engage and embrace the temptations of Jesus, which are the temptations of us all.

However you choose to reflect on these things, my prayer is that they will help you recognize your fundamental strengths and weaknesses to more fully surrender into God's loving hands. I'm sure that by doing so and through the counsel and encouragement of the Holy Spirit working through others, you will be able to grow in your walk with Jesus.

Appendix 3.
Spiritual Health: The Heptagon

As you come to him, the living Stone—rejected by men but chosen by God and precious to him—you also, like living stones, are being built into a spiritual house to be a holy priesthood, offering spiritual sacrifices acceptable to God through Jesus Christ.

1 Peter 2:4-5

Church health and growth is all about life—the body of Christ being an organism rather than an organization. And life gets messy sometimes, doesn't it? So it's easier for us to deal with organizations because we can control organizations. Think of it this way: organisms are to organizations what the horse is to the cart. Many churches put the cart before the horse, building facilities and programs before they have adequately taken care of the needs of the people. It's not the cart that will get things moving—it's the horse that provides the power to move the cart. We need to feed and care for the horse, but instead our energy goes into the cart, so the horse ends up too weak to pull the cart. There are other analogies that can be drawn from this metaphor. Like organizations, carts have interchangeable parts—if a wheel breaks, you can replace it. The parts of an organism are inextricably interdependent.

We are told in Scripture that we have life in the Spirit, but what does that really mean? Jesus gives us pictures of this life through many of his stories and teachings that deal with biological life. Life in the Spirit resembles organic life, just on a different plane.

Jesus started off his ministry by clearly declaring what he came to do. He was here to help us understand our covenant identity as sons and to plant the Kingdom of God into our hearts, literally to inaugurate the rule of God in our lives. To show us what the Kingdom life looks like, Jesus used stories involving snapshots from ordinary life: agriculture, parents and children, the relationship between friends, money matters, coins that are lost, sheep that are found.

When you track these stories through Scripture you find that Jesus often relies on the subject of biological life. The Kingdom of God is a seed, it is the sowing of seeds on various soils, and it is a vineyard. Take this beyond the Gospels to the rest of the New Testament. What is the community of believers called? The body of Christ. God often uses biological life as a metaphor for what he wants our lives, and the lives of those we lead to look like.

The Seven Signs of Life

Biology—the study of life and all living organisms. In school you probably learned about the seven processes of life that identify all living organisms. These seven signposts

Appendix 3. Spiritual Health: The Heptagon

of life are:

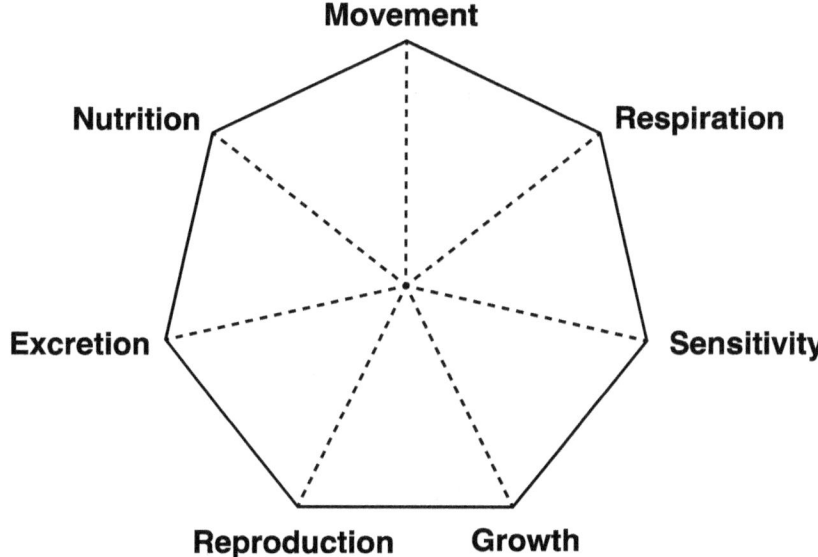

These make up our seven-sided shape, the Heptagon—seven signs of life in the kingdom of God. These seven processes can be a useful diagnostic tool for assessing the spiritual health of those you disciple and the ministries they lead.

Movement: Show Your Not Dead

Movement is an indication of life and usually occurs in response to stimuli. Consider animals in the wild. They prefer to lie in the cool shade of a tree or in a den dug into the ground. But when threatened by a predator, they move—quickly. And when they are hungry or thirsty, they must move to hunt or they will die.

Animals move when stimulated by an outer (danger) or inner (hunger) force. Plants exhibit movement through growth, so the effect is sometimes so slow it is hard to detect.

The Old Testament is a series of stories about patriarchs, prophets, and people on the move. We see this principle at work in Exodus 14: the children of Israel have left Egypt, but hesitate at the crossing of the Red Sea. Behind them lies a life of slavery to Pharaoh, but before them they see only a very, scary unknown. They stop moving. How much easier it seems to stand still in what we know, regardless of how unfulfilling, than to move into the unknown!

You would think that seeing Pharaoh's army rushing after them would be sufficient stimuli to get them moving again, but they allow fear to paralyze them. Their leader tells them to stand firm, but God says, "Move on!" It is not until they get moving again that they see the miraculous power of God in their midst.

The alive disciple is a disciple on the move. God uses many different methods to stimulate movement—his Word, his Spirit, and sometimes persecution—because his desire is to see his followers reaching out to our dying world. What about you? Are you moving? Don't be afraid to move on, even if you don't know yet where you will end up.

Respiration: Breathing God's Breath

Respiration is not synonymous with breathing. Every cell in your body has a powerhouse called the mitochondrion that releases energy. This is respiration. The powerhouse is dependent on oxygen that is brought into the body through breathing. So breathing is absolutely necessary for respiration, and the respiration process is essential for energy to be released for the body to function. A living organism cannot "make" energy, it can only release it.

Appendix 3. Spiritual Health: The Heptagon

Breathing may be natural for most living organisms, but for many humans in the Western world, breathing correctly is a dying art (no pun intended). Several studies indicate that our ability to breathe effectively has significantly diminished over the last few decades, resulting in loss of vitality and quality of life. In general, we are bad breathers and it's killing us.[96]

Bad breathing can be the result of many factors: illness, lack of exercise, fear, pollution. Sometimes it's just us holding our breath—like a child throwing a temper tantrum—in a vain attempt to exert control. In the same way, many of us are bad spiritual breathers. Just as our breathing oxygen releases energy in our bodies, God's breathing into us releases the energy of his Spirit in our lives. When we breathe deeply of the breath of God, we discover that the energy of God to complete the task at hand is released within us.

As Christian leaders we need to encourage our people to breathe deeply again. Ole Hallesby says that prayer is to the soul what breathing is to the body. Prayer is the breath of God filling us up again. What might be making your disciples breathless, robbing them of vitality? How can you encourage them to practice a life of prayer—inhaling God's Spirit and exhaling his will? God wants the very power of heaven to be loosed in our lives, and it comes by spiritual respiration.

Sensitivity: The Pentagon At Work

Your body is not a bunch of independent parts randomly stuck together. It all works as one unit. The first function we looked at was movement. We said that living organisms move

---

[96] Mike White, "Clinical Studies about the Importance of Optimal Breathing," *Optimal Breathing*, breathing.com, 19 November 2004.

according to stimuli. Sensitivity is what enables the body to sense the stimulation and know that it must move. Thus, sensitivity plays a vital role in life.

Sensitivity is vitally important to the life of any Christian community. There is sensitivity to sight, hearing, touch, smell, and taste and these are reflected through the fivefold gifts Paul mentions in Ephesians 4—what we refer to as the Pentagon.

A healthy, living community needs disciples who are sensitive to the needs and pains of others, believers who can laugh with those who laugh and cry with those who cry. This is the sensitivity of touch and is found in believers whose base ministry is pastor. We also need those who are sensitive to sight, in this case foresight given by God. These are the prophets.

We need people who will be sensitive to hearing others, listening actively, and then instructing them on how to proceed. These are our teachers. Those sensitive in speech, being gifted to share the Good News on any occasion, are the evangelists. And those who can sniff out staleness and know it is time to move forward are the apostles, sensitive to the move of God to explore new territory for the kingdom. God wants us all to be sensitive to his stimuli so that we will move and act as he directs.

Growth: The Inevitable Result Of A Healthy Life

Growth is a natural process of living things. It is an expression of life. Are you growing? Sometimes it is hard to tell. We don't see growth every day. It comes through the natural rhythms of life. But growth must always be occurring in a living being. When you stop growing, you die. It's that simple.

Appendix 3. Spiritual Health: The Heptagon

What about you and the leaders in your Huddle? Are you still growing? It's a good question to ask because anything that stops growing will eventually die. As a Christian leader, you must constantly be aware of who or what is showing signs of no growth and thus decay and death. As we see in the Semi-Circle, growth takes place as we swing in the rhythm between abiding and fruitfulness.

We are not told to work for our growth. God is the one who causes us to grow. (Look at 1 Corinthians 3:6–9 and Colossians 2:19.) But there are things we can do to create a growing environment, both individually and corporately. As a matter of fact, if the other six aspects of the Heptagon are operating properly, growth will occur spontaneously. So let us move on to reproduction.

Reproduction: Creating The Future

Reproduction is different from growth in that it is a multiplication of a life. All living things reproduce by bringing together two disparate elements and then fusing them together into a new element. A sperm and an egg, living cells unto themselves, come together to form a new life, in appearance like that of the "donors" of the sperm and egg. Reproduction has taken place.

In our role as leaders, God takes the raw materials of our lives and fuses them with the heart of a disciple who is open to receive the investment we are making. By his grace we are able to multiply our lives into others. As we multiply our lives into those imitating us and encourage them to repeat the investment process with their own Huddles, something wonderful begins to happen.

Reproduction is a sign of life. There seems to be a mechanism within the created order that prevents unhealthy specimens from being multiplied. The unhealthy ones generally don't multiply; it is the healthy that carry on the species. It is the goal of a species to create a healthy next generation, the most important target of their lives. For leaders, creating a healthy next generation is the most important challenge we have.

If we look at Europe, children, teenagers, and young adults don't attend church any longer. Why is that? It is because Christians in Europe have forsaken the reproduction of themselves into a new generation. There really is not a "next generation" of Christians in Europe. Perhaps it is because the older generations of Christians were not healthy. God is doing new things—sparking new growth and raising up new leaders committed to costly discipleship. Our primary cry must be for the leaders to come. We must say with the psalmist, "Don't let me die, Lord, until I speak of your power to the next generation."[97] It is possible! A growing number of leaders around the world are rediscovering the joy of ministry as they disciple others using LifeShapes and variations on the 8:6:4 Huddle principle. Reproduction is the definitive signal that you are alive!

Excretion: A Cleansed Life

"OK," you say, "I can see how the other six biological processes can be applied to the discipleship process, but not excretion. That's just gross!" Well, you would be wrong. We see this natural part of life in the proclamation Jesus made at the beginning of his ministry: "Repent and believe the

---

97 Paraphrase of Psalm 71

Appendix 3. Spiritual Health: The Heptagon

Good News."

Every heart builds up a collection of junk throughout the day that needs to be emptied through the process of repentance. If we do not get rid of these sins, they will act just like a toxin does in the human body, causing illness and, eventually, death. Jesus made it clear: Forgive others so God can forgive you. Research is now showing that unforgiveness causes increased blood pressure, hormonal changes, cardiovascular disease, and impaired brain functions, including memory loss. Not excreting what others have done to us is just as unhealthy as not getting rid of our own sins. If you don't excrete in your natural life, aside from looking really nasty and feeling very uncomfortable, you will die. That's just a medical fact. Toxins build up within you and cause vital organs to stop working. Eventually your entire body shuts down—permanently. The writer of Hebrews calls these toxins building up within us "the root of bitterness." We are told to remove it—rip it out.

For Christians, excretion comes in the form of repentance and discipline. Oswald Chambers says that "The entrance into the Kingdom is through the panging pains of repentance crashing into a man's respectable goodness," and that it is the Holy Spirit "who produces these agonies."[98]

In some cases, church discipline requires that an unrepentant brother be expelled, as Paul instructs the Church at Corinth, in order to give him the opportunity to come back to the life of faith. Whether in our individual lives or in the lives of our churches, we must not embrace wickedness, and we cannot accommodate sin in any form. It must be excreted for us to

---

[98] Oswald Chambers, *My Utmost for His Highest* (Uhrichsville, OH: Barbour and Company, Inc., 1935) 342.

remain healthy.

Nutrition: The Obedience Diet

Finally, we have nutrition. All living things must take in nutrients or they will die. In this era of carb-free this and fat-free that, we have an even greater awareness of what proper nutrition is. For the spiritual diet, there is but one main course.

"I am the bread of life," declares Jesus. To live, we must dine on his words, his actions, his commands. We can break this down even further. When Jesus met with the woman at the well in John 4, his disciples had gone off to a nearby village to buy food. When they came back, they offered some to Jesus.

"I have food to eat that you don't know about," he said. The disciples wondered just where he got this food and what it was. Perhaps they were jealous, thinking it was probably better than what they had to eat. Then Jesus spelled it out clearly for them. "My food is doing the will of my father," he told them. Obeying God is our nutrition. When we obey the commands of Jesus, our souls are fed. We feel full and fulfilled.

Without nutrition, you will die. There is no way around that. Without the right kind of nutrition, you will die slowly. In the same way, leaders die if there is not a regular feeding on Jesus, the very Word of God. We must clearly and consistently proclaim his teachings. But we can't stop there. We must obey his commands to get our fill of nutrition vital for our growth.

A Healthy Self-Examination

So now the question is, what do we do with the Heptagon?

Appendix 3. Spiritual Health: The Heptagon

Knowing that Jesus often used biological illustrations in his storytelling does not mean we will automatically apply the teachings to our lives and the lives of those we lead. We must make a conscious effort to compare our lives with the healthy life described by Jesus. Today's leaders are giving birth to the leaders of tomorrow. Many leaders are in the transitional phase of birthing a discipling culture, often the most painful and discouraging phase. It is important during this time of transition to closely monitor the vital signs of those you are discipling. The seven signs of life represented by the Heptagon can help you do just that.

Doctors say that most cancers can be completely cured if they are found in time. Thus, we are taught how to check our bodies for potential signs of cancer or other disease so we can catch it, cure it, and continue living. Just as we conduct self-examinations on our physical bodies, we need to perform self-exams spiritually. The seven processes of the Heptagon make a thorough exam possible. Go through each of the seven processes of life in this way, "checking your own pulse." When you find an area you have been neglecting, give it more attention. Don't wait until disease sets in and you need emergency-room care. Teach these principles for a vital life to those you disciple. If every follower of Jesus were to maintain all seven functions of life in their spiritual life, there would be no need for pastors to be counselors. Imagine that!

Growth Cycle of Church Groups

God has designed us to live as social creatures, so it would be difficult for us to be living beings in any genuine sense without authentic community. It would appear from a study of the Scriptures that we can draw certain conclusions about groups, their sizes and functions, and how we as leaders should build community. Scripture is also instructive on how the proper use of groups can alleviate the overwhelming burden of ministry so many pastors are experiencing.

> *Moses' father-in-law replied, "What you are doing is not good. You and these people who come to you will only wear yourselves out. The work is too heavy for you; you cannot handle it alone."*
>
> *Exodus 18:17-18*

Ever feel like Moses in this passage? Trying to lead a consumer-driven, staff-driven, program-driven church organization is a sure prescription for burnout. Like all good father figures, Jethro tells his son-in-law Moses, "Hey, man! You can't do it all and you can't do it alone. For your sake and the sake of your people, you need to try something different. God has a better plan." Yes, God has a plan for the healthy distribution of leadership among groups and it looks something like this:

- Nation
- Tribe
- Thousands
- Hundreds
- Fifties
- Tens

Appendix 3. Spiritual Health: The Heptagon

- Twos and threes

Jethro advised Moses to establish leaders of thousands, hundreds, fifties, and tens along with the leaders of the twelve tribes. Above the twelve tribes was the nation of Israel itself led by Moses under God's authority. Following Jethro's advice, Moses identified qualified and equipped men[99] over these various size groups. The tens may have represented the average expected size of the nuclear family at that time and for that culture, but in today's society the smallest group would be a couple formed by marriage.

From any reading of the books of Moses, we can see that the national and tribal leaders of Israel were already in place, and marriages were happening all the time. What Moses had failed to recognize was that there was a need for a more complete infrastructure of leaders and groups in order for the people of God to be in effective relationship with God himself, with each other, and with the world at large.

Interestingly, Jesus seemed to follow a similar pattern: he sent out disciples in pairs (obviously not married pairs). He called together a team of twelve out of a team of seventy-two. Then on the day of Pentecost, there were about 120 waiting as Jesus had instructed for the promised Holy Spirit, after which the Church had thousands in its community. These may have been organized naturally along ethnic lines. This would provide one explanation for why the apostles had to intervene to make sure that the least prominent group within the Church had a fair share of the church's resources.[100]

It is not our intention to argue for an overly tight application

---

99 See verse 21
100 See Acts 6

of these insights into the development of Christian community, but to offer a reflective tool as we seek to develop living communities within our shifting western culture. One of the Kingdom tasks assigned to God's people is to rebuild human community wherever we can. Again, our experience leads us to conclude that this will involve the emergence of a spectrum of groups in different shapes and sizes. If we are to be strategic as leaders, we need to know where to begin. Many sociologists and anthropologists think that the most important component of human society is the extended family.

Our experience confirms that churches should focus on the development of clusters, or mid-sized Missional Communities, the extended family-size group between twenty and seventy. To do this we will need to disciple leaders who carry this vision and are capable of overseeing these groups and the long-range task of rebuilding our communities and culture. A discipling culture is one typified by low control and high accountability. Huddle provides the perfect context for high accountability; your leaders will feel empowered to push out kingdom boundaries if they know they have a safe place to return to on a regular basis. Life in community is what the Church is all about. Looking at your ministry in the light of the Heptagon helps identify trouble spots before they become full-fledged illness and incurable disease. As we maintain openness to the Holy Spirit, the bringer of life, we will exhibit more of the life that he brings.

Appendix 4.
Relational Mission:
The Octagon

In chapter 11, we spelled out the Person of Peace strategy that Jesus taught his disciples as a means of reaching out. Now, using the Person of Peace as the first point, let's go around the Octagon to provide more depth to this strategy. Remember: The Person of Peace is key. Now, let's look at the other seven principles in the Octagon, aiming to build and equip our people for this mission.

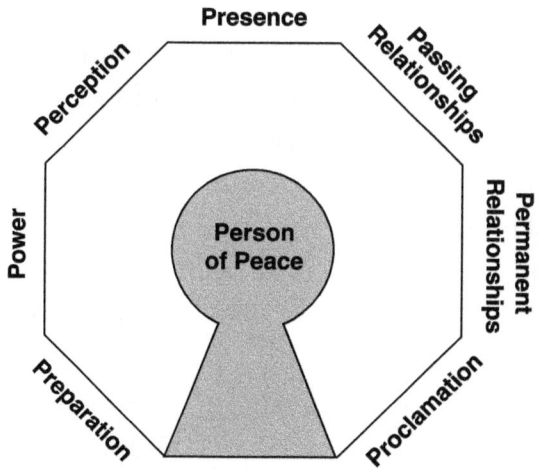

Presence: Jesus Is Where You Are

Presence evangelism occurs when you are present in a situation or with an individual or group. Where you are is always an opportunity to model Jesus, acting as he would act, speaking as he would speak. As you show kindness and speak encouragement, a Person of Peace may become evident to you. Perhaps you are in a committee meeting and you speak in a positive way where others are complaining. After the meeting another committee member comes up to you and thanks you for remaining positive. This could be a Person of Peace making himself known. An opportunity to share why you are upbeat is open to you because you are present. As the wise man said, "Wherever you go, there you are." And wherever you are may be an opportunity to meet with a Person of Peace.

Passing Relationships: The Sprint

People we meet only once or twice are what we would call passing relationships. The clerk at the gas station. A stranger standing in line at the bank. The person we happen to sit next to on a plane. Most likely, even if they show themselves to be a Person of Peace at that moment, we are not going to lead them into a personal relationship with Christ in our brief encounter. But we may be used to take them closer to that point. Paul said that some plant, some water, and God gives the harvest.[101] In a passing relationship, you may be called on to plant a seed or to water what has already been planted. Just because you do not see the end result does not mean you are not a vital part of the process.

---

101 See 1 Corinthians 3:6

Appendix 4. Relational Mission: The Octagon

Permanent Relationships: The Marathon

Permanent relationships are those in your family and with close friends. If a passing relationship is like a sprint, permanent relationships are a marathon. You are with these people often and for extended periods of time. It is important that you do not force the Gospel message when this person is not ready. You may have to wait for a long time before he or she is a Person of Peace for you, but until that time their heart is not ready to hear you. It seems we have the hardest time sharing our faith with those closest to us. Perhaps this is in part due to our impatience. We want so much for them to live in the incredible kingdom life we are experiencing that we rush them before God has prepared them to hear us. Pray, wait, and watch. God is never in a hurry, and he is never late.

Proclamation As Identification

Most pastors love opportunities to proclaim the Gospel to those who are not believers. Weddings and funerals are two gatherings of nonbelievers with whom we can share a salvation message. This is fine, as long as we understand we are not going to convince those who are not ready to receive. That is not how it works. Our proclamation should be used to identify those who are Persons of Peace, then enter into relationships with them, or connect them with others who can walk with them in the initial stages of discipleship. This is what evangelism really is: inviting a person to walk the walk of faith, not just pray a prayer.

Preparation: Moving People Along The Scale

Preparation is similar to cultivating soil and planting seed in advance of the harvest. Often our words will be one turn of a person's soil. Another comes along and, sensing an opportunity with a Person of Peace, turns the soil once again. The next week, the soil gets turned over one more time. Then yet another comes and plants seed. A few more come and water the seed. None of these individual workers sees what the others have done, and perhaps none will be there for the harvest. But all have had a hand in making a disciple.

Dr. James F. Engel at Wheaton Graduate School developed a model that is helpful for those engaged in the communication of the Gospel. Known as the Engel Scale, this model gives insight into the decision-making process of the unbeliever. On this scale, a person who asks forgiveness of sin and is born again spiritually would be at the "zero" point of the scale. To the right of this point are positive numbers— +1, +3, +5, etc. As the disciple grows and matures in his walk, he progresses to the right of the scale.24

To the left of zero are corresponding negative numbers. A person who is open to listening to your experiences with God and is asking questions about the Kingdom could be said to be a -1. This is a Person of Peace. Someone who is not interested at this time in spiritual matters could be a -5. And the one who would rather knock your teeth down your throat than hear about Christ is a -10. If, in the preparation phase of the Octagon, you move a person from -5 to -3, is this not evangelism? We may not be there for the zero hour, but we will have been used by God in the process.

Power: Awe As Evangelism

Jesus often used demonstrations of the power of God to

identify the Person of Peace. Praying for the sick and seeing a miraculous healing will often reveal a Person of Peace, whether the one prayed for or simply one watching. Our God is, truly, an awesome God. He will do things to create awe in those who have yet to commit their hearts to him. We do not create these miracles, nor can we box God up and manipulate when and where miracles will occur. All we can do is be ready when they do happen. The Person of Peace for our life may be revealed at that moment, and we should be ready for this time.

Perception: Feeling The Temperature

Perception is what Peter Wagner called "testing the soil." We need to be spiritually perceptive to situations and circumstances, as well as to individuals, in order to identify the Person of Peace. For instance, in a presence evangelism setting, you are golfing with three other men you just met on the first tee. As you complete your round and are shaking hands after the eighteenth hole, ask yourself, "What was the temperature of the soil? Was it hot, warm, or cold?" If the temperature was cold—none of the men exhibited any signs of being open to you sharing the Good News with them—move on. Shake the dust from your cleats, as it were, and wish them well. But if you sense any warmth in the soil, pursue a further relationship with that person. He is a Person of Peace for you. The eight principles of the Octagon provide a comprehensive but not exhaustive approach to evangelism that, along with the other LifeShapes, have proven to be incredibly effective teaching tools.

Appendix 5.
Fivefold Ministries Questionnaire

Read through the statements and decide as honestly as you can whether they apply to you often, sometimes, or rarely, and check the appropriate box. Do not linger on each item, as your first thought is likely to represent the most accurate response.

1. I am good at listening and taking in what people say.

   ☐ A. Often   ☐ B. Sometimes   ☐ C. Rarely

2. People say I am good at presenting information and ideas.

   ☐ A. Often   ☐ B. Sometimes   ☐ C. Rarely

3. When I'm excited about something, I get others interested in it too.

   ☐ A. Often   ☐ B. Sometimes   ☐ C. Rarely

4. I can accurately assess a person based on first impressions and know instinctively if they are being real with me.

   ☐ A. Often   ☐ B. Sometimes   ☐ C. Rarely

5. I can be counted on to contribute original ideas.

   ☐ A. Often   ☐ B. Sometimes   ☐ C. Rarely

6. I see more value in building up something meaningful and useful than always striking out into new territory.

   ☐ A. Often   ☐ B. Sometimes   ☐ C. Rarely

7. I try explaining things in different ways if people are finding a concept difficult to grasp or understand.

   ☐ A. Often   ☐ B. Sometimes   ☐ C. Rarely

8. People with different value systems have said that they feel comfortable when they are around me and that I have a positive effect on them being open to new ideas.

   ☐ A. Often   ☐ B. Sometimes   ☐ C. Rarely

Appendix 5. Fivefold Ministries Questionnaire

9. People comment that I am unusually creative.

   ☐ A. Often ☐ B. Sometimes ☐ C. Rarely

10. People describe me as entrepreneurial.

    ☐ A. Often ☐ B. Sometimes ☐ C. Rarely

11. When I communicate truth (even hard truth) to others I see resulting changes in their knowledge, attitudes, values or conduct.

    ☐ A. Often ☐ B. Sometimes ☐ C. Rarely

12. I love to share information with others.

    ☐ A. Often ☐ B. Sometimes ☐ C. Rarely

13. I like to tell stories, especially my own.

    ☐ A. Often ☐ B. Sometimes ☐ C. Rarely

14. I have just suddenly known something about someone.

    ☐ A. Often ☐ B. Sometimes ☐ C. Rarely

15. I'll be the first to try new things out if it will encourage others to do the same.

    ☐ A. Often ☐ B. Sometimes ☐ C. Rarely

16. I like to create safe places for people to flourish and grow.

   ☐ A. Often ☐ B. Sometimes ☐ C. Rarely

17. People have told me that I have helped them learn important truth in a meaningful way.

   ☐ A. Often ☐ B. Sometimes ☐ C. Rarely

18. I like to share what I believe.

   ☐ A. Often ☐ B. Sometimes ☐ C. Rarely

19. Sometimes I just intuitively know things that others seem to miss.

   ☐ A. Often ☐ B. Sometimes ☐ C. Rarely

20. I can clarify goals, develop strategies, and cast a vision to accomplish tasks.

   ☐ A. Often ☐ B. Sometimes ☐ C. Rarely

21. I remember names or at least where I first met someone.

   ☐ A. Often ☐ B. Sometimes ☐ C. Rarely

22. I generally appreciate hard facts more than theories.

   ☐ A. Often ☐ B. Sometimes ☐ C. Rarely

Appendix 5. Fivefold Ministries Questionnaire

23. I have enjoyed relating to a certain group of people over a period of time, sharing personally in their successes and their failures.
    ☐ A. Often ☐ B. Sometimes ☐ C. Rarely

24. I sometimes get frustrated and even depressed at the lack of faith or understanding of others around me.
    ☐ A. Often ☐ B. Sometimes ☐ C. Rarely

25. I like change even when it makes others uncomfortable.
    ☐ A. Often ☐ B. Sometimes ☐ C. Rarely

26. I get concerned, and maybe even upset, at other people's difficulties and problems even if I haven't experienced them myself.
    ☐ A. Often ☐ B. Sometimes ☐ C. Rarely

27. I share what knowledge I have with others.
    ☐ A. Often ☐ B. Sometimes ☐ C. Rarely

28. I think I would do well selling a product I really believed in.
    ☐ A. Often ☐ B. Sometimes ☐ C. Rarely

Building a Discipling Culture

29. I am sensitively able to discern the real meaning behind things.

☐ A. Often   ☐ B. Sometimes   ☐ C. Rarely

30. I love new challenges that require me to stretch and change.

☐ A. Often   ☐ B. Sometimes   ☐ C. Rarely

31. I am quick to help when help is needed and often do things which I see need to be done without even being asked.

☐ A. Often   ☐ B. Sometimes   ☐ C. Rarely

32. I love to show people how to do things that I do well.

☐ A. Often   ☐ B. Sometimes   ☐ C. Rarely

33. I mix easily with a wide variety of people without having to try to be one of them.

☐ A. Often   ☐ B. Sometimes   ☐ C. Rarely

34. I sometimes feel compelled to speak the truth even if it makes others feel uncomfortable.

☐ A. Often   ☐ B. Sometimes   ☐ C. Rarely

Appendix 5. Fivefold Ministries Questionnaire

35. I enjoy coming up with new and original ideas, dreaming big and thinking about visions for the future.

    ☐ A. Often   ☐ B. Sometimes   ☐ C. Rarely

36. I like to provide a safe and comfortable environment where people feel they are welcome, that they belong, are listened to and cared for.

    ☐ A. Often   ☐ B. Sometimes   ☐ C. Rarely

37. I enjoy relating stories and sharing my experiences.

    ☐ A. Often   ☐ B. Sometimes   ☐ C. Rarely

38. People say I get passionate about the things I believe in and it shows.

    ☐ A. Often   ☐ B. Sometimes   ☐ C. Rarely

39. I enjoy meditation and thinking deeply about spiritual things.

    ☐ A. Often   ☐ B. Sometimes   ☐ C. Rarely

40. I've always wanted to build a business/organization from the ground up so I can give my specific vision to it.

    ☐ A. Often   ☐ B. Sometimes   ☐ C. Rarely

41. I am faithful in providing support, care and nurture for others over long periods of time, even when others have stopped.

☐ A. Often ☐ B. Sometimes ☐ C. Rarely

42. I get great satisfaction in accomplishing the details of a task.

☐ A. Often ☐ B. Sometimes ☐ C. Rarely

43. I look for opportunities to socialize and build relationships with people that are different from me.

☐ A. Often ☐ B. Sometimes ☐ C. Rarely

44. I have expressed my spiritual feelings as pictures or analogies.

☐ A. Often ☐ B. Sometimes ☐ C. Rarely

45. Others have suggested that I am a person of unusual vision.

☐ A. Often ☐ B. Sometimes ☐ C. Rarely

46. I find that people trust me and come to me regularly, wanting to chat, and looking for my advice and help.

☐ A. Often ☐ B. Sometimes ☐ C. Rarely

Appendix 5. Fivefold Ministries Questionnaire

47. I enjoy taking notes when someone is speaking and pay close attention to the details of what they are saying.

    ☐ A. Often   ☐ B. Sometimes   ☐ C. Rarely

48. I don't mind getting on a soapbox for things that are important to me.

    ☐ A. Often   ☐ B. Sometimes   ☐ C. Rarely

49. I have had dreams that I know were more significant than regular dreams.

    ☐ A. Often   ☐ B. Sometimes   ☐ C. Rarely

50. I like to help organizations, groups and leaders become more efficient and often find myself thinking about how things function.

    ☐ A. Often   ☐ B. Sometimes   ☐ C. Rarely

51. I have a real aversion to gossip and often stop it when I hear it.

    ☐ A. Often   ☐ B. Sometimes   ☐ C. Rarely

52. Friends often ask me to help clarify a situation or issue.

    ☐ A. Often   ☐ B. Sometimes   ☐ C. Rarely

53. When I like a movie or a restaurant, everyone will hear about it.

☐ A. Often ☐ B. Sometimes ☐ C. Rarely

54. I sometimes have an urge to share my thoughts with people, and I have been told they meant something or were relevant to the person's current situation.

☐ A. Often ☐ B. Sometimes ☐ C. Rarely

55. People tell me that the things I say often help them to try new things.

☐ A. Often ☐ B. Sometimes ☐ C. Rarely

56. People sometimes tell me that I care too much for others.

☐ A. Often ☐ B. Sometimes ☐ C. Rarely

57. I enjoy coming up with the best, most efficient way to do a task right.

☐ A. Often ☐ B. Sometimes ☐ C. Rarely

58. I find myself talking about things I'm passionate about to the people I meet.

☐ A. Often ☐ B. Sometimes ☐ C. Rarely

Appendix 5. Fivefold Ministries Questionnaire

59. Social justice for the poor and marginalized means a great deal to me.

　　☐ A. Often　☐ B. Sometimes　☐ C. Rarely

60. Despite not enjoying the nitty-gritty details of leadership, I still often end up leading.

　　☐ A. Often　☐ B. Sometimes　☐ C. Rarely

61. I think before I speak.

　　☐ A. Often　☐ B. Sometimes　☐ C. Rarely

62. I like to create safe environments where people can learn and mature.

　　☐ A. Often　☐ B. Sometimes　☐ C. Rarely

63. I don't shy away from controversial subjects if they are important to me.

　　☐ A. Often　☐ B. Sometimes　☐ C. Rarely

64. I often have a strong sense of what to say to people in response to a particular situation.

　　☐ A. Often　☐ B. Sometimes　☐ C. Rarely

65. When in a group, I am the one others often look to for vision and direction.

☐ A. Often   ☐ B. Sometimes   ☐ C. Rarely

66. I am willing to challenge or confront people in order to help them mature.

☐ A. Often   ☐ B. Sometimes   ☐ C. Rarely

67. I enjoy digging out information and ideas or metaphors to explain a concept.

☐ A. Often   ☐ B. Sometimes   ☐ C. Rarely

68. Sometimes, in my enthusiasm, I push my views too far with people.

☐ A. Often   ☐ B. Sometimes   ☐ C. Rarely

69. My inspired thoughts surprise me with their clarity and unexpected direction.

☐ A. Often   ☐ B. Sometimes   ☐ C. Rarely

70. I have a clear vision and others have said that they feel confident to go along with me.

☐ A. Often   ☐ B. Sometimes   ☐ C. Rarely

Appendix 5. Fivefold Ministries Questionnaire

71. I sometimes have difficulty setting boundaries with needy people.

   ☐ A. Often ☐ B. Sometimes ☐ C. Rarely

72. I try to think of different ways of expressing the truth.

   ☐ A. Often ☐ B. Sometimes ☐ C. Rarely

73. I am interested in living and working overseas or among people from a different culture.

   ☐ A. Often ☐ B. Sometimes ☐ C. Rarely

74. I regularly like to be alone for long periods of time to reflect and think.

   ☐ A. Often ☐ B. Sometimes ☐ C. Rarely

75. I get frustrated when I feel I'm not experiencing new things in my life.

   ☐ A. Often ☐ B. Sometimes ☐ C. Rarely

76. I empathize with those who are hurting or broken and can support them through their pain to wholeness.

   ☐ A. Often ☐ B. Sometimes ☐ C. Rarely

77. People have told me that I have communicated timely words or pictures that must have come directly from some higher plane.

☐ A. Often ☐ B. Sometimes ☐ C. Rarely

78. I love to meet new people and get to know their story.

☐ A. Often ☐ B. Sometimes ☐ C. Rarely

79. Sometimes I am able to reveal specific things that have then happened or meant something at a later date.

☐ A. Often ☐ B. Sometimes ☐ C. Rarely

80. When reading, it is easier for me to grasp the wider picture or message than the specific details.

☐ A. Often ☐ B. Sometimes ☐ C. Rarely

Place a tick against each item number for which you answered "Often" or "Sometimes" (the "rarely" answers are not counted but you may wish to use the column marked "C" for "Rarely" so as to keep tabs on which answers you have transferred from the question sheet).

Finally, add up the number of "often" ticks, double the answer and add to the number of ticks for "sometimes."

Appendix 5. Fivefold Ministries Questionnaire

Legend: A = OFTEN B = SOMETIMES C = RARELY

Item	A	B	C	Item	A	B	C	Item	A	B	C	Item	A	B	C	Item	A	B	C
1				2				3				4				5			
6				7				8				9				10			
11				12				13				14				15			
16				17				18				19				20			
21				22				23				24				25			
26				27				28				29				30			
31				32				33				34				35			
36				37				38				39				40			
41				42				43				44				45			
46				47				48				49				50			
51				52				53				54				55			
56				57				58				59				60			
61				62				63				64				65			
66				67				68				69				70			
71				72				73				74				75			
76				77				78				79				80			

Total of items marked "often"	Total of items marked "often"	Total of items marked "often"	Total of items marked "often"	Total of items marked "often"
Multiply by 2	Multiply by 2	Multiply by 2	Multiply by 2	Multiply by 2
Total of items marked "sometimes"	Total of items marked "sometimes"	Total of items marked "sometimes"	Total of items marked "sometimes"	Total of items marked "sometimes"
Grand Total	Grand Total	Grand Total	Grand Total	Grand Total
PASTOR	**TEACHER**	**EVANGELIST**	**PROPHET**	**APOSTLE**

Letters to the Reader

A Personal Word

As I referenced in the opening chapter of the book, and as you may have heard, in 2023 it became public that I had an affair. I want to acknowledge that sin to anyone who reads this book, but further to demonstrate my process of confession, repentance, and restoration.

Throughout this book, we have looked at the process of discipleship by seeing how Jesus led the 12. During my process of repentance and restoration, I have reflected on how Jesus restored Peter with gentleness, healing, and a re-centering on mission. After repeating the question "Do you love me?" three times, Jesus ends with a call to mission: "Follow me."[102]

To show you what that has looked like in my life, I want to share key messages from some letters I wrote during this process to my community, as well as a report from the leaders who discipled me through the restoration process. I've edited these letters slightly to connect them to what you've already read in this book, in order to help them make the most sense in the context of what we have been learning here.

I hope that these will give you a picture of what restoration

---

102 John 21:15-19

can look like thanks to the grace and forgiveness of our Savior Jesus who calls all of us to follow him and make disciples, no matter what we have done.

Letter 1

Let me begin by saying thank you for all the kind words and encouragement you have sent in recent weeks.

I'm so sorry for any pain I have caused. I'm sure my behavior has caused confusion and disappointment for many of you. I'm very sorry.

Sally's kindness and grace have been wonderful, and the way in which my children and the whole family have stepped forward to offer support, help, and guidance has been incredible. It is beyond my ability to fully express how grateful I am to all of them. Sally and I are together in the UK and doing well, and the children and the grandchildren are all thriving. Thank you so much for all your prayers—they have been a blessing to us all.

I'm planning to share my journey of restoration with you through a series of letters. I hope you find them helpful both in understanding my situation and that of others going through similar experiences.

In future letters I hope to share some of the healing process that Sally and I are engaged in, but for the first couple of communications I thought I would share the beginnings of my personal journey of restoration and recovery.

The counsel I have received suggests that all restoration and healing occurs in community, so I have invited a group of wise, mature, and experienced women and men—whom I call the Restoration Team—to walk with me. Their main tasks have centered around asking me hard questions and listening carefully to what I'm saying. Meeting with them every two weeks has been truly transformative for me, providing not only helpful pointers for the journey but also uncovering and confirming a therapeutic process I've been in for a while. This process is helping me answer some really important questions.

Questions like: "How did I become emotionally and physically involved with someone during the COVID pandemic when for most of my adult life I've only ever loved one woman—Sally?"

And, "Why would I ignore all the warning counsel from my family, who felt concerned when they saw changes in my behavior?"

To be honest these questions are only the latest in a series of questions I have been wrestling with for some time, prompting a quest for a deeper understanding of my inner life. This quest has led me to start a doctoral research program into the intersection of neuroscience, communication, and spiritual formation and to seek therapeutic solutions to my struggles.

These struggles have often left me exhausted and overwhelmed with feelings of abandonment, rejection, and isolation. During these times I have found myself losing track of my thoughts mid-sentence, flooded with unexpected emotions. I've even fallen asleep mid-sentence while talking to friends.

Letter 1

This reminds me of the story of falling asleep while driving my truck that I shared in the prologue of this book. As in that situation, all the struggle and trauma I had experienced leading up to COVID (not all due to the pandemic) had taken its toll. I was bumping along the bottom of my physical and emotional capacity. But I just kept going, because that's what I thought I should do. It was what I had been trained to do from when I was a small boy, and if I'm honest it's something I still have a tendency to do even now. Keep calm and carry on!

These kinds of inbuilt mechanisms have given me great resilience over the years, but have also left me with real frailties. The layers of loss and grief have been laid down into my soul year after year, and I have simply ignored them and moved on to the next challenge. I honestly thought I was processing these things well, but most of the pain was unresolved. Even now the inner workings that lie behind these tendencies still beset me.

I offer none of this as an excuse for my behavior or as a request for a free pass. I share them simply as a way of inviting you to understand how the Lord is bringing about change in the midst of my journey of restoration and recovery.

I have come to realize that I am one of those people that Jesus spoke of when he saw that they were "harassed and helpless."[103] Fortunately for me I'm not "a sheep without a shepherd." I, like you, have a wonderfully caring and compassionate Shepherd who understands my frailty and is able to meet me in my need.

Knowing this has brought me afresh to the scriptures particularly John's Gospel where I see Jesus counseling frail

---

103 Matthew 9:36

failures like me: the woman at the well[104], the woman caught in adultery[105], and Peter[106]. In his compassion Jesus says and does really unexpected things. In John 4 he sends the woman at the well as a missionary to her village. In John 8 he tells the woman he's not there to condemn her. In Peter's restoration he asks him repeatedly "Do you love me?"

Jesus understands trauma, grief and the thoughts, feelings and behaviors that will support their healing, and he seeks relational connection rather than anything else. This is perhaps what Paul means by "restoring someone gently" when we've fallen into sin.[107]

This is the process that I'm in, and I'm deeply grateful to the Lord for all the ways he has shown me his kindness in all of this.

Thank you for all your prayers and kindness.

Mike

---

104 John 4
105 John 8
106 John 21
107 Galatians 6:1

Letter 2

Thank you to everyone who was so kind and encouraging after my last letter. The support I have received from you and all my family and friends has meant more to me than I could ever say. Bless you! Your encouragement helps me to continue to seek the deep repentance and faith-filled journey I need as I receive the Lord's restoration in my discipleship from him.

As I indicated in my last letter, I have been pressing into a process for some time, trying to understand what lies at the heart of my struggles. Sally and I have been best friends for 50 years, and so it was a real shock when I realized I wasn't functioning well in our relationship.

In my last newsletter, I related the strange experience of falling asleep and running off the road on a journey (a story I repeated in the prologue of this book). The experience mystified me for many years, and I tried several different interpretations to explain what happened. But it wasn't until a retreat that I took last year with the Onsite therapeutic team that I began to understand what it all might mean.

Onsite, the gold standard of therapeutic organizations, offers retreats at their locations in several places around the United

States. There was a place available for me at their horse ranch in the mountains of San Diego County in California, and so I traveled there in the hope of finding some help and guidance.

The therapeutic team and the personal therapist assigned to me offered a variety of different therapeutic processes, including conversation, meditation, art, foraging, and EMDR (eye movement desensitization and reprocessing). It was an incredible experience that has continued to provide resources for reflection and healing that I return to on an almost daily basis.

During one session I was invited into what I think experts in the field call a "psychodrama". I was among a very small group of fellow travelers, and we were helped to understand what neuroscience and psychotherapy are beginning to uncover about the connection between behavior and trauma. Three of the participants were asked to sit one behind the other on seats, each holding a different toy representing different parts of the brain. The person in the back seat held a reptile, representing the brain's survival instincts. The middle seat was occupied by someone holding a teddy bear, representing our need for intimacy and comfort. The person in the front row was given an Einstein doll representing the part of the brain, such as the frontal lobes, that offer us rational thought.

The Onsite team of clinicians positioned themselves around the chairs. One stood on one side describing how the various parts of the brain react in response to trauma. Two others stood opposite each other on either side of the front and middle chairs near a sheet that laid on the floor. After giving a detailed explanation of the structure of the brain, the narrator said, "And this is what happens as a result of trauma…." At this moment, the two other clinicians picked up the sheet and cut off the

Letter 2

front-row seat from the other two. The narrator explained, "The rational part of the brain is cut off from the other parts of the brain. In trauma the brain focuses on the instincts for comfort and survival."

I found this idea very challenging, but as I reflected with my therapist, things began to fall into place. In the end the insights I gained proved enormously helpful.

In my desire to understand what was going on in my life, I had the beginnings of an explanation of what was going on inside of me. I had always assumed reason would guide my actions, and yet these recent discoveries in neuroscience suggested that my brain (like everyone else's) was likely to take a different path than the one I might have expected, one that connected to much deeper instincts than reason.

It would appear that our brains have deeply ingrained strategies of attachment that are automatically activated as a trauma response as a quest for survival.

My pattern of attachment is what the specialists in the field call "Anxious Attachment". This tends to lead me to look toward new places of security and comfort, particularly if the ones I previously relied on no longer appear to offer me the nurture and protection I hoped for.

For most of my life I have experienced what I would call "manageable trauma." Although this was at times quite extreme, I was able to find a way through. But in recent years I have experienced multiple layers of unresolved trauma that have overwhelmed me. It's difficult to write this, but I found myself struggling with such a sense of loss and abandonment that I looked outside of my marriage for comfort and security, even though this was a "self-sabotaging" strategy (an apparently common behavior in those who have experienced multiple traumas). It wasn't a rational or even a conscious decision; it was something that happened as an unexpected response to what I understand now to be overwhelming circumstances.

In saying this I'm not suggesting that I'm not responsible for my actions or that what I did was anything other than sinful. But it does help me to understand where and how the Lord wants to heal and transform my heart and mind.

In all of this I take great comfort in the knowledge that the apostle Paul—reflecting on the internal, irrational battle that existed within him—seemed to understand his own behavior from a similar perspective:

> *For I do not do the good I want to do, but the evil I do not want to do—this I keep on doing. Now if I do what I do not want to do, it is no longer I who do it, but it is sin living in me that does it. So I find this law at work: Although I want to do good, evil is right there with me. For in my inner being I delight in God's law; but I see another law at work in me, waging war against the law of my mind and making me a prisoner of the law of sin at work within me.*[108]

I fully identify with what Paul is saying here and the next statement is very similar to things that I've expressed through this whole experience:

> *What a wretched man I am! Who will rescue me from*

---

108 Romans 7:19-23

Letter 2

this body that is subject to death?[109]

And of course I also fully embrace what Paul says next…

Thanks be to God, who delivers me through Jesus Christ our Lord!…[110] *There is now no condemnation for those who are in Christ Jesus, because through Christ Jesus the law of the Spirit who gives life has set you free from the law of sin and death.*[111]

In my next letter, I hope to share more on this important process in my life. My hope is that it will help you to pray for Sally and I, and I pray that it might perhaps help you with some of the things with which you wrestle.

Much love,

Mike

---

109 Romans 7:24
110 Romans 7:25
111 Romans 8:1-2

Letter 3

Charlie was an amazing dog. So many of you mentioned our highly relational and lovable black Labrador when you sent messages of thanks after visiting Sally and I in Pawleys Island, South Carolina. You also invariably mentioned Betty, Sally's mum. It was as though meeting Betty and Charlie made you feel that you had connected with us as a family when you came for training with us and our team.

After we left Pawleys Island and went to live in Greenville, South Carolina, Charlie struggled with health problems. You will perhaps remember how he miraculously recovered from illness a couple of times. But the day finally arrived when Charlie would not recover again. I knew it as I knelt beside him to pray one more time. Charlie just lifted his sweet noble head and looked directly at me. It was as though he was trying to tell me something. Perhaps he was trying to say his time had come and he was going to be taken from us.

I loved Charlie, but the deep sense of loss I experienced took me by surprise. I wept and wept. After we laid him on the back seat of the car and took him to the vet for his final journey, I spent the whole day not able to do anything other than sit alone and cry. It was as though his death opened a fault line within me, and the unanticipated flood of emotions rushing through the fissure in my heart was overwhelming.

I wasn't ready for this at all. I had held it together with the loss of my parents and even the tragic death of our grandson, but somehow Charlie's death circumvented my defenses and knocked me to the ground. All the old wounds of struggle, rejection, and hurt seemed to be laid bare.

Questioning why this was the case, I sought help. The therapist, after a few sessions, suggested that I might be the subject of what he called "compounded loss"—a condition created by a continuous experience of the trauma of loss without the opportunity to process it through the natural patterns of grief. I learned a fundamental axiom of life that grief heals trauma. Each of the five processes of grief (denial, guilt, bargaining, depression, acceptance) takes us deeper into our inner life and helps us to settle and naturally heal old wounds and the losses associated with them.

I've learned that this is because the emotions connected to each stage of grief attract deep, often hidden hurts and feelings and help us to process them. The stages of grief are not necessarily connected to feelings that can be rationally explained but are internal processes seeking a reason to be there. So they connect to unresolved feelings and wounded memories, and with this the miracle of healing takes place. And so, the processes of grief (if embraced) heal past traumas. In the death of my dear canine friend Charlie, the Lord revealed that I needed to find a journey of healing for the wounds that remained unresolved within me.

But unfortunately the healing would have to wait a little while. Sally and I moved from Greenville to Dayton, Ohio,

Letter 3

hoping that working in a local church would promote our healing journey. We had drifted apart in our struggle for emotional survival, and we both hoped the move would bring us closer and offer a path of recovery from the burdens we carried.

Unfortunately, the opposite happened. In our first year, we were plunged into a vicious church fight in which I was again pilloried and persecuted for my theology of mission and discipleship. In our second year we were thrown into the COVID crisis with all of the complications and challenges associated with it. I reverted to type, pushed down the pain, and activated my familiar patterns of duty and discipline. Sally and I were again coping separately with our struggles, and into this immensely complex and difficult set of circumstances I was offered an illicit relationship which I foolishly and wholeheartedly embraced like a drowning man grasping at anything to stay afloat.

Though it offered an anesthetic to the pain, the relationship could not of course bring healing. When it ended I pressed further into therapy in the hope of finding answers to the deep needs that were being exposed within me. I discovered that for me duty and discipline have functioned as what the apostle Paul calls "the law," and my compensating strategies for the effects of the law are often expressions of what he calls "the flesh". Together they have conspired to bring about "death."[112] Of course with death comes grief, and with this grief, I have rediscovered the life axiom I learned with Charlie's death: grief heals trauma.

For me, the deep grief I have experienced over these last months has begun to produce a fruit of healing I could never

---

112 Compare with Romans 7:7-8:8

have anticipated. I'm so grateful to all those who have been brave enough to share the journey with me. And I realize that those who have rejected me in this time have been used by God to increase the grief and so deepen the process of healing.

I, like many of you, have been conditioned to avoid the process of grief from my nurturing experience onward. I now understand how the Lord intends the stages of grief to heal all our losses. Loss is common to all and is no doubt the direct result of us leaving paradise. But in his kindness, the Lord has provided within the stages of grief a way we can all find healing and an emergence of hope that we might reclaim the paradise lost.

In my letters, I have attempted to share a transparent picture of what's been going on with me. In some ways, the first was simply an attempt to share what happened, offering my sincerest apologies. The second tried to explain the irrationality of my behavior and the therapeutic process I've been in to help me understand how such things happen to ordinary people. I concluded with a reference to Paul's plaintive cry at the end of Romans 7: "Who will deliver me from this body of death!" and his expression of gratitude to begin Romans 8: "There is no condemnation for those in Christ Jesus." I have felt the depth of both of these simple expressions of faith, and they continue to be the deepest cry of the heart.

May you continue to know the Lord's pleasure and his loving presence in all things.

Much love,

Mike

Letter from Restoration Team

Dear Ministry Partners and Friends,

I hope this letter finds you well. We are reaching out to provide an update on the accountability and reconciliation process that Mike Breen has undertaken, as well as to offer insight into the journey of restoration that we believe is essential not just for Mike, but for all of us. This letter reports on the process Mike has been through, the journey of the restoration and accountability team, and how we see this as a pathway for future growth and healing for the entire body of Christ.

Goal: To communicate the restorative process and the benefits of a grace-based approach to dealing with mistakes, sins, and failures. Our aim is to encourage a restorative, rather than a legalistic, response to failure, following the teaching of Galatians 6: "Restore with a spirit of gentleness."

The accountability process, co-chaired by Dr. Reginald S. Screen and Dr. Mike Rayburn, has been a thorough and prayerful journey. Over several months, Mike has been engaged in deep reflection and accountability, working to understand and address an inappropriate relationship that took place. This moral failure has been a source of pain for Mike, his family, and many others who were impacted by his actions.

Dr. Mike Rayburn offered the following perspective on Mike's journey:

"In my opinion, Mike has made a thoughtful and sincere effort to make himself accountable to a panel of Christian leaders (both men and women). I believe his purpose was to be honest and transparent about what happened between him and a woman, which amounted to an inappropriate relationship and a moral failure. I think he saw this as a necessary step in the process of healing for him and his family, as well as a need to understand himself. He recognizes that the weaknesses in his own personality, which led to his mistakes, need to be understood and corrected if he is to be less susceptible to the same failures in the future.

"I see in him a determined effort to address these things with the help of professionals as well as with a rather insightful group of praying friends.

"Quite frankly, I have not seen such a comprehensive effort to deal with sin in most Christians, or in the Church at large. In my experience, the effort rarely goes beyond repentance before the Lord, and occasionally an attempt to apologize or make restitution to those who have been hurt. In terms of an outlook for the future, all that is offered is hope—tempered with a reality check. We are usually told, 'Since we are all flawed, we need to accept the fact that we'll probably do it again';

"There is no attempt made to understand why we make bad decisions. How are we deceived into doing what we hate (Romans 7)? How can we tear down the strongholds of lies and vain arguments in our minds that our enemy uses to control our behavior (2 Corinthians 10)? How do we learn how to be like the young men in 1 John who have overcome the evil one?"

Additionally, Robert Pitman, who has been closely involved in the process, shared the following:

"I have seen a broken Mike and a vulnerable Mike that I have not seen before. Mike is learning things about himself

Letter from Restoration Team

that have led to brokenness, but it's what's been needed that is leading him to healing and the restoration of his marriage and family!"

Mike Smith, a long-time friend and spiritual mentee of Mike Breen, offered his reflections:

"Mike has been a spiritual mentor in my life for over 10 years, which made this moral failure[113] extremely difficult for me to comprehend and even humanize. However, being a part of his restorative process has reminded me that none of us are ever beyond the threat of temptation and failure, NOR the latitude of grace. The whole of this process has allowed Mike to see the progression and the mindset that ultimately produced this failure and, at the same time, reclaim the life and commitment to Christ that he originally embraced as a spiritual leader. I have seen him recalibrate his life through remorse, consideration, and a genuine desire to return to being the man God called him to be."

Ryan Snow also shared his perspective, highlighting the tangible growth and accountability Mike has embraced:

"Mike is slowly growing, healing, and changing. He has been submitted to a consistent process of connection and some level of tangible and regular accountability with this group, his wife, and family. I am thankful in an age of leaders who hide and are not culpable, that Mike is seeking restoration in a tangible, honest, and humble way."

Mike Ely, another member of the reconciliation team, offered his encouragement based on what he has witnessed:

---

113 See https://www.vanderbloemen.com/blog/5-deadly-states-of-mind-that-can-lead-to-moral-failure

"I've been a part of the reconciliation team for Mike, and I've been encouraged by his candor and honesty in dealing with his own brokenness and healing. His humility to not brush over his own issues but deal with them head-on, and to submit to those whom he was leading and mentoring for years, is a difficult and courageous task. But Mike pushed through. It's refreshing to be a part of a healthy healing process, and I believe Mike is moving forward himself and with Sally into a healthy future."

Finally, Mike's wife, Sally Breen, shared her personal reflections on their marriage and this journey of restoration:

"We are digging deep into the foundations of the good marriage and good friendship we have had over these last 50 years. Good soil always eventually grows good fruit, even if it's been dormant for a while or ravaged by storms.

"During the worst of times, I was still very clearly hearing God's voice, audible at times, and it led me through. One time, when I was pleading with the Lord and in a very low, desperate moment with all my emotions coming out, I said to my Father, 'I love Mike so very much.' He replied, 'But I love him more. Hand him over to me. I will take very good care of him. I know his heart.' So that's what I did."

The accountability and restoration process has brought about significant personal transformation for Mike. He has faced his own failures with a depth of honesty that is rare and has taken meaningful steps toward restoration through professional help, spiritual guidance, and support from close, praying friends. We, as the Church, can take away valuable lessons from this process, not just for Mike, but for all of us.

Letter from Restoration Team

The future pathway for Mike is one that continues to prioritize grace over judgment, healing over shame, and accountability over hiddenness. His journey reflects the biblical call to restore with a spirit of gentleness (Galatians 6), and we believe this is the model the Church must adopt as we walk with those who fall into sin. This is not just about Mike's restoration, but about our collective journey toward grace-filled living—acknowledging that we all stumble and that restoration is possible for everyone.

Thank you for your ongoing prayers and partnership as we continue to support Mike through this process. We hope that this letter not only informs you of the steps taken but also encourages all of us to embrace a grace-based approach in our personal and communal lives.

In His Grace,

On behalf of *The Accountability and Restoration Team*:

Dr. Reginald S. Screen and Dr. Mike Rayburn

$24.97
ISBN 978-0-9998981-3-0

www.ingramcontent.com/pod-product-compliance
Lightning Source LLC
Chambersburg PA
CBHW050848160426
43194CB00011B/2075